Growing Up
and Growing Old
in Italian-American
Families

Growing Up
and Growing Old
in Italian-American
Families

Colleen Leahy Johnson

Rutgers University Press

New Brunswick, New Jersey

Library of Congress Cataloging in Publication Data

Johnson, Colleen Leahy, 1932–
  Growing up and growing old in Italian-American families.

  Bibliography: p.
  Includes index.
  1. Italian American families. 2. Italian Americans—
Ethnic identity. 3. Life cycle, Human—Psychological
aspects. I. Title.
E184.I8J64   1985   306.8'08951   84–9760
ISBN 0–8135–1064–3

Contents

List of
Tables and Figure

Tables

Preface

This study of Italian Americans explores dimensions of ethnic group membership as it is manifested in family organization. Interviews were conducted with over four hundred individuals in a northeastern city, here called Easton. Participants in the study were either Italian, married to Italians, or part of a Protestant control group selected to measure group differences. Middle-aged and elderly Italians provide a description of family life both in its traditional immigrant form, stemming primarily from southern Italy, and its contemporary organization. Compared to these were Italian families in which intermarriage had taken place, which provide a measure of change in today's family. White Protestant families form a second comparison group. This group, whose histories in this century date back at least three generations, illustrates how Italian families differ from a core American reference group. In order to account for the strong attachments found in Italian families, continuities in socialization practices are also explored.

The research focuses on a critical point in the family cycle when family loyalties are being tested. The majority of the families are in the middle stages of the family cycle, when middle-aged couples are dealing with the changing bases of attachment with both their parents and their children. At that point, older parents are becoming dependent and the middle-aged children are attempting to fill the void created by their parents' retirement, declining health, and diminishing resources. Also, at this stage, their own children in adolescence and early adulthood are at the age when independence from the parental home is generally the norm. Thus, it is a description and analysis of the dilemmas of dependence and independence between family members and how solutions are sought that must balance personal interests and the interests of the nuclear and extended family.

The research findings are also used to address practical concerns on the viability of the family as a social support system in old age. During a period when the public sector is reexamining its commitment to social programs addressed to the needs of older people, many assumptions are being made on the nature of the American family and its resources for caring for its elderly members. The study of one ethnic group, long noted for the strength of its family ties, is one approach in examining this widespread problem: it can provide insights into dimensions of family life associated with supportive behaviors.

Numerous individuals contributed to this research. In addition to co-authoring chapters, Jessica Field Cohen and Patricia Quinn Pirro conducted many interviews and assisted in the analysis of the data. Tore Mita interviewed most of the elderly Italians. Without his fluency in Italian and several southern dialects, we would have had to omit numerous individuals. Maureen Giovannini and Judy Alamprese conducted interviews and functioned as excellent interpreters of the family. Carol Marshall was of invaluable assistance in helping me to understand the internal workings of the Italian family. Sharon Cooke provided much assistance in the earlier version of the manuscript, and Barbara Barer provided help in editing the final version. Finally, the research certainly would not have taken place without funding by the National Institute of Mental Health (MH 26417).

I wish to thank the many members of the Italian community who agreed to be interviewed and who shared their lives with us. To protect their anonymity, their names have been changed and the name of the city has been disguised. Their cooperation and enthusiasm for this study made the research personally as well as professionally rewarding for the entire staff.

Part 1
Background

Chapter 1
Introduction

In one sense, all American families today face similar problems and have available a similar range of options for their resolution. All families have had to face rapid social change which directly affects the performance of family roles. The high rate of divorce threatens the stability of marriage at all levels of society, and the women's movement has stimulated a reevaluation of the roles of wife and mother. The young are more prone to question basic values of parents and to seek lifestyles in contradiction to the best-intentioned parental goals. Older family members are not immune to these changes, which usually are at odds with their more traditional values.

Not surprisingly, the families we interviewed shared these widespread concerns. The middle-aged respondents in this research were born in the 1920s and 1930s; they married in the 1950s and continued to live in the same city in the mid-1970s when we interviewed them. They were in their forties and fifties and dealing with transitons of their children into adulthood and of their parents into old age. In relationships with their children, they were wrestling with determining the degree of autonomy or control that would be optimal, or in some cases they were standing by, realizing helplessly that parental influence was quite ineffective. These respondents also faced decisions as to the degree of support they could extend to their aging parents with the increasing likelihood of illness or physical dependency. They expressed concerns about how this support to parents would compete with the needs of their nuclear families.

The White Ethnic Family

In reading descriptions of Catholic families of European origin, one finds parallels between these groups that differ from the dominant model of the middle-class family in the United States (Mindel and Haberstein 1976). The concept of traditionalism probably best summa-

rizes these parallels, but it is a traditionalism that must repond to en-
croaching changes. This commonality was evident in the respondents'
comparison of the past and the present: old people had been respected
and esteemed, but they no longer are. Families were patriarchal, but
now women are treated as equals. Children were reared strictly, but
now parents are so permissive that children do as they please. In the
past, relatives helped each other and today everyone is out for him or
herself. Essentially, what is described is a traditional family system
of rural or preindustrial society which can be contrasted to a modern
form common in industrial society.

Certainly Italian Americans and other groups of relatively recent
immigrant background have viewed the events around social change
through a lens somewhat different from more established groups.
Those in middle age with roots in southern and eastern Europe are
likely to be children of immigrants who witnessed the many difficulties their parents faced in establishing a toehold in this country. During their childhood, the depression years imposed even greater economic hardships for their families than for other groups, since many
already had marginal economic status (Elder 1974). Prejudice and discrimination and frequent epithets such as "wop," "dago," or "grease-
ball" reminded them further of their marginality in the broader society.

Having been through a war and a period of economic prosperity,
most of the respondents have achieved home ownership, a stable family, a secure job, and a solid position in the community, only to find
that respected middle-class values are broadly questioned. After a lifetime of balancing the contradictions of the Old World culture of their
parents with the American value system, many find themselves out-
dated. Just when college education for their children is feasible, access
to the higher status jobs is cut off by a depressed economy. The neighborhoods they have long maintained against urban blight are breaking
up or deteriorating by forces quite beyond their control. Finally, their
initial attempt to resolve confusions of ethnic identity by some assimilation into the wider society clashes with the rise in ethnic conscious-
ness that is the clarion call of the day. Even though being ethnic is in
vogue these days, being a white ethnic can also mean one is labeled as
conservative, traditional, and an intolerant hindrance to affirmative action. Thus, confusion over one's ethnic identity is likely.

The responses of white ethnics to this uniformity of events imping-
ing upon families today vary from the dominant group, most likely because of the greater traditionalism they share. I assume that these ethnic groups also vary among themselves as problems are filtered further

through a cultural lens stemming from their parents' specific cultural background. More systematic research is needed on the extent to which these cultural determinants continue to influence behavior and in what direction.

The Study of White Ethnics

Among students of ethnicity, there are three points of view on the Catholics of European origin, the white ethnics. One popular view, which has struck a responsive chord among white ethnics themselves, describes contemporary times as a period of "the rise of the unmeltable ethnics," a rise that suggests the growing importance of ethnicity (Greeley 1974; Novak 1972). A second view, common among sociologists, suggests that social class determinants rather than ethnic group membership are more significant. Their conclusion, then, is that white ethnics have become submerged into their respective social class subgroups (Duncan and Duncan 1968; Yancey, Eriksen, and Juliani 1976). Finally, a third view assumes that ethnic groups persist in a new and identifiable social form, unlike either the country of origin or the dominant group in this country, but one which is salient in fostering personal and social adjustment (Glazer and Moynihan 1963). The growing acceptance of this view is evidenced in a recent encyclopedia of American ethnic groups which catalogues the many subgroups in this country (Thernstrom 1980).

Despite the widespread popular interest in ethnicity, it is surprising to find that a review of 165 years of publications from the three most widely read sociology journals (Kitch and Egon 1976) yielded only thirty-one articles on the European Catholic groups. Moreover, there are few intensive studies of ethnic families, the institution in which ethnic behaviors are most likely to be expressed. Reports of ethnic variation are found in studies of rates of alcoholism (Wechsler et al. 1970; Zax, Gardner, and Hart 1967), mental illness (Rabkin and Struening n.d.), achievement levels (McClelland, Pandlesbacker, and de Charmes 1955; Majoribanks 1972; Psathas 1968; Rosen 1959), and patterns of juvenile delinquency (R. Stein 1971), all of which potentially have their source in family processes. Also in recent years, histories of ethnic families have contributed insightful descriptions indicating variation in the adaptation of European groups (McLaughlin 1971).

Upon closer examination of conceptions of ethnicity, some of which are tinged with the ideological or polemical, one can only agree with Andrew Greeley (1974) who describes it as a murky subject on which there is little agreement on concepts and methods of study. In the same vein, Irving Howe comments that "No one quite knows what ethnicity means: That's why it's a very useful term" (1977:68). Understandably, ethnicity is a complex phenomenon because its study potentially can include psychological, sociocultural, historical, economic, and political factors. Definitions of ethnicity and the focus of research also vary depending upon the group one is studying. For example, studies of the first and second generations in this country usually examine traits of the country of origin, such as language, religion, customs, and rituals. Today, however, after most European groups have been in this country three generations, such characteristics as language are no longer a mark of distinction. As these traits disappear, manifest characteristics of ethnicity are less observable, whether or not assimilation has taken place.

Moreover, the extent to which these manifest characteristics of ethnicity act as a determinant of behavior or a principle of social organization is questionable. The Japanese American who studies the tea ceremony or the Italian American who takes an art appreciation course on the Italian Renaissance, will learn little of her parents' background and its effect on her own life. Additionally, these ethnically based activities do not necessarily indicate the extent ethnic group membership acts to organize social roles and regulate primary relationships (Barth 1969). By implication, traits and customs as indicators also imply that ethnicity is an ascriptive, static status rather than one that can be used selectively and voluntarily according to varied situations.

Certainly spokesmen for the new ethnics conclude that the meaning of ethnicity goes beyond manifest characteristics to include subjective and psychological meanings.

> The new ethnicity entails: first a growing sense of discomfort with the sense of identity one is supposed to have— universalistic, "melted," "Like everyone else"; then a growing apprehension for the potential wisdom of one's gut reactions (especially on moral matters) and their historical roots; a growing self confidence and social power. . . . (Novak 1974:19)

The white ethnics' repeated insistence on the importance of their heritage has drawn responses from the academic community which imply that the new-found identity could be a superficial return to something one had lost, rather than a manifestation of continuing group membership. As a consequence, this new expression of ethnicity has been dismissed as a mere political maneuver copying the techniques of the blacks (Horowitz 1975; H. Stein and Hill 1973), a regression in a psychological sense (T. Parsons 1975), or a sentimental search for roots as an antidote to alienation (Bell 1975; Isaacs 1975). Thus, the emblematic uses of ethnic group membership, still observable on bumper stickers, lapel pins, or celebrations of national holidays, have been described by Isaacs (1975:30) as a search for "primordial affinities and attachments." He goes on to describe the process as a "massive retribalization running sharply counter to the globalizing effects of modern technology and communications."

Most systematic studies make a distinction between the cultural and social-structural dimensions of ethnic group membership. Milton Gordon (1964) has isolated and specified the major variables that distinguish cultural from structural assimilation. On one hand, structural studies today identify trends in residential concentrations, intermarriage, social mobility, and the presence or absence of discrimination. Recent evidence shows structural realignments in our society which indicate assimilation is taking place. Old ethnic neighborhoods are dispersing, intermarriage is increasing, and the intensity of exclusionary tactics against white ethnics is declining (Duncan and Duncan 1968; Yancey, Eriksen, and Juliani 1976).

The study of cultural variables, on the other hand, usually suggests the persistence of ethnic behaviors. The evidence, however, is more elusive, most likely because of the varied and unspecific nature of the definitions of the concept. Gordon includes a trait index composed of intrinsic factors such as religious beliefs, values, musical and recreational tastes, and so on. His extrinsic factors are such traits as dress, manners, and language usage. As noted above, however, selected extrinsic and intrinsic traits disappear after several generations in this country, although the more personal and subjective meanings of group membership undoubtedly remain. Certainly fiction, personal reflections, and scattered descriptive studies present a convincing picture of the persistence of a common heritage and shared meanings. Of those by Italian Americans, for example, Richard Gambino's book, *Blood of My Blood* (1974), and Elizbeth Stone's *New York Times Magazine* feature, "It's Still Hard to Grow Up Italian" (1978), provide cultural material suggesting a strong ethnic identity, but one which might escape detection through standard sociological techniques.

In contemporary anthropological studies, the cultural dimension of social behavior is studied systematically. The focus is on the standards of evaluations observable in norms and values, common beliefs, sentiments, shared experiences, and a sense of a common past. Usually, evidence of these dimensions is found in the less institutionalized forms of behavior and values as they are expressed in day-to-day interaction among primary relationships. Because they are more difficult to define and observe systematically, these more subtle and less easily measurable behaviors are more readily identified through phenomenological methods.

If ethnic phenomena today are less amenable to standard sociological methods, a combined approach is warranted, because few would question the significance also of structural variables. Unfortunately, as William Yancey and his colleagues (1976) point out, the distinction between cultural and structural factors all too frequently form two mutually exclusive focuses of investigation which result in conflicting views on the persistence of ethnicity. Nathan Glazer (1981) in a review of three books on ethnic mobility points out that sociologists have been expert in denying that differences really exist, even though the average person on the street can readily see that they do. He traces this situation to the current research emphasis on structural variables and a neglect of cultural material.

In this study I have attempted to combine both approaches. I assume that the significance of ethnicity rests upon the extent to which ethnic group membership acts as a determinant of one's status and roles and the composition of the social network. In other words, is ethnic group membership used as a basis of social organization? If it is used for this purpose, one can assume the process is associated with cultural material evident in the norms and values, sentiments, and meanings, which are transmitted across generations. These factors interact with structural variables such as patterns of marriage and social and geographic mobility.

The study of ethnic families provides an excellent source of understanding of these issues. First, the family is an institution that bridges other social institutions and the less institutionalized units of study, such as face-to-face interactions, emotional expressions, and lifestyle (LeVine 1973). Second, the family system is the primary socialization agent for the social patterning of behaviors, norms, and values and the formation of the basic personality structure. Not only does the family initially socialize the young, but it also is the most likely setting for the expression of adult behaviors that might be ethnically derived. Third, the study of family systems can reveal the degree to which ethnic membership acts as a constraint on the behaviors or as a vehicle for change. Whether these constraints, or their absence, are adaptive to individuals or to society in general then becomes an important research question.

Issues of Dependence and Independence

The dilemma of dependence and independence is one area in which there are predictable ethnic differences. It borders on a truism to state that core American values extol independence, individualism, and self-reliance. These widely endorsed values can result in a tendency to view dependence as adults upon either parents or children pejoratively. Robert Hunt (1971:121) calls adult dependency a "red herring of considerable stench to most Americans." In this same view, David Schneider and Raymond Smith (1973:52) describe such dicta as "stand on your own two feet," "be independent," and "make your own way in life" as a string of clichés through which these truths are held to be self-evident and expressed over and over again.

Although such a value orientation historically has served Americans well in the settlement of the frontier and in industrial development, the extent to which they receive widespread endorsement by all subgroups is uncertain. Moreover, social critics are only now beginning to examine the costs of such an orientation (Lasch 1979). As Phillip Slater (1970) has pointed out, certain basic needs for engagement and community are continually frustrated in the quest for individualism. From a cross-cultural perspective, researchers are indicating that some universal events in the life cycle, such as aging, present greater problems when group attachments are minimal (Cowgill and Holmes 1972). Even more salient are the tentative conclusions by Bertram Cohler and Henry Grunebaum (1981) that the norm of independence is incongruent, because, in reality, children remain bound to parents well into their adulthood. Research in aging also documents that a large majority of related nuclear households live near one another and are in frequent social contact (Shanas 1979). Likewise, family therapists point out that dependence rather than independence characterizes family relationships and should be considered in treatment procedures (Boszormenyi-Nagy and Spark 1973).

While dependence throughout the life cycle may be the reality of family life for many individuals, in contradiction to our value system, this condition generally is negatively sanctioned in American society except during early childhood. The aged, as they experience declining physical capacity and economic resources and increasing social and psychological dependency, are particularly prone to find themselves forced into a socially disapproved role, a role that in fact contradicts their own social expectations. Margaret Clark (1969) points out that individuals in this stage of life are presented with two equally unsatisfactory choices: the denial of dependency or self-recrimination for being dependent. Talcott Parsons (1953) notes that dependency with illness is a form of alienation, because to be ill is to be socially undesirable. Although these problems affect all Americans as they age, it is apparent that not all subgroups uniformly endorse the value of independence. Presumably, the problems of dependent elderly become magnified in family systems that value highly the independence of individual members and the autonomy of the nuclear family from its kinship extensions (Clark and Anderson 1967).

Developmental approaches suggest that dependency needs are not relatively fixed throughout the family cycle. For example, Cohler and Grunebaum (1981) in their case studies of mothers and daughters in four Italian-American families find that the dependence of daughters upon their mothers during their years of raising children is a source of ambivalence to middle-aged mothers. In other words, there might be a shift in the needs of these women who, after a lifetime of family interdependence, want to seek some independence from family obligations. Issues of dependence and interdependence in adult life are only now beginning to be addressed (Munnichs and van den Heuval 1976; Troll and Smith 1976). One productive route of inquiry, which is used here, is an analysis of how variations in values on independence are translated into the ongoing relationships between three generations in a family: the elderly parents, their middle-aged offspring, and the adolescent children.

The Research Problem

This study is based upon the assumption that if ethnicity continues to be relevant to members of an ethnic group, it will be expressed in one or more of the following: the value system and more specific norms regulating interaction, the patterning of family roles, the socialization of the young, the relationship between generations, and the ethnic characteristics in the networks of social interaction. These dimensions of the family have been used here to explore the potentials families have to generate their own internal support system. By use of the variable of ethnicity, a key question asked is the following: Does the family system of this subculture resolve the dependence-independence dilemma differently from the dominant American pattern?

If an ethnic group retains this capacity, then it is worthwhile to examine its effectiveness in fulfilling the needs of its members. We need to know more of the configuration of the families with high potentials and how they function at several stages of the family cycle.

In identifying components of the family that facilitate the satisfaction of dependency needs of the elderly, it is apparent that the dimensions of the traditional family system have this potential. Using this traditional family system as an ideal type, several patterns are relevant to the research problem: The elderly have relatively high status in the family, which assumes a hierarchy not generally found in the modern nuclear family. There is a pool of available relatives to share in the caregiving, which assumes an actively functioning kinship group. Likewise, there is a value system that places a priority on family interests over individual interests. Finally, traditional socialization mechanisms pressure members to conform to family goals. This constellation of characteristics is termed interdependence, a concept used here to describe a form of family integration characterized by intimacy, need satisfaction, and group allegiances. It connotes a reciprocal, ongoing quid pro quo in family relationships. In contrast to dependence, interdependence generally connotes gratification of needs that are not dominated by guilt, resentment, or conflict on the one hand or dysfunctional passivity and dependence on the other. Where the mechanisms are culturally elaborated and given positive significance, it is logical to assume that the dependency of individuals is considered a natural human condition to which the family can accommodate.

Interdependence in families described here connotes a high priority given to the family, often at the expense of personal interests. For example, if a middle-aged family member rejects his firm's offer to move to another city and take on a more lucrative job because he wants to be able to see relatives often, that is interdependence. If a woman quits her job without complaints to have more time for a sick mother, that is interdependence. If a young adult foregoes taking an apartment with friends because of parental objections, that is also interdependence. This propensity to conform to family expectations over individual priorities also is likely to be evident in the relationship to older parents.

In order to examine these family processes and determine how they vary according to ethnic background, three comparison groups were used: Italian families in which both spouses were Italian, intermarried families in which only one spouse was Italian, and a white Protestant control group. A research instrument tapped both behaviors and cultural directives on the problem areas that all families must resolve: how to raise children, care for an elderly parent, deal with one's spouse, define male and female roles, and maintain kinship relationships. The categories used for comparison included the following items for measurement.

Network Connections

The family's social activities were examined to determine the degree of age integration in family activities and the extent of participation of kin and ethnic peers. It was assumed that a social network that includes grandparents, parents, children and their children, their relatives, and friends from the same ethnic background encourage a normative consensus which serves to perpetuate ethnic features of the family.

Filial Relationships

Questions probed both the attitudes and behaviors of middle-aged children toward elderly parents, the amount of aid extended to them, and the expectations respondents have for their children in the future. These were compared to the expectations of the elderly parents so continuities and discontinuities in intergenerational relations could be identified.

Kinship Solidarity

Kinship relations were investigated to determine the extent of social contact, the number of socially significant relatives, and the attitudes on the desirability of reciprocal kinship relations. Presumably, kinship-dominated networks logically reaffirm and perpetuate ethnic norms and behavior.

Marital Relations

This measure included items on communication patterns, power distribution, mutual support patterns, and the degree of marital segregation in social activities. This analysis examines how priorities to the marital dyad were balanced against the demands from the families of origin.

Socialization

Independence training, social control, and levels of nurturing or need satisfaction were examined, as well as the values that tap egocentric versus sociocentric orientations. It was assumed that for interdependence to be incorporated acceptably into family processes when one is dealing with aged parents, it is elaborated at other stages in the family cycle and perpetuated through socialization practices.

In interpreting the results, the works of Fredrik Barth (1969) and Elizabeth Bott (1971) have been used. First, following Barth, the ethnic group is conceptualized as a category of self-ascription and ascription by others. Ascription to a shared category assumes common agreement on norms and strategies for interaction. While these boundaries are fluid, which permit movement across them, it is assumed that greater rewards accrue to an individual whose behaviors are reinforced by the values of primary relationships.

Second, for practical research purposes, the boundary of an ethnic group is a social network consisting of sets of social relationships between family members and others (Bott 1971). Where these networks are connected, meaning individuals in the network also have relationships with each other, they tend to agree on the norms that govern family relationships. If consensus is present, individuals are pressured to conform to family expectations. Where members of the same ethnic group constitute a family's network, one can predict a persistence of some dimensions of ethnicity in the performance of family roles.

Third, over time, the socialization processes are colored by the character of the social network. Parental role functions and values in childrearing result from multiple factors, but an important one stems from the social environment of the family and the extent to which the activities of the nuclear family are observable to relatives and friends. Where the social network is connected by relatives who share the same views and who are in frequent interaction with each other, it is proposed that the potential for change is minimized. Further, when this family type is enclosed by a consensual network, the family remains an important agent of socialization for individuals well into their adulthood, making the persistence of ethnic factors more likely. In contrast, where the networks include individuals with diverse norms and values, socialization techniques can be predicted to change. Such an interpretation would explain how elements of socialization have been transmitted from generation to generation.

I also assume that at some point the relationship between middle-aged offspring and the elderly parents must be redefined if the parent becomes dependent. If an offspring assumes a high commitment to the parent, that individual will call upon the previous patterns of the family in determining what supports to provide. It is predicted that an exchange process takes place in which parents must give up power in exchange for their dependency. As middle-aged offspring take over caregiving, the dependence and power in the relationship are renegotiated, and the offspring reach a stage of filial maturity. These processes are viewed as being associated with continuity in socialization where issues of authority and dependence, although under negotiation, stem from earlier patterns in the family.

Change is conceived here as originating from two sources. First, the structural sources of change come from the influence of geographic and social mobility and intermarriage, which usually expand the social network to include nonethnic members. The expanded horizons resulting from education establishes some distance between the individual and the ethnic community. However, one can also assume that structural variables alone provide only a partial explanation that omits the more dynamic processes taking place on a day-to-day basis.

A second source of change stems from the transmission of values over the developmental cycle of the family. Interdependence varies according to the stage of the life cycle and changes resulting from marriages, births, and attrition by deaths. Dependency needs and independence strivings fluctuate in a manner that is presumed to vary by ethnicity because behaviors are regulated by variable values. The identification of this variation comes through group comparisons in which both ethnic background and social class placement are made both within and between groups. Thus, the varied effect of both social class and ethnic background can be determined.

If, in Italian families, childhood dependence changes to an interdependence on the family of origin after marriage and parenthood, rather than independence and the formation of a private, nuclear family, then this family type differs from the model family system of the urban, middle class. Interdependent families in middle age logically would shift their attention from the dependency needs of their children, who are entering adulthood, to the dependency needs of their parents who are in old age. Certainly these processes are complex and tend to be studied from the perspective of one academic discipline at a time. Nevertheless, an attempt is made to integrate these diverse perspectives in the hope that the descriptive accounts that follow, and the inductively derived explanations, will provide a basis for future theory building and hypothesis testing.

Methods of Investigation

The research was designed to collect both qualitative and quantitative data on the family. On the one hand, it was desirable to have an accurate picture of the structure and functions of the family and its extensions in order to make systematic comparisons between groups. On the other hand, since the research problem also centered on the processes by which close family relationships were maintained, relatively open ended techniques were required. Consequently, the methods borrowed features from both sociological and anthropological research. It required adherence to systematic sampling procedures, sample sizes large enough to be subject to statistical analysis, and techniques to transfer qualitative data to measurement. At the same time, every attempt was made to avoid survey techniques with a forced-choice form of questioning.

This book includes quotations from the respondents, so the terminology often follows their usage. For example, Italian Americans usually refer to themselves simply as Italians, so this usage has been followed. Where Italians in Italy are mentioned, it is specified. Also following the respondents, the word *family* is used in many contexts. It refers to a specific constellation in a household, an extended group of relatives, or, in the broadest sense, the blood ties with many individuals in this country and in Italy. Also the term *the family* on occasion took on symbolic, almost mystical meaning.

In selection of the Italian families in the middle stages of the family cycle, marriage records covering 1948 through 1960 were used. Initially, a list of almost 100 common name changes was compiled so that names could be used reliably for identification of ethnic background. Since immigrant status of parents and the mother's maiden name were recorded on marriage licenses at that time, few Italians were omitted from the list. Later contacts indicated that less than 5 percent were incorrectly identified. For the in-married families, 160 names were randomly selected using a table of random numbers and, of these, 47 percent were interviewed. Slightly less than 20 percent refused to be interviewed and 13 percent could not be located. The remaining 20 percent were omitted because of divorce or widowhood. Also, those who had married in middle age were not included, for they were in old age themselves when we contacted them. Every effort was made to interview all of those who were randomly selected by repeated phone calls and home visits.

The intermarriage sample was chosen using the same technique. However, in order to have a matched sample by education, occupation, and family size, some randomly selected families were passed over in order to match them with the in-married families. Of those contacted, the refusal rate was approximately the same.

For the Protestant control group, name identification on marriage licenses could not be used, so wedding announcements in the newspapers during those same years were used. Since they included church affiliation and information on education and occupation, matching with the in-marrieds was facilitated. This group is similar, although there were more high-status families among the Protestants. While there has been no attempt to account for the effects of those social class differences on every measure, the general trends are reported in chapter 3.

A small opportunity sample of middle-class, geographically mobile Italian families was selected through personal contacts and church and suburban directories. Although these twenty-eight families differed in some ways from the geographically stable families, they have not been used in the statistical analysis. For one thing, it was difficult to match them in socioeconomic variables because many wives were college graduates. Also, over half of them had relatives who had followed them or preceded them to the city, so they could not be termed isolated nuclear families. This finding is important in itself, for it suggests chain mobility not totally unlike the emigration from Italy.

The elderly Italian Americans were randomly drawn from voting registers. Since there were time and money limitations, it seemed to be the only source where both age and ethnicity could be identified. We were assured by Italian politicians that Italians have the highest percentage of registered voters of any subgroup in the city. They felt that this applied to the elderly as well. Nevertheless, the results on the elderly must be interpreted carefully, for this subgroup excludes non-citizens and those who have never voted.

Initially, all interviews were with the wives, although in many cases the husband or another family member was present. Husbands were interviewed separately in twenty-six of the in-married families, and twenty-three of the Italian husbands were interviewed in the intermarried group. Most husbands were quite willing, but after forty-nine interviews it was determined that this number provided sufficient data on the male point of view. In a case-by-case analysis, there were few differences between husbands and wives in their descriptions of their families. There were significant differences, however, in the values: husbands tended to have more conservative values on dependency and authority patterns in the family. Otherwise, their reports on the family coincided with their wives. Male informants in the community also discussed the family in detail and these corresponded with those more systematically selected.

In all, 414 individuals were interviewed, of whom one-quarter were used for comparative purposes. These include the following:

In-married Italian families	74 wives and 26 husbands
Intermarried Italian families	98 wives and 23 Italian husbands (Of the wives, 52 were Italian and 46 were non-Italian women who had married Italian men)
Protestant control families	56 wives
Italians over 65 years of age	66 (28 males and 38 females)
Geographically mobile Italian families	28 wives
Informants	43 (community leaders, lay historians, identified as "experts" on the group)

The Italian samples are representative of the geographically stable Italian community. The Protestant families are well matched to the Italian samples. There are three reservations, however. First, since most middle-aged respondents had remained in the same community in which they married, the statistical findings do not reflect the effects of geographic mobility. Second, the elderly were selected from voting registration lists, so noncitizens were excluded. Third, the respondents are predominantly of southern Italian origin—90 percent, which reflects the emigrant distribution nationally, but the interpretations cannot apply to the families of northern Italian origin. These potential sources of bias need to be taken into consideration in an interpretation of the findings, but any potential distortion is far outweighed, in my mind, by the representatives of a sample that is systemically selected. Table 1.1 reports on the social class distribution of these groups and Table 1.2 compares them on other key family variables.

Interviews lasting from two to three hours combined both open-ended and structured questions. Attempts were made to elicit spontaneous responses and to tap qualitative aspects of family life. Thus, the interviewer had considerable leeway in letting the respondent determine the order of topics to be discussed, as long as he or she covered all areas and included all structured questions. If too many digressions took place, the respondent was led back to the pertinent areas.

The format was designed to counteract the problems of "halo effect" through the use of multiple questions in various areas. Projective stories, attitude questions, and the independence measures were particularly useful in addition to the open-ended discussion. Since no great discrepancy was found, however, these are not reported here. The frequent and relatively spontaneous reports of problems and con-

Table 1.1.

Social Class Distribution of Sample Families
(Hollingshead two-factor index, by percentage)

	In-married Italians, n = 74	Out-married Italians, n = 98	Protestant control group, n = 56
Upper middle class	8	6	17
Lower middle class	34	29	45
Upper lower class	50	57	36
Lower lower class	8	8	2

Table 1.2.

Characteristics of the Samples (by means)

	In-married Italians, n = 74	Out-married Italians, n = 98	Protestant control group, n = 56
Age			
husband	47 years	46 years	48 years
wife	42 years	40 years	43 years
Number of children	2.9	3.2	2.8
Age of children	14 years	13 years	16 years
Length of residence in house	11 years	11 years	11 years
Years married	21 years	21 years	21 years

flicts by the respondents suggested that, in most cases, the interviewers were obtaining a fairly accurate and candid portrayal. Notes were taken throughout the interview, which were transcribed in detail after the interview and distributed into the appropriate categories.

In preparation of the data for measurement and statistical analysis, two types of data were used. The factual data, that is, demographic information and objective facts on social contact and assistance patterns among family members, were transposed into measures for analysis. In contrast, the qualitative data were collected through a focused interview in which the respondent talked freely about his or her family. Much of the material on attitudes and values was buried in extensive discussions. Using their notes, the interviewers placed these data into the appropriate category soon after the interview. Then each interview was "blind" coded by two individuals who were not familiar with the research questions. Using this technique, a measure could be attached to such important categories as filial responsibilities or values on discipline. Since the coders agreed an average of 80 percent of the time, their coding sheets were alternated in obtaining the measures.

In constructing this coding sheet, all items on the interview form were examined for their relevance to our research questions. The items that contributed logically to the interdependence measure were

assigned numerical values with a higher number signifying higher interdependence. As an example of how the data were measured, a high
score for the relationship of a son or daughter with elderly parents included residence with respondent, positive values on obligation to parents, high level of services to parents, no perception of problems if
parents should live with them, rejection of the nursing home option,
high expectations for their children's future obligation, and rejection
of mobility for oneself or one's children. These measures could then
be correlated with other variables both within and between samples.

Of course, any work is fraught with the biases of the interviewers
and the investigator who analyzes the data and reports it. I have tried
to keep mine to a minimum by letting the respondents speak for themselves. Where I might have erred is in the deemphasis of negative
views of the Italian family. However, criticisms more often came from
non-Italian spouses, so most are contained within one chapter on intermarriage. In any case, an emphasis on strengths over weaknesses is
probably overdue in family studies, particularly with ethnic or blue-
collar groups where depictions too frequently are less flattering. Furthermore, a discussion of types of families best equipped to serve their
elderly members inevitably places more emphasis on positive rather
than negative dimensions.

Overview

The first part of the book includes a description of the research setting.
Chapter 2 provides the history of immigration and the slow but steady
integration of Italian Americans into the institutions of the broader
community as their educational and occupational skills increased.
Chapter 3 examines the major structural variables associated with family differences. Social class and intermarriage are used to examine
variations in various dimensions of the family. The small sample of
geographically mobile Italians is also described to indicate the patterns
of family organization of those who moved away from the family of
origin. Finally, generation level is examined as a possible source of
variation on the Italian family.

Part 2 includes six chapters describing the dominant characteristics
of the average Italian-American family as it differs from the intermarried and the Protestant families. Most descriptions are based on a
modal type reflecting the largest percentages of respondents, and vari-

ations are discussed from that point of view. The section begins in chapter 4 with the kinship system and the sentiments and supports exchanged between nuclear households. One family's genealogy is used to indicate the demographic changes that have taken place over the past four generations and the types of interaction found among its two hundred members today. The life passage and calendric rituals are described in chapter 5, while chapters 6 and 7 deal with marriage. Chapter 6 describes families in which both spouses are Italian, and chapter 7 reports on intermarriage and the considerable adjustments that must be made to cultural differences. This section concludes with a discussion of aging and the Italian family. Chapter 8 describes the elderly Italians, their old-fashioned ways, and their expectations for their children and relatives. The responses of the children as they accommodate to these Old World ways are described in chapter 9.

Part 3 contains an analysis of the processes by which ethnicity continues to determine the configuration of the Italian-American family. The childrearing practices used with adolescent children are described in chapter 10, concentrating on the parental role and its patterning of affection and authority. Continuities in these socialization processes are traced in the relationship between elderly parents and their middle-aged offspring in chapter 11.

The final chapter synthesizes the findings and suggests some practical applications. Throughout this book, generalizations are based on statistical confirmation of tests of significant group differences or correlations. However, many statistical findings have gone unreported because my intention has been to provide a description and interpretation that best approach the qualitative side to Italian-American family life.

Chapter 2
The Old World
and the Immigration
Experience

Origins in Southern Italy

The places of origin of at least 80 percent of the Italian immigrants to the United States were the provinces east and south of Rome. This region is referred to as the *Mezzogiorno*, which is freely translated as "the land that time forgot" (Gambino 1974). Long noted for its insularity, these provinces were relatively immune from wars of unification and the social and political changes taking place elsewhere in Italy. Adverse environmental features such as the mountainous terrain, the paucity of arable land, soil erosion, low rainfall, and intermittent droughts contributed to the absence of economic development (Lopreato 1970). The peasant class, who made up the bulk of those who later emmigrated, were the primary victims of these physical forces. Around the turn of the century, their condition was described as destitute. In their ceaseless struggle to survive, these peasants referred to their lives as *La miseria* or misery.

In addition to these physical factors, the social and economic conditions in southern Italy further compounded their problems. Until late in the nineteenth century, southern Italy remained a collection of warring states often dominated by a foreign power (Nelli 1980). A feudal social structure persisted with political power resting upon the hereditary ownership of land. Absentee landlords, sometimes with the support of the clergy, tended to exploit the peasants. For example, the average worker received daily wages averaging only sixteen to thirty cents. Those peasants who owned their land were no better off, for they were subject to heavy taxation as well as to the subdivision of the land with each generation (Lopreato 1970).

Late in the nineteenth century after unification of the country, the peasants' situation was worse in some ways. The northern-dominated central government used discriminatory practices in trade, industry, and agriculture. Problems were compounded by a rapid population growth and a subsequent decline in per capita income in the south. The peasants were affected by crop failures, increasing competition for agricultural markets, and the failure of absentee landlords to improve the land or to adopt more modern agricultural methods. One of the few options open to many peasants was emigration so, not surprisingly, they were receptive to the labor recruiters who first came to extol the riches of the New World (Iorizzo and Mondello 1971).

For centuries, southern Italians lived in small villages usually perched on hillsides above their fields. Referred to as the *companilisimo*, or those who lived within the sound of the church bells, town living protected the inhabitants from roving bands of marauders and from the malaria-breeding swamps below (Iorizzo and Mondello 1971). Houses were described as hovels or huts in which families were densely packed in a few rooms above the ground floor, where livestock was housed. Males were often forced to walk miles to their small plots of land each day.

A typical village consisted of four major classes. The highest class, 1 or 2 percent of the population, consisted of gentry, landowners, physicians, lawyers, and the priest. Below them, the craftsmen, shopowners, and minor officials made up a middle class of less than 10 percent. The remaining 88 percent were the peasants, of whom only 15 percent owned small plots of land (Lopreato 1970). The domination of so many by so few prevented social mobility, education, and the acquisition of skills needed for the modern economy developing elsewhere.

These characteristics have been found to persist today. A popular interpretation of the world view which grew out of this social structure is espoused by Edward Banfield (1958), who terms it as an ethos of "amoral familism." In his words, "The extreme poverty and backwardness of which is to be explained largely, but not entirely, by the inability of the villagers to act together for the common good or, indeed, for any end transcending the immediate material interests of the nuclear family" (pp. 9–10). He hypothesized that in the village he studied, the rule was, "Maximize the material, short-run advantages of the nuclear family; assume that all others will do likewise" (p. 83). Since individual actions were geared only to the advantage of a small number of people, the development of more integrative social and political organizations did not materialize.

This view has been used extensively by economists and political scientists in more recent studies of southern Italy. Constance Cronin (1970) also explored its implication for the extended family system in Sicily. In agreement with others, she concluded that the nuclear family is the basic social unit. Relationships with kin are peripheral and primarily cemented by the concept of *onore*. She found that associations with relatives largely center upon decisions about marriages of children. Since family honor rests upon the virginity of its unmarried females, relatives work together to maintain the chastity of its women and to further the formation of marriages that enhance the family's reputation.

This ethos has also been associated with the southern Italian value system, which is characteristic of peasant cultures in general. In their subjugation to nature, individuals attribute their situation to fate and the erratic forces beyond their control. Since fate determines one's life chances, life is seen as immutable and uncertain. At the mercies of the government, the clergy, and the landowners, peasants tend to develop a mistrust of those outside the nuclear family. Basic human nature is also suspect, so that even one's relationships with the family require constant vigilance and control (Cohler and Grunebaum 1981; Giovannini 1978; Papajohn and Spiegel 1975; Schooler 1976). In most respects the value system of the Italian immigrants differed markedly from New World values which prized self-direction, optimism, and individualistic achievement.

Immigration to the United States

Between 1810 and 1820, the decade when immigration statistics were first compiled, 439 came to the U.S. from Italy (Nelli 1980). By 1860, only 14,000 Italians had been recorded, the majority of whom came from northern Italy. After 1880, however, large numbers of men came from southern Italy, and by 1901 southerners comprised 83 percent of the Italian immigrants. Of all European immigrants during those years, Italians had the smallest percentages of women and children. These men were described as "birds of passage," whose goal was to stay for a few years, save their money, and return to their villages. Over one-half, in fact, did return; while 3.8 million came between 1899 and 1924, 2.1 million departed during those years. The peak immigration was between 1901 and 1910, when over

2 million arrived, many of whom were women and children (Nelli 1980). Thus, for those who remained in this country, immigration was stabilized as families began to form.

Most of the immigrants in the early twentieth century settled in urban areas of the Northeast, although settlements of Italians eventually were formed throughout the country. During the peak years of immigration, 97 percent of the Italians entered the United States through New York City and, according to Humbert Nelli (1980), those who remained there gave the city the largest Italian population of any city in this country, and even larger than the combined populations of Florence, Venice, and Genoa. Of all immigrant groups from 1820 to 1967, Italians ranked second highest with over five million individuals. The present population is more difficult to ascertain because third-generation descendants are not counted in the national census. Estimates range greatly from seven million to twenty million, but Italian Americans are identified as the largest ethnic group of European heritage (Monticelli 1967).

Over 80 percent came from southern Italy, where conditions prevented the acquisition of education or skills. For example, around one-half of the immigrants were illiterate, most of whom had known only farm labor, and few knew any English. In comparison to other immigrants, Italians comprised a very small percentage of skilled laborers. In 1907, Italians were only 1 in 150 arriving plumbers, 1 in 26 plasterers, 1 in 74 locksmiths, and 1 in 38 machinists (Foerster 1919). Considering the fact that, in 1901, the average amount of money the Italian immigrants declared to immigration officials was $12.67, settlement in America presented great challenges.

The Italian immigration to this country has been described as a chain migration (McDonald and McDonald, 1964) in which the earliest members of a town facilitated the immigration of fellow townspeople. Letters home or return visits spread information on the New World and others decided to follow. Fellow townspeople, or *paesani*, assisted later arrivals in finding jobs and places to live until they were self-sufficient. This chain migration fostered a sense of cooperation and sociability which seems alien to the ethos of amoral familism described for southern Italian towns. Some observers conclude that as *paesani* became more interdependent and reciprocal in relationships with each other in this country, old suspicions and mistrusts broke down (Cohler and Grunebaum 1981; McDonald and McDonald

1964). Certainly these chain migrations are evident in Easton, the site of this research, in the residential concentrations of townspeople and in the formation of mutual aid societies.

The shared identity among *paesani* suggests that the social organization in this country developed into a different form than that found in southern Italy. The growing significance of the extended family is another expression of wider sources of identity. Since early patterns of marriage were endogamous to urban neighborhoods (Lalli 1969), this bond was reaffirmed as customs, beliefs, and values growing out of the New World experiences, rather than the country of origin, were transmitted to subsequent generations. For this reason, those doing research on Italian Americans have difficulty applying Banfield's concept of amoral families to Italians in this country. The following description of the immigration experience in Easton suggests that the Italian immigrants initially formed units of solidarity with relatives and *paesani* in a form quite divergent from that described in Italy.

Settlement in Easton

Easton is a northeastern city that has a population of 180,000 in the city itself and a slightly larger population in the surrounding suburbs. Like other cities in the region, it has a large proportion of European ethnic groups which contributes to a population in which the majority (54 percent) is Catholic. The largest of these groups is Italian, estimated to be 20 to 25 percent of the city's population. The black population is approximately 10 percent, while 7 percent are Jewish. Thus, in the city itself, only 29 percent are white Protestants, although they are a majority in many suburbs.

The history of this city has been amply documented by the local historical society, newspapers, and several theses and dissertations. The area was originally settled by the veterans of the Revolutionary War who were mainly British and Scotch-Irish. By the 1840s, Irish and German immigrants began to arrive to work on transportation projects and a small Jewish community was formed of middle-class German immigrants. By 1880, the city had over fifty thousand residents, of whom only twenty-seven had Italian surnames. Among the occupations listed for these early Italian residents were musician, vendor, and organ grinder.

The Italian immigration to the city paralleled the national pattern. A large influx of Italians began around 1890 when laborers were recruited to build a railroad. When the need for additional laborers arose, an Italian foreman became an agent to recruit cheap labor. For the newly arriving Italians, predominantly men who came alone, he assumed the role of *padrone,* or "il bosso," arranging for their housing, banking, and assorted services. Unlike the proverbial picture of a *padrone* as one who acted as a slave master over helpless underlings, this *padrone* in Easton apparently served more to facilitate adaptation. He opened boarding houses, a saloon, a grocery store, and a bank to help channel money back to Italy or arrange for passages for other family members. In the early 1900s, his bank reported the average savings account of an Italian laborer to be sixty-three dollars, which equalled over two month's pay for the average immigrant. The *padrone* was paternalistic, however, for he did not pay interest on these accounts because of the added services he provided.

The thousands of Italians who arrived in Easton in a relatively short time settled on the north side of the city. They had a lifestyle sufficiently different from the rest of the residents to interest the city considerably. Early newspaper accounts described the new "Little Italy" as a "densely populated life-teaming corner of our city." To one reporter, it was like entering a foreign country where only Italian was spoken. He reported in 1899 that there were two individuals who were kept busy reading letters and writing news home for the illiterate immigrants. They generally functioned as the communication link between the old country and the new.

During this period, the newspaper accounts of the growing population were mostly prejudicial and condescending. The Italian neighborhoods were described as a "source of suffering and sorrow and sin," as reporters attempted to provide a "glimpse of Italy that's not so fair as the sunny clime we read of." Another reporter concluded that "They are, on the whole, a simple-minded race, primitive in their emotions and passions . . . easily led by their feelings." Italians were also referred to in these newspapers as "dark," "dusky," and "dirty." There was a repeated complaint about what was perceived as their resistance to learning English. The men who immigrated without their families did not escape the notice of the journalists. According to one reporter, the boarding houses in which they lived were viewed as less than human. "One hundred and fifty men pay five cents a day for a diet of bread only. Then they wrap themselves in their blankets or shawls and lie down on the floor at night and huddle together like hogs."

As male immigrants found jobs and their economic prospects became more secure, they turned to the expansion of their families. Between 1900 and 1910, wives and prospective brides began to arrive in large numbers, so that the ethnic community changed markedly from one of single men to two- or even three-generation families.

A newspaper article during this era described a typical family dwelling as simple and overcrowded. A large family might live in two rooms, with the kitchen also serving as a dining room, parlor, and work room in which women and children made dresses and overalls for nearby factories to supplement the father's pay. The second room was reserved for sleeping and for the repository of the family's valuables, including crucifixes and pictures of the Virgin Mary and patron saints that hung on the walls. It was reported that these rooms housed not only the mother and father and their children, but also other relatives, especially new arrivals from Italy.

Interviews with older respondents suggest that the means by which they immigrated, formed families, and settled were quite varied. Some men sent home to the village in Italy for a bride; others returned to the village to look for one; still others met and married the sister of a *paesano* living in Easton. Married men often sent for family members one at a time or made intermittent trips to Italy for them until all members were reunited.

In some cases there were permanent separations. For example, Antonio Tomasino came here with his father in 1921 at the age of thirteen, while his mother, brothers, and sisters stayed behind in Italy. With the ban on emigration of males in 1924, his older brothers were unable to come, so his father returned permanently to Italy, leaving Antonio here with other relatives.

Occasionally wives resisted leaving their families. Rosa Nestino reported that she remained in southern Italy after her marriage in 1921. Except for his intermittent visits, she and her husband were separated for twenty-seven years. When she finally joined him in Easton in 1948, she came with their three adult children (who had been conceived on his periodic visits). This belated immigration was encouraged by a cousin who warned her that if she did not settle with her husband in America, he would find another woman.

Financial resources, wars, and political conditions sometimes kept families separated for years. The examples above of the sporadic breaking up and reunification of some families indicate that immigration was not an irreversible break with the Old Country. Nevertheless, the majority of families expanded through the arrival of wives, children, and relatives. New arrivals often lived with kin until the men found jobs; then they usually settled in houses or apartments nearby. (This chain migration is illustrated in more detail in chapter 4 through a history of one extended family.)

The expansion of the Italian community from single men to families took place over three decades. During these years the community at large gradually accepted the Italians. For example, credit was given to Italians for early signs of patriotism to their new nation when Italian women sacrificed their wedding rings for the war effort in 1917. In 1929 an article concluded that "some of the fairest maidens of the city are of Italian background, who typify an amalgamation of the races which make them indistinguishable from Yankee girls."

Adaptive Responses to the Immigration Experience

The early Italian settlers had to fashion institutions to fill the vacuum created by their break with the tightly knit, family-based society in Italy. The paternalistic *padrone* provided some community supports until his death in 1905. He housed many single men, fed them, and saw to their material needs. Like the *padrone* described by Luciano Iorizzo and Salvatore Mondello (1971), he provided the buffer until families were formed, and he also acted as a cultural broker to the dominant group. In the meantime, Italians had other resources in their *paesani*, their fellow townspeople, and the *compariggio*, their godparents. These relationships were particularly important because of the insular character of southern Italian culture which made this immigrant group less prepared than most in Easton for adaptation to the urban environment. Instead of amoral familism, however, some observers conclude that primary relationships outside the nuclear family expanded with immigration, so that the extended family was more significant in this country (Cohler and Grunebaum 1981).

Using a rough measure based on a random sample of Italian Americans who married in the 1950s, one can estimate that in Easton approximately 90 percent of their forebears came from southern Italy, an area south and east of Rome. Of these, 20 percent came from Sicily. Older respondents report that settlement in the city was made by

immigrants from a limited number of towns in southern Italy. One elderly historical buff reported that, in the early years, people from eight
towns in Italy made up the bulk of the community. Even today some
streets and neighborhoods are still informally identified by the names
of the village of origin of the first Italian residents. Certainly such a
concentration of *paesani* from the same towns strengthened the link to
the Old World.

A second result of this settlement pattern is evident in the mutual
aid societies among the *paesani* which developed spontaneously to
provide both the material and psychological support to new arrivals.
After the family, these loose organizations were the major unit of support for newcomers. Marriages were formed among the townspeople.
Regional dialects were maintained and, in fact, persist today. Nelli
(1967) concludes that these support systems, which developed in response to the new urban environment, were interim institutions that resembled neither an American community structure nor a southern Italian one.

In addition to the *paesani* network, the *compariggio*, or the godparent system, also expanded the family resources of the early immigrants. This system performed a useful function in creating quasi-kin
relationships out of friendships. In the early years, godparents for
one's children were usually selected among the *paesani*. If a married
couple came to America at a young age, they sometimes selected new
godparents for themselves as well as for their children to substitute for
those left behind in Italy. One elderly respondent told of how important this tie was:

> *My husband and I were the only ones of our family to come
> here. My new godmother became a second mother to me. Any
> time we visited, it was a big feast. If it hadn't been for my* com-
> pare *and* comare, *I would have been lost in those early years
> in America.*

Godparents were selected according to several principles. One
might select a close friend, usually a *paesano,* who could immediately
perform kinship roles of support and sociability. Others selected persons of importance in the community who could further the family's
interests. Still others used the custom not only to select a godparent
for a child, but also to create a special relationship for themselves.
One respondent described the southern Italian tradition of having sev-

eral different kinds of godparents. For example, the *comare* of the *capola* was the one who cut the baby's fingernails for the first time and purchased the first hat. In other cases, two adults made an informal vow to be godparents to each other. Women might send each other flowers and then begin calling each other *comare*.

Of greatest interest is the process by which the *compariggio* created quasi-kin relationships among the immigrants to help them through the period of adaptation. The older respondents often emphasized the importance of this source of support in the early years as a compensation for the loss of family. Once the extended family was established, however, the selection of godparents was more likely to be confined to relatives. (This important institution in its contemporary form will be described in chapter 5.)

The first nationality or ethnic Catholic parish for Italians, St. Paul's, opened its doors in Easton in 1893. The parish began by serving an immigrant population and, in fact, today continues to serve immigrants who had come decades ago. A second church, St. Teresa's, was founded some years later only a few blocks away. While these churches are a source of cohesion in the community today, it is uncertain how important they were in the early stages of adaptation. For one thing, many people were only nominal members of the church. A survey in 1910 showed that St. Paul's had 5,900 members, which represented 84 percent of the Italian population at the time. However, a local history of the diocese reports that, despite the large numbers of members, only 800 were regular churchgoers. This report also states that attempts to proselytize among Italians were unsuccessful and recommended that they be abandoned.

Italians, however, remained overwhelmingly Catholic. By 1936 there was one Protestant Italian church, but its members totalled only 1 percent of the population. Older respondents reported early Protestant missionary activity in Italian neighborhoods, which included charitable works for needy families. Some conversions were made, and one affluent Protestant Italian family attributed their success to early assistance by their church.

Clashes with other immigrant groups most likely hindered the influence of the Catholic church. The church in this country was dominated by Irish clergy (Herberg 1955) who were often unresponsive to the needs of the Italian immigrants. In any case, many Italians were limited to their own national parishes. In fact, older respondents recount outright exclusionary practices in some German Catholic parishes on the Northside, a condition that further discouraged assimilation.

Political organizations as an ethnic interest group came somewhat later, probably delayed by the persisting insularity of the informal societies based on village origins. Once formed in the 1920s, however, these organizations acted as a source of integration into the wider community. One ninety-six-year-old former leader in the Italian community described the events that led to the first effective political interest group. In 1924 he was approached by a highly placed Republican, he recounted, "who told us to get busy and do something for ourselves." It so happened that the Republicans were facing a tight race for the mayor's election. Thirty-six Italians responded by forming a political club that solicited 700 members at dues of one dollar each. When the Republican candidate won by 700 votes, city jobs for the first time became open to Italians in sufficient numbers. This leader concluded that "It put a fire under everyone and eventually it led to a place of power for us in the community." His report is confirmed by a survey in 1933, which reported a high percentage of Italian voters in the city and no less than fourteen active political organizations.

Occupational and Educational Patterns

The rural background of most of the immigrants left them ill-prepared to find work in their new urban setting. Many of the earliest immigrants were recruited specifically for work on big projects such as the railroads. When these projects ended, the men had to rely on their relatives and *paesani* for contacts that would lead to jobs. In any case, Italian immigrants generally got the hardest, lowest paying jobs. The older men remember the rigorous work well. "We had the worst jobs—the pick and shovel type—we worked in ditches. We had the dirtiest jobs, but we survived." "We had to fight for everything. Nothing was handed us on a silver platter." "We Italians suffered to make America great. We built your railroad, bridges, highways. We worked like animals and earned very little money."

It was common for the men to hold many different jobs over the years as they sought better opportunities or, more adversely, were subject to periodic layoffs. There are many success stories. For example, the Italians came to dominate in the produce business, which had previously been a stronghold of the Germans. Some enterprising Italians formed their own small businesses, which later grew into large enterprises. One respondent gained experience helping a man lay linoleum. At the age of seventeen, he went into business for himself and later expanded his work to include carpeting. Eventually, the concern employed seventy people.

A few immigrants changed careers several times, moving back and forth between the Italian community and the city at large. One successful respondent went to Easton in 1904 at the age of twenty-three and began working nights at a chemical factory, cleaning out vats. He went to school in the afternoons and even started a grocery store. This store failed, but he continued his schooling despite reporting a difficulty in learning English. Nevertheless, this enterprising man went on to finish college and, in the meantime, went slowly up the ladder of a bank. By 1927 he became an officer, at which time he concluded that, as an Italian, he could go no further. Even though he brought the bank five million dollars of business from the Italian community, he reported that he and his wife were never completely accepted by the bankers. Consequently, he formed his own insurance company to serve the ethnic community and, at the age of ninety-five, enjoyed a prosperous and prestigious position among Italians.

Most immigrants, however, were neither as ambitious nor as fortunate. Mr. Germinio had four years of education in Italy before immigrating in 1910. He reported that his first job was in a shoe factory at $3.50 a week. He went on to a casket company at $6 a week, after which he made steady advances by changing jobs. He earned $16 a week as a machinist. By the mid-1920s, he was working at the Franklin Car Company at $75 a week. This prosperity suddenly ended when the company closed in 1927, and it took years to recover the losses, particularly during the depression years. After advances and reversals, he was able to retire as a foreman in 1950.

While most men now in old age stayed within blue-collar jobs, their occupational histories showed progressive acquisition of skills, leading them to more remunerative employment. Three-quarters of the respondents over sixty-five retired from skilled jobs, while only 6 percent had risen to white-collar or professional positions.

Since the average wages of the day were too low to support a family, women and children had to work as well. Piecework in the needle trades done in the home was the most preferred form, although women and older daughters also went to work in smaller enterprises outside the home, such as a knitting mill, a men's suit factory, and a glove and pocketbook factory. Their work histories were sporadic and, as children came, more and more of them endeavored to remain at home. Interestingly, Italian women rarely worked as domestics, an occupational choice typical of other immigrant groups (McLaughlin 1971). In the summer, women and children often went into the fields and, under the supervision of a male relative, picked fruit and vegetables. In general, when women worked, the jobs available to them were closely identified with their traditional activities, and they rarely went far from home or the watchful eye of the family.

As early as possible, children replaced the mother as the earner of a supplemental income. At seven or eight years of age, some children began selling newspapers or doing odd jobs. As they moved into adolescence, work took increasing priority, school became less important, and many children dropped out of school as early as the laws would permit. If the child continued in school, his life was often hard. Vincenzo Mantaro arrived in this country when he was eight years old and began selling newspapers immediately:

My day began at 4 A.M. and at 7:45, I had to be back home to get ready for school. After school at 3:30, I was back on my corner and sometimes stayed until midnight. My sister gave her unopened pay envelope to my parents until the day she got married. I gave them everything I earned, too. Family cooperation was an absolute necessity for survival in those days. The twelve cents I earned each day went to my mother for food. At that time, bread was three cents a loaf, five cents bought five pounds of potatoes, and for a penny a pound we could buy in a load of tomatoes for sauce. Our food didn't make a rich man's meal, but it was delicious.

The insularity of the Italian community and the high commitment to work for the economic success of the family often clashed with educational institutions of the community. Schools in those early days prided themselves in being agents not only of social mobility but also of assimilation, a force often at odds with the goals of the family.

There have been studies of achievement that place Italians near the bottom in comparison to other European groups (Rosen 1959). In the early years, educators blamed deficient racial or cultural background or deficient parenting, which permitted and even encouraged truancy. Later analyses assigned the blame more objectively to cultural factors originating in southern Italy, which posed value conflicts to American patterns of achievement (Psathas 1968; Rosen 1959; Schooler 1976; Strodtbeck, McDonald, and Rosen 1957; Ulin 1968).

Schooling in America differed markedly from that of southern Italy where any education past three to five years was necessary only for training in the priesthood or the professions—goals that were out of reach for the peasants. School officials and social workers in this country were highly critical of the tendency of Italian parents to take their children out of school at a young age to work (Odenkrantz 1919). Leonard Covello (1967), a New York City school principal, concluded that the acculturative functions of education posed a threat to the family-centered Italians, a conclusion also reached by later observers (Cordasco and Bucchioni, 1974: 479–565; Lopreato 1970; Nelli 1970).

A discrepancy between Old World and New World values has been traced to the fact that work for the average Italian, not education, was more than a basic necessity; it was also the major source of respect. In the relentless drive for the family's economic independence, all family members were expected to contribute. If a choice had to be made between a mother or a child working, family goals dictated that it be the child since the mother played a far more central role in the maintenance of family integration. Thus, it was not so much that schools were rejected, but that work had more meaning. Richard Gambino (1974:80) has noted that,

> To Italian immigrants and their descendants today, work involves more than questions of economics. Work is regarded as moral training for the young. And among adults, it is regarded as a matter of pride. To work is to show that one has become a man or a woman, a full member of the family. So strong is the ethic that it governs behavior quite apart from considerations of monetary gain.

In the adult-centered immigrant family, adolescence as a separate and distinct time of life was virtually unrecognized (Ianni 1961). At an early point in their teens, children were thought to have reached maturity and thus a time for work and contribution to family income. The fact that schools incorporated athletics and social activities into the curriculum seemed incomprehensible to parents who viewed work as the primary goal.

Even younger men have told of having difficulties in adapting to school because they lacked the knowledge and understanding of

American institutions in general. Anthony Manzi, a successful man in his forties who holds a doctoral degree, describes his earlier education:

> *Here I am, an American success story and I can't figure out how I got here. After running wild with slick greasy hair and the teenage gangs, something happened to me. I mean I began to look for role models. I got out of the Italian neighborhood and sought out Jews for friends.*

> *In high school I was president of the honor society, student council member, and voted outstanding senior in the country. I had many scholarship offers, even one from Williams. But then I didn't know the prestige of the school. I found out in graduate school. I went to a small college because my girlfriend went there. I wandered into graduate school without even knowing what a master's degree was.*

> *No one in my family knew anything about this. "Only Americans do such things," they said. I could have gone into medicine if my family knew how to do it. Italians didn't use banks, other institutions, because they didn't know how—that was for the Americans. When I was in trouble in school, mother just spanked me for being disrespectful to the teacher and never questioned it. It was a foreign environment to her.*

In summary, historical reports and life histories of Italian immigrants suggest that the lines were clearly drawn between the world of the family, with the ethnic community, and the outside world. Often the outside world was viewed in terms of "some kind of ominous threat out there" (Stone 1978:42). This orientation has been traced to the culture of southern Italy which, in its insularity and traditionalism, made the immigrants ill prepared for adapting to American institutions and for transmitting adaptive strategies to their children. Nevertheless, as the following section indicates, selective changes have modified the immigrant culture markedly.

The Italian Community Today

From almost every perspective, the Italian community today differs from that of the immigrants, yet ethnic characteristics remain observable. The Italian population still tends to be concentrated on Easton's

Northside and in adjacent suburbs. There is still a distinct Italian section of the city, a "Little Italy," which retains much of the flavor of
the old country. There are two active Italian churches in the neighborhood, along with numerous Italian cafés and restaurants. The area
gives a good impression of stability; houses, however modest, are well
maintained and lawns and gardens flourish. Patterns of sociability are
observable on the streets, even well into the evening when one might
expect residents who are fearful of crime to stay at home. One's first
impression is that the ethnic neighborhood has been retained through
the generations in this country as the basis of solidarity and continuity.

On closer examination, however, one finds that the Italian flavor of
the neighborhood is created, not only by second- and third-generation
Italian Americans, but by recent immigrants from Italy. Each month,
the largest numbers of new citizens settling in the city come from
Italy, and these individuals tend to live around the Italian-speaking
churches, cafés, schools, and businesses. Some observers have commented that today the Northside looks more like the early 1900s than
it has in any intervening decade.

Residential segregation suggests a centripetal force in maintaining
ethnic affiliation. In locating the sample families sixteen to twenty-
eight years after their marriages, we found that almost one-third had
remained in the old Italian neighborhood near their parents and the
childhood home. Another 37 percent had moved to the suburbs that
bordered the Northside, a short ten minutes away by car. An additional 18 percent lived in the western suburbs near the original area of
settlement of a second group of Italians who came from the northern
areas of Piedmont and Tyrolia. All told, only 12 percent of the families in the sample settled in neighborhoods outside these two original
areas of settlement and their adjacent suburbs. One can conclude that
those who remained in the region after marriage have a marked propensity to stay near the old family home and childhood friends. As a
result, very few older parents are without children and relatives nearby.

The two nationality parishes are also flourishing today. The older one
serves the new immigrant population and many elderly Italians. It has
an active senior citizens' group and is raising funds to build senior citizens' housing on its property. The second church, St. Teresa's, with its
many second- and third-generation families, maintains a school and an
active calendar of social activities. Of the younger Italians who moved
to the suburbs, many still return to this parish each Sunday, and, at great

inconvenience, some families even continue to send their children back
to the parochial school.

The respondents remain predominantly Catholic; only 4 percent are
Protestant. In the intermarried families, this percentage increases to 10
percent, which signifies no great movement to the religion of the dominant group. In other indicators of religiosity, the Catholic schools are
used by 35 percent of the families, a higher proportion than Catholics in
general (Greeley 1977). Comparisons of church attendance today with
past attendance estimates that Italian Americans in this research attend
church more regularly than their parents did.

Increased church attendance sometimes is used as an indicator of assimilation of Italians into the mainstream of American Catholocism
(Russo 1969). However, in an examination of the level of religiosity of
the sample families, church attendance was not found to be associated
with other variables of family life except that regular church attenders
were more conservative in values on authority and independence. This
suggests that the church stands for more conservative values on family
life and thus is more compatible to Italian views than are most other institutions. Those living in the older sections of the city find the church
and its schools particularly important as islands of stability in rapidly
changing neighborhoods.

Italian Americans also maintain active, ethnically based political interest groups. Their effectiveness is documented by the numerous Italians who have been elected to state and local offices. The importance of
politics to the average Italian American is evident as well. On election
days, St. Teresa's school is dismissed and the cafeteria is used for a
large spaghetti lunch where voters can meet Italian candidates.

The mutual aid societies among *paesani* were one of the first casual-
ties of assimilation because they were essentially first-generation institutions (Juliani 1973). Replacing them today are such organizations as
the Sons of Italy and the Daughters of Columbus, which are highly visible service clubs although they do not have wide appeal to the average
Italian.

These social patterns greatly increase the likelihood that a family's
social network will be dominanted by other Italians. The fact that Italians remain residentially concentrated means that one's neighbors are
likely to be Italian, that one finds fellow Italians at church, and that
one's children meet them at school. Even Italians who intermarried
were not found to differ significantly in this settlement pattern.

Although Italian Americans still prefer living in or near the old neighborhoods, their standard of living and lifestyle are far different from that of the immigrants. For one thing, the most visible insignia of ethnicity has been diminishing over the years: the Italian language is rarely spoken by the second generation and is virtually incomprehensible to the third. Clothing and house styles are no longer easily distinguishable. Although Italian Americans still call out old card games, music, and other ethnic entertainments for annual festivals, these patterns are not usually evident at other times. What remains uniquely Italian is food; most prefer pasta over potatoes and wine over beer or hard liquor.

Centrifugal forces, on the other hand, can be found in the high rates of social mobility in the second- and third-generation families. Greeley (1977) reports that, for the country as a whole, Italians are near the national average, being slightly lower in education levels and slightly higher in income. These national figures are reflected in the sample characteristics reported in Table 2.1, although rates of occupational mobility are somewhat higher in Easton. Among Italian men in Easton, 42 percent remain in blue-collar or unskilled occupations in comparison to 52 percent of Italian Americans nationally. Another 39 percent are in white-collar positions or are small-business proprietors, while 13 percent are now working in professional or managerial occupations. Of the women who work, only 2 percent hold professional positions such as teaching or nursing. The early opposition by Italian men to women working apparently has less effect today, for over half of the women in the sample hold a part-time or full-time job. One can conclude that as their children mature, Italian women, like others today, seek positions outside the home.

These dilemmas in regard to education are also less prominent. Nationally, Italian Americans stand slightly below the average in education (Greeley 1977), where one-half of the Italian-American males have not completed high school. In this sample, half of the males in their forties had graduated from high school. While 20 percent had also gone on to college, only 7 percent had received college degrees and 5 percent had completed graduate training. Italian women were considerably behind in education in comparison to non-Italians participating in the research, for only 10 percent had gone to college.

When schooling and jobs remove individuals from the ethnic community for large segments of time, it is inevitable that the Old World ways begin to diminish. One of the earliest effects can be seen in the rates of intermarriage (Abramson 1973). The sampling procedures required an examination of all marriage licenses involving Italians in the

Table 2.1.
Social Class Indicators

	Occupation, by percentage	
	Italian men, n = 120	Italian women, n = 126
Professional, managerial, proprietors	13	2
White collar (clerical, sales, technician), small proprietors	39	40
Blue collar (skilled workers)	39	11
Unskilled workers	3	4
Retired/Unemployed	6	43
	Education, by percentage	
Graduate degree	5	1
College degree	7	2
Partial college training	11	7
High school diploma	50	63
Partial high school	18	21
Grammar school or partial	9	6

even years between 1948 and 1960. In 1948, 42 percent of all marriages took place with non-Italians, a rate that increased to 59 percent in 1960. Whereas in 1948 the proportion of men and women marrying out was equal, over the next twelve years 10 percent more women than men were choosing non-Italian spouses. In a casual reading of recent wedding notices, one can tentatively conclude that intermarriage rates are even higher today.

Nevertheless, the Italians in the sample overwhelmingly chose other Catholics; only 7 percent married Protestants. The most frequent choice (24 percent) was the Irish, while an equal percentage married those of no identifiable ethnic background. Thus, at least one-half selected marriage partners from a more assimilated segment of society. Italians who did marry out, however, chose mates of similar socioeconomic status. Respondents from blue-collar families married those of blue-collar status, and the same holds true for those in the middle class.

This analysis of social mobility and intermarriage indicates forces for assimilation. The structural variables can operate as centrifugal forces to loosen boundaries around the ethnic group. Through the formation of relationships with outsiders, Italians are exposed to differing values and lifestyles. In one sense, the decades since the first immigrants arrived in Easton have witnessed a progressive diminution of the most visible insignia of ethnicity, such as language usage. Over the years, the insularity of the Italian community has also diminished. As involvement in American institutions has increased, the mistrust of the outside world has lessened; and thus today few parents or children view educational and occupational aspirations as a threat to the family.

As a result of the other structural variables, however, centripetal tendencies continue to tighten the boundaries around the group. The residential pattern discussed above is one of the more important, for it assures that one's primary relationships remain dominated by relatives and other Italians. Additionally, church affiliation, important to many Italians today, is likely to signify a greater statement of ethnic identity, at least as it serves to perpetuate traditional values. Religious participation also provides a vehicle for keeping up with traditional rituals and celebrations.

There was some observational and anecdotal evidence that Italians still face prejudice and discrimination, but the degree to which these restrictions deter assimilation is difficult to determine. When asked directly, respondents rarely discussed prejudice in detail, even with Italian interviewers. Those incidents reported were the more subtle forms of discrimination, such as an unfriendly reception when one moved into a new neighborhood. Some executives in local businesses concluded that being Italian excluded them from the upper echelons of management. Some children were exposed to ethnic epithets at school. There was also a general consensus that several prestigious clubs had never admitted Italian members. Even a country club that is largely Catholic is said to discourage Italian applicants. One Italian banker noted that after being called "Italian," "wop," and "dago" all his life, he had to go back to Italy to be called "American" by his relatives there. In comparison to incidents reported by older Italians, however, these restrictions have apparently diminished.

As will be demonstrated throughout the book, the significance of ethnic group membership to those who participated in this study usually was traced to a family-centeredness that they saw as being different from others. The next chapter will examine this family system from two perspectives. First, it provides an overview of the southern Italian antecedents of the family and evidence of changing configuration in this country. Second, the major structural determinants are examined statistically through a series of group comparisons.

Chapter 3
Contemporary
Sources of Stability
and Change

The Family System of Southern Italy

All literature on the family system in southern Italy points to the conclusion that it is the fundamental unit of social structure. The important concept of *onore della famiglia* (honor of the family) refers to family solidarity and maintenance of traditions through service, respect, and devotion (Covello 1967). According to Cronin (1970:85), the mandate of service to family means "the extent to which the individual—his desires, plans and ambitions—is subjugated to the interest of the family." Within this cohesive unit, there is little individuality apart from the family, and members are expected to support male authority, sacrifice for the family, respect parents, and avoid bringing shame on the family (Barzini 1964; Moss and Thomson 1959). Consequently, there is widespread agreement on the supreme importance of family, the submersion of the individual within the family, limited options for nonfamilial interests, and strong means to enforce conformity to family goals.

The hierarchy of male authority is also prominent in Italy, but it exists in the context of role segregation where families, while father-dominated, are mother-centered. The functional importance of the mother as the center of the family who rules over the hearth and home has led Luigi Barzini (1964:210) to describe the family as a *"crypto-matriarchy."* Nevertheless, the firm basis of male authority is generally not questioned, despite the power the mother exercises at home.

The family in both the United States and Italy is usually described as adult centered (Covello 1967), meaning that children are expected to conform to adult demands. To enforce these standards, parents use an explicit system of rewards and punishments. Because the honor of the family rests upon maintaining the virginity of its unmarried females and the fidelity of its married females, the activity of females is quite constricted (A. Parsons 1969). Male children, on the other hand, are granted considerable freedom to form associations outside the family. Consequently, the segregated sex roles within an adult-centered house have resulted in a hierarchical structure with males at least nominally over females and the parents over children.

The status of the old is subject to mixed views, suggesting that there is some discrepancy between norms and reality. Cronin (1970) reports no great reverence for the aged in Sicily, while Leonard Moss and Walter Thomson (1959) as well as Covello (1967) place some emphasis on their high status. One point of agreement is the widespread endorsement of the norm of *respecto* for elders. However, with the loss of the work role, the status of the male appears to decline even though the female, if she continues to be active in the home, suffers no such losses (Covello 1967; Cronin 1970). Since work is the central attribute of status and a source of respect, growing old in southern Italy has more effect on the status of men than of women. Nevertheless, old people continue to remain actively involved in family life and are not usually segregated from the activities of younger members (Covello 1967).

While there is consensus on these features of the family, there is considerable disagreement on the unit to which one is referring when one speaks of family. *La famiglia* refers to the nuclear family of procreation, and it is this unit that is the focus of most research (Banfield 1958; Cronin 1970; Douglas 1984; Moss and Thomson 1959). The degree of importance of the extended family is subject to continuing debate because of the long-standing conceptions on the social atomism of southern Italian village life. As noted above, Banfield (1958) minimizes the importance of any social unit other than the nuclear family, while Cronin (1970) found that involvement with the extended family in Sicily was largely limited to marriage arrangements. Others have associated the dominance of the nuclear family to demographic factors such as rates of immigration, age of marriage, patterns of land tenure, and family size (Douglas 1984; Silverman 1968). In any case, the extended family system generally functioned largely as a social rather than economic unit (Covello 1967; Gans 1962).

The Italian-American Family

After an extensive review of the literature on both sides of the Atlantic, Cronin (1970) concludes that the pronuclear writers did their research entirely in Italy (Banfield 1958; Moss and Thomson 1959), whereas the proextended adherents also studied the immigrant groups in the United States (Covello 1967; Day 1929; Pisani 1959; Williams 1938). Such a division suggests that the extended family as a unit of functional importance developed as an adaptive solution to the immigrant situation. For example, Covello's excellent study (1967) in Brooklyn in the 1930s finds that a social exclusiveness of family and relatives submerged the individual in the family and deemphasized individual interests. More recently, Gambino (1974) describes major categories of relationships for contemporary Sicilians as family (or "blood of my blood"), godparents (*compare* and *comare*). and friends to whom one says hello (*amici*). Others are strangers (*stranieri*), even though one might see them daily.

Works on southern Italy suggest notable continuities with the immigrant family in this country. Virginia McLaughlin's (1971) historical study of Buffalo's (New York) Italians between 1900 and 1930 found continuity and stability in family organization with immigration. For one thing, patriarchal controls continued, particularly in the protection of female honor. Sex segregation also persisted. A woman had great prestige and control in the home, but she continued to be under the rule of her husband or other male relatives. Few women worked outside the home, a factor she associates with Italians having the lowest percentage of female-headed households and the lowest desertion rates of all immigrant groups in Buffalo. Another historical study in Providence, Rhode Island, suggests family cohesiveness (Smith 1977). Comparisons of records from 1890 and 1930 indicate that the children of Italian immigrants were more likely than those of Jewish families to remain in the city; of the married children in 1930, 60 percent lived at the same address as that of their parents.

These pictures of stability can be contrasted with research on Italians in this country before World War II in which conflicts between the first generation and their children were usually emphasized (Lopreato 1970). For example, Paul Campisi (1948) describes the first generation as in a transition period when Italians were coping with the new environment. A picture of confusion, conflict, and disorganization emerges, as well as a deep rift between generations (Ward 1971). Irvin Child's (1943) study of the "second generation in conflict" describes types of adaptation as the "rebel," the "apathetic," or the "in-group." In keeping with these themes of the time, conflicts of the second generation were more often associated with a rejection of the Italian background and self-conscious Americanization. Presumably, they also rejected the family by changing one's name, moving away from old neighborhoods and marrying non-Italians (Firey 1947; Kennedy 1952).

In contrast, Herbert Gans's (1962) later study of second- and third-generation Italians in a working-class neighborhood in Boston presents observational accounts of the family in the 1950s. He found the family structure to fall in between the nuclear and the extended types. The dominant pattern was high sociability among selected relatives, a close bond between mothers and daughters, segregated sex roles, and a marginal status for the aged. He found the families to be adult-centered with children expected to conform to adult authority. Although these features suggest a continuation of southern Italian culture, Gans instead associates it with a working-class subculture.

Since Gans's research there have been few in-depth descriptions of the modern Italian family. Scattered reports in the literature present a mixed view. For example, there have been recent studies of the contemporary Italian-American value orientations (Cohler and Grunebaum 1981; Kluckhohn and Strodtbeck 1961; Papajohn and Spiegel 1975), which suggest a continued insularity, suspicion of the outside world, and other features of peasant values.

Gambino (1974) also suggests retention of important dimensions of ethnic background. His book, *Blood of My Blood,* was being widely read by Italians during the time of the interviews, and it generally struck a responsive chord and elicited positive evaluations. His purpose was both personal and scholarly, but ultimately aimed at recording and interpreting the Italian-American identity for third-generation Italians. He emphasized the persisting conflict between the old way (*la via vecchia*) and the new way (*la via nuova*) through a detailed analysis of Italian family roles and the socialization experiences.

Scattered contemporary accounts present a mixed view of the family. Of the more objective evidence, Francis Femminella and Jill Quadagno's review in 1976 of census and survey research indicate widespread family stability. In a 1973 census report, only 10 percent of the Italian-American households had female heads. Divorces were rare: only 3 percent were divorced, a percentage not significantly higher among younger Italian Americans. However, the family structure has changed in size. Fertility rates have declined, with the second generation averaging half the children of the first generation. Ethnic endogomy is high; Harold Abramson's (1973) analysis of National Opinion Research Center data on the Catholic population finds that 66 percent of Italian-American marriages are with other Italians. A report by Richard Alba (1976) is in agreement with this research and reports high rates of intermarriage. Residential stability for Italian Americans is also widely reported, so Italians usually remain the largest population of white ethnics in our cities today (Lieberson 1963; Lopreato 1970). In a study of a Chicago neighborhood, Gerald Suttles (1968:105) describes Italians as leading a double life: "During the daytime, they leave the neighborhood and do their work without much thought of their ethnicity. When they come home in the evening, however, they are obliged to reassume their Old World identity."

One area of the family that appears to be changing today is the role of women, but reports on this factor are also mixed. For example, Cohler and Grunebaum (1981), in a detailed description of four middle-aged Italian mothers and their daughters, found that these women preferred more freedom from family responsibilities and obligations. Although one cannot generalize from this small number, a larger study of personality changes of white ethnics also suggests changes in the female role (Cohler and Lieberman 1979). Among Italian women, there is a shift with age toward more active mastery and concerns for achievement. In contrast, Jessica Cohen's (1980) comparison of college-educated Jewish and Italian mothers indicates that Italian women tend to have more traditional conceptions of the female role, which suggests that education does not act as a leveler in how gender roles are determined in the family.

Notably absent from this review of research on the Italian-American family are comprehensive, in-depth studies. Instead, there are fragmented reports on various dimensions of the family and, even then, there is little agreement on the major configuration of the contemporary family. The descriptions and analyses in later chapters are intended to clarify some of the inconsistencies and add to our understanding of ethnic family processes.

Structural Sources of Change

Sociologists generally assume that European Catholic groups are changing from their traditional family systems because of structural changes such as social and geographic mobility and intermarriage, all factors associated with assimilation (Alba 1976; Yancey, Eriksen, and Juliani 1976). Gans (1962), in his study of a Boston Italian neighborhood, emphasized social class determinants. From this perspective, family variation is seen as resulting more from social stratification processes than from ethnic background. Certainly many of the dimensions of the Italian-American family described in the following chapters resemble working-class families irrespective of class level. The family structure tends to be hierarchical, sex roles are segregated, and kinship solidarity is prominent (Komorovsky 1962; Rubin 1977; Young and Willmott 1957). Children are raised in patterns identified with the working class, with an emphasis on social conformity rather than self-direction and external rather than internal controls (Kohn 1969). The question then arises, to what extent are these dimensions of the family a function of social class placement rather than ethnicity?

In order to determine the structural sources of change, two groups were used as a basis for comparison. First, the control group of white Protestants provided one basis for comparison. This sample differed in both religion and in the generation length in this country. All were at least the grandchildren of immigrants from predominantly Protestant countries of northern and western Europe. They were matched to the Italian groups on the basis of stage in the family cycle, education, and occupation. Each group has both middle- and working-class families, so comparisons can be made in class differences both within and between groups. Second, a matched sample of Italian Americans who had married non-Italians provided the basis for comparison of the effects of intermarriage. Since the non-Italians were mostly Catholic, it was possible to examine how intermarriage with other white ethnic groups affects the Italian family.

Frequency distributions, t-tests, and analyses of covariance were used to determine the differences within and between groups in kinship solidarity, the relationship between the older parent and middle-aged offspring, socialization techniques, and marital roles. These areas of family life were selected on the assumption that they would identify the extent that traditional family practices have persisted. These findings can also be weighed against larger-scale studies of the American family. For example, the ongoing debate on the American kinship system can be found in Bert Adams (1968, 1971), Geoffrey Gibson (1972), Eugene Litwak (1965), and Marvin Sussman and L. G. Burchinal (1962). Recent articles on the family life of older people include Elaine Brody (1981), Alan Kerkoff (1965), Helena Lopata

(1978), Ethel Shanas (1979), Marvin Sussman (1976), Judith Treas (1977), Lillian Troll (1971), and Vivian Wood and Joan Robertson (1978).

In looking at class differentiation within each group, the variable of kinship contact was used as one indicator of differentiation. Reviews by both Adams (1971) and Troll (1971) report that working-class families have more contact with relatives. Troll suggests, however, that these differences might even out if geographic mobility is controlled. Such an analysis is possible here since, with the exception of twenty-eight geographically mobile families, the others have remained in the same city in which they were married. Thus, differences between social class and ethnicity can be discerned without the confounding variable of geographic mobility.

These comparisons of kinship measures in Table 3.1 indicate interesting and unanticipated results. Social class comparisons in the wives' frequency of contact with parents find that all working-class wives have about the same weekly contact with parents, although in-married wives are much more likely to have daily contact than are the Protestants. More variation is found among middle-class families, with almost twice as many in-married Italians having daily contact with the parents. Most in-married wives have weekly contact, three-quarters of the intermarried do and only slightly more than half of the Protestants do.

The interaction with siblings also varies markedly by ethnicity. In-married Italian wives are much more socially engaged with brothers and sisters, with almost two-thirds having daily contact. In direct contrast, 60 percent of the Protestants do not see a sibling weekly. The intermarried families fall in between, but one can discern the tendency for blue-collar families to have more contact than white-collar, intermarried families.

The wives' report of their husbands' contact with relatives indicates that men, in general, have less contact than women with parents and siblings. In fact, the differences between the husbands in weekly contact with parents are not large. Again, however, the pattern of higher engagement with siblings is apparent among in-married Italian men.

In order to determine class differences in kinship involvement with each comparison group, a composite measure was made of kinship solidarity which combined both social contact and mutual aid. The t-tests run between the class division in each group found unanticipated results. Among the Protestants, the predictable class divisions appeared with the working class significantly more involved with kin

Table 3.1.

Percentages Reporting Contact with Parents and Siblings, by Social Class and Ethnicity

	In-married Italians		Out-married Italians		Protestant non-Italians	
Wives	Middle class	Working class	Middle class	Working class	Middle class	Working class
Parents	n = 29	n = 31	n = 27	n = 45	n = 26	n = 17
Daily	52	58	26	44	27	18
Weekly	41	32	52	38	31	65
Total	93	90	78	82	58	83
Siblings	n = 29	n = 42	n = 31	n = 61	n = 24	n = 17
Daily	62	64	16	39	8	18
Weekly	28	24	45	39	33	35
Total	90	88	61	78	41	53
Husbands						
Parents	n = 26	n = 25	n = 24	n = 36	n = 26	n = 14
Daily	31	44	21	19	12	36
Weekly	46	32	50	42	46	36
Total	77	76	71	61	58	72
Siblings	n = 27	n = 37	n = 29	n = 47	n = 21	n = 16
Daily	33	27	24	19	—	19
Weekly	48	43	24	34	33	38
Total	81	70	48	53	33	57

NOTE: The n's differ from that of the total sample because only those with a sibling nearby are recorded. Also 22 percent had deceased parents and were not included here.

$\tau = 2.07$, df 54, p<.05). There are no significant class differences among the intermarried families. However, in those families where both husband and wife are Italian, the middle-class families have significantly higher kinship solidarity ($\tau = 3.26$, df 72, <.002).

This finding is in agreement with the percentages in Table 3.1. Kinship involvement is higher in middle-class, in-married Italian families, while in the intermarried and Protestant families the predictable class differences appear with working-class families being more actively involved with relatives.

In order to find the comparative effects of social class and intermarriage in in-married and out-married Italian families, analyses of covariance were run on composite measures of the parent-child relationship (contact and aid extended), kinship contact and reciprocity, the degree of traditionalism in the marital relationship (power relations and role segregation), and childrearing patterns (discipline and parental surveillance). The findings are revealing.

Table 3.2 indicates that in the relationship Italian Americans have with their elderly parents, neither social class nor intermarriage alone is a source of significant variation. However, the two-way interactions indicate that these variables working together do exert some effect. With middle-class status and intermarriage, individuals established more social distance from the parents.

Table 3.2 also indicates that kinship relationships are significantly affected by intermarriage when contact and mutual aid decline. As the frequencies in Table 3.1 indicate, intermarried families at both class levels are less involved with siblings than are in-married. However, the analysis of covariance finds that it is intermarriage, not social class, that accounts for the most variation. These findings indicate that the highest kinship solidarity is found in middle-class, in-married Italian families. Kinship contact declines with out-marriage, irrespective of social class.

A childrearing score was derived from measures on discipline techniques and parental supervision, with strict discipline and parental protectiveness as indicators of traditional techniques. Here again, Table 3.2 shows that intermarriage, not social class, accounts for more variation. With intermarriage, Italian parents apparently relax their vigilance and social control and grant their children more independence.

In the marital relationship, Table 3.2 demonstrates that social class, not intermarriage, is the determinant of how roles are defined. As

Table 3.2.

Analysis of Variance for Intermarriage and Social Class:
In-married and Out-married Italian Respondents

	Social class		Intermarriage		Interaction effects	
	F-ratio	Sig. level	F-ratio	Sig. level	F-ratio	Sig. level
Parent-child relationship	3.00	<.086	2.91	<.091	4.20	<.05*
Kinship relationship	2.73	<.101	28.78	<.0000*	5.53	<.02*
Marital relationship	7.47	<.007*	2.61	<.109	.18	<.676
Childrearing	.772	<.381	9.65	<.002*	.001	<.975

described in previous research, marriages in blue-collar families are more likely to be emotionally distant with explicit segregation of roles, separate leisure activities, and lower levels of communication (Komorovsky 1962). In agreement, both in-married and out-married Italians in the middle class have marriages that resemble the American companionship model, with husbands and wives interchanging roles, sharing in activities, and communicating frequently.

From this analysis of Table 3.2, several conclusions can be made on this sample. Social class differences alone in contact with parents and relatives account for less variation than does intermarriage. Italians have more frequent contact with parents and siblings than the comparison groups, but in contradiction to conceptions on class and kinship involvement, the middle-class Italians have more contact. This pattern is also found in childrearing practices where intermarriage accounts for more variation than social class.

One explanation is that, with intermarriage, the nuclear family is removed in part from the closely knit social network of other Italians. Perhaps as a consequence, other dimensions of family life begin to change. The most prominent change, observed in the interviews and reflected in these statistics, is that of childrearing techniques, where the traditional practices are relaxed. In the relationships with the elderly parent, however, neither social class nor intermarriage alone are sources of differentiation, but in combination they are structural variables associated with change.

The marital relationship, which is prominently influenced by class position, is not greatly affected by intermarriage. This finding probably is due to the fact that the patterning of sex roles in Italian working-class families is similar to that of other working-class groups intermarrying with Italians. Whether an Italian woman marries within or outside of her ethnic group is of little consequence in determining the character of her marital role. The importance of social class has also been pointed out by Schneider and Smith (1973), who suggest that class differences are more clearly reflected in sex roles. Thus, class differences are probably more manifest in marital roles than other family roles.

Bott's (1971) important work on the social network effects on the patterning of marital roles is of relevance here. In her theory, families who are embedded in a closely knit network are more likely to have more segregated marital roles. Her theory generally applies to the findings reported here. Among the out-married Italians and the Protestant families, kinship involvement is higher in working-class families and marriages are more segregated. Among in-married Italians, however, marriages follow predicted class models, but kinship involvement is significantly higher in middle-class families. The question arises, then, as to why middle-class, in-married Italian families do not follow the predicted association between the network characteristics and the patterning of family roles.

One possible explanation concerns the role of women in maintaining kinship activities. Kinship relationships involve reciprocity, whether it be material aid, shared meals, services, or just sociability. If these exchanges are frequent, a family needs resources of time, money, and even a house adequate to accommodate visiting relatives. Obviously these resources are more likely to be found in middle-class families. The wives are less likely to work, their income is higher, and they most likely have their own car to visit or chauffeur a parent. In other words, women are freed from work responsibilities and this freedom is most likely to be directed toward family and kinship activities, rather than personal pursuits outside the family.

In summary, the social processes that affect intermarried families can be explained at least in part by network theory. The traditional values of parents, while diluted with the younger generation, are still of some influence, because the social networks connecting the nuclear household to other social relationship remain dominated by relatives, other Italian friends of long-standing, and numerous members of the older generation. The influences from the American culture come from secondary relationships, not usually primary ones. These outside influences are more prominent among men who, in any case, are not the primary custodians of kinship solidarity. Women, who have the major responsibility for raising children, extending services to parents, and maintaining kinship relationships, are not as likely to be presented with other options from members of their social network. Once they are exposed, however, as they are with intermarriage, they begin to adopt other family practices at odds with the Italian way.

The Generation from Immigration

There has been a long-standing assumption that the generation level from point of immigration is an effective predictor of family change. Presumably, each generation assimilates to some degree the culture of the hosts, so that once these individuals move away from the immigrant setting the influence of the culture of origin will have a diminishing effect. This model, by its very simplicity, has had great appeal and has led to gross generalizations with little empirical basis. For example, Campisi's (1948) model of generational change is continually cited in the literature on Italian Americans to support blanket assimilation, even though he bases his model on little actual research. At a more general level, Marcus Hansen's (1952) principle of third-generation interest describes a sentimental return to the culture of the grandparents by individuals whose second-generation parents had rejected it in favor of assimilation. Although few observers would deny that there are progressive changes with each generation, both of these models of generational change undoubtedly obscure other sources of variation. The major question, then, is whether there is a progressive change in the family by generation or whether there is. a symbolic return in a search for roots.

In contrast to some ethnic groups like the Japanese Americans (Johnson 1976), it was somewhat surprising to find that Italian Americans rarely referred to their generation level. When asked, most respondents had to think about it and discuss the place of birth of their grandparents before determining their own status. There was some confusion in their minds as to whether the first generation born in this country was the first generation sociologically or whether the immigrants were the first generation. Some of this confusion could be due to the fact that there was a great deal of movement back and forth between Italy and the United States in the early 1900s, so their descendants today cannot readily categorize the immigrant status of their parents and grandparents.

Furthermore, Italian Americans rarely conceptualize generation level as a reference to explain behavior. For example, parents are not usually labeled by generation in order to justify their differing values. Generation level meaning parents and grandparents, of course, is used within the family, but the eldest generation to Italians does not always refer to the immigrant. To many, the first generation might refer to grandparents who never left Italy, or to the one of greatest genealogical distance that one can remember.

By the common sociological definition, most of the Italians interviewed are in the second generation, the children of immigrants. The proportion does not change with intermarriage; 80 percent of the in-married and 76 percent of the out-married are in the second generation. Most of the remainder are in the third generation. Although this distribution is skewed, *t*-tests were run on differences between middle-aged respondents in the second generation—that is, the children of immigrants—and the third generation, their grandchildren. By using global measures, the total score for interdependence finds that the groups are virtually the same. Only one dimension of the family, the kinship system, varies significantly, but this difference is not in the predicted direction. Rather than finding that the second generation is closer to the country of origin, it is the third generation who has a more closely knit group. Since Bartolomeo Palisi (1966) also reports this increase in kinship activity with the third generation, these combined findings suggest that the kinship system continues to develop and expand in this country into a form that differs from the extended family in Italy and the immigrants.

A Note on Geographic Mobility

Since these families were selected from records of marriages dated years before we contacted them, they are limited to those who did not move from the city where the marriage took place. Geographic mobility inevitably would have changed the frequency of social contact with the extended family and, according to the explanatory model used here, other dimensions of the nuclear family. In order to determine the nature of these changes, a small sample of geographically mobile families (n = 28) was selected through informal references. These families had lived in their present house a mean of eight years, but both husband and wife had grown up in another area.

These families were not included in the statistical analysis because they posed several methodological problems. First, while a decision was made to limit the selection to middle-class families, there was too much discrepancy in educational level between them and the middle-class, geographically stable Italian women. Sixteen, or 57 percent, had attended college in comparison to 10 percent of the geographically stable women from middle-class families.

Second, many of these geographically mobile nuclear families proved not to be isolated. Seven, or 25 percent, had a relative in the area who had either preceded or followed them to Easton. Another eight families were in close and frequent contact with their relatives because they were less than two hours away by car. Three families had parents living with them before their deaths. From this distribution, one can tentatively conclude that, in many cases, geographic mobility for Italians might be a transplantation of the extended family system, rather than a relocation of the nuclear family.

Nevertheless, geographic mobility is associated with a common pattern of adaptation. First, the move was described as stressful and requiring a long period of adjustment. Only two families made a conscious choice to establish a family of procreation away from parents and relatives. The remainder had to move because job opportunities lay elsewhere. Since the men had a college education preparing them for more specialized positions, they apparently only sought employment elsewhere after exhausting the possibilities in their home towns. Although a move to better oneself was overtly applauded, the reaction of the parents was invariably negative. "There was such a fuss made, you'd think I had moved to Russia [rather than 200 miles away]." "My husband's mother was broken-hearted—she made us feel guilty." "My parents did everything to keep us there." "My parents said, 'Why are you doing this to us? Don't you love us?'"

Most wives reported a difficult adjustment initially. "We felt very much alone—we had nobody." "We had lived a closed life there. I hated being away at first." "My house had been like Grand Central Station there, and here, it was empty." Respondents described the early period as one of making attempts to counteract loneliness through frequent visits back and forth. Three families tried commuting initially. When the move was finally made, parents would come to stay for a month at a time or the family would spend their entire vacations back in their home town. Over time, some relatives followed them to their new homes. In other cases, distant cousins in the new area were introduced. One wife who had moved seventeen years earlier reported that all members of her nuclear family, even her younger children who had never lived in the home town, called that place home. However, most wives reported a conscious attempt to replace their intimate family relationships with new friends, usually of Italian background.

By the time they were interviewed, some years had elapsed since their relocations and in most cases the families had adapted well. Only one wife concluded that her life would have been happier if she had not moved. In fact, virtually all of the wives reported that the move had made them independent, autonomous individuals for the first time in their lives: "Until I moved, I never thought for myself or made decisions—my parents did that for me." Some tended to view siblings who had remained at home as being too dependent or narrow in their perspectives. The change in lifestyle was seen as an opportunity for personal growth. It was also described as an event that enlarged the horizons of their extended family. "They have an excuse for traveling for the first time. Coming to visit us is a big adventure for them."

Another advantage cited was that the distance provided a buffer from periodic family crises. "Now there are so many things I want to stay out of. For example, my brother has just left his wife. If I were there, I'd be on the phone most of the time." After a period of adjustment, the privacy of the nuclear family was viewed positively as a preferred lifestyle. To return to a situation where one was involved with others' problems had become distasteful.

Respondents identified the marital relationship as the family dimension most affected by geographic mobility. All but one wife described their marriages as companionate, as indicated by open communication with husbands, joint problem-solving, and shared activities. (The one exception is a family where the move was made in an attempt to reconcile a broken marriage.) Most others would agree with the following comments: "We've learned to grow together"; "I now take my problems to my husband rather than my mother or sister. It makes us much closer"; "There's less friction between us without our parents around." In other words, dependence on or interdependence with family has been replaced by interdependence between husband and wife.

On measures of childrearing techniques and attitudes toward authority and dependency, this group is more conservative and traditional than middle-class Protestants or the out-married Italians. They tend to use stricter discipline techniques and more supervision of adolescent children. However, because of methodological constraints described above, statistical confirmation is lacking.

This analysis indicates several important points. First, geographic distance from relatives created by a move in adulthood usually is compensated for by frequent visiting. Also, in some cases, relationships with distant cousins are formed as a substitute for the primary relatives left behind. Second, after a difficult period of adjustment, roles with the family assume the modal type described for the middle class as the marital relationship comes to take on functions formerly fulfilled by kin. Third, over time, these families have adapted well to their middle-class family style; they are satisfied and prosperous. Certainly the influence of the extended family remains; all families have retained

high involvement through frequent and sometimes lengthy visits, telephone calls, and letters. In other families, a chain migration has taken
place as other relatives join them in the new city. Nevertheless, in all
measures on childrearing and values, these geographically mobile Italian families have remained more traditional than the Protestant groups.
Although statistical confirmation is lacking, one can suggest that traditional values regulating childrearing are more culturally determined
and less responsive to structural pressures, while the marital roles take
on class-based characteristics.

Summary

Through a quantitative analysis, this section has identified structural
sources of change in the sample families through comparisons of subgroups of in-married and out-married Italians with a control group of
white, Protestant, non-Italians. The basic factors examined are those
associated with traditionalism. The traditional family here refers to a
hierarchical family system, segregated sex roles, childrearing practices
encouraging conformity to and dependence on the family, a strong
sense of filial obligation, and high kinship involvement. While it is
uncertain if all of these factors were prominent in the family system of
southern Italy, they have been noted in the early immigrant family.
They were also described as part of the "old-fashioned way" extolled
by the older Italians interviewed.

The structural factors of social class, generation level, and intermarriage, variables commonly identified as sources of change within
groups, were analyzed so that some generalizations could be made for
this group of Italian Americans. First, social class alone does not appear to exert significant changes in the family as long as husband and
wife are both of Italian origin. Second, intermarriage exerts more
influence than social class, particularly in decreasing the influence of
the extended family. When both intermarriage and social mobility
have occurred, even more changes occur as greater social distance is
established between the middle-aged Italians, their parents, and their
relatives. Third, generation level was not found to be an important
source of family variation. Fourth, while the methods do not permit
generalizations on the effects of geographic mobility, one finding is
quite prominent: unlike the other Italian groups, the marriage relation-

ships in the absence of the extended family becomes more central in the family.

The following chapters will augment these statistical findings through more detailed descriptions of the family system. Largely through the phenomenological approach, the meanings of family membership are described and the processes by which individuals adapt to the demands as well as the benefits of this solidary family system will be explored.

Part 2
A Description of Family Life

Chapter 4
Relatives: Circles
of Sentiment and
Support

If one were to conceptualize the Italian family as a circle enclosing a series of concentric rings, the individual would be in the center, first surrounded by the nuclear family, and then by rings of relatives of increasing kinship distance. The point at which the primary group
relationships become secondary relationships differs among groups as
does the number of socially significant individuals. However, the extent
to which these individuals or these rings are connected to each other has
some influence on the roles within the nuclear family (Bott 1971). The
stage in the life cycle also determines the characteristics of these relationships, because individuals conceivably can move out of the circle at
some points or deemphasize some relationships from time to time.

In the organization of this section of the book, I begin with the outside rings of this circle, the kinship system, in order to illustrate how
Italian Americans define family and relatives and how they maintain relationships with them. This choice was made because Italians and their
nuclear families are generally enclosed by a connected series of relatives, a situation that has an impact upon most other dimensions of their
nuclear families.

Kinship and Aging

The support of any parent in his or her old age is easier if there are several adults to share the responsibility. An only daughter can become
burdened with a disabled parent if she is faced with competing demands
from her husband, her children, or a job. If, however, she also has
brothers and sisters, or aunts and uncles, they can provide relief to her
and her parent. Thus, in beginning with a description of the extended
kin network of Italian Americans, several questions arise. Do relatives

who maintain frequent contact with each other also mobilize to assist in taking care of the sick and dependent members? Can they bolster the caregiver who is supporting the elderly person?

One example comes from Lucy Parotte who faced many demands at the time of the interview. The health of both her parents was deteriorating. Her father, who had been recuperating from a stroke, suddenly became confused and occasionally incontinent. Her mother had a mild heart attack and could not overexert herself to care for him. Lucy brought both of them into her home where she also maintained a beauty parlor. Since she was an only child, these responsibilities could easily have become burdensome. However, she did have some cousins and married children who immediately rose to the occasion.

Her daughter Beverly had married into a large Italian family. Beverly's mother-in-law, Mrs. Liparulo was also an old friend of Lucy's and a regular client of the beauty parlor. This overlapping friendship and affinal kinship relationship also extended to Mrs. Liparulo's sister. They both brought in meals and, even more important, became available to babysit each day, so Beverly could go to her mother's.

The support of several first cousins was also invaluable. Mary was always considered the family's good luck charm. She accompanied Lucy or sat with her in the hospital or in the doctor's office while a parent was being treated. Nina's help was equally welcome. As a beautician herself, she came in to work in the beauty parlor so business could go on as usual. Gina, another cousin, cleaned the house and cooked so Lucy was free of these daily chores.

This example points to certain prerequisites in a kinship network that facilitate its functioning as a social support system. The first requirement is a pool of relatives who are potentially available. The usual contact with relatives through occasional visits, letters, and long-distance phone calls might bring a pleasant interlude to a day, but it does not necessarily provide support. Families whose members are scattered over great distances cannot function as a social support system, however much affection and sentiment is exchanged. In the above example, the kinship network includes a daughter and cousins in proximity. It can also be expanded to include affinal relatives.

The second requirement is the adherence to the norm of reciprocity. Even if relatives are available, they must be willing to participate. In this country, kinship relations are usually optional and expectations are not well defined. The provision of social support usually must go beyond sociability and enjoyment of each other's company to include some willingness to provide more practical help. Such supports usually are regulated by norms specifying what one should do.

The third requirement is a minimum of competing commitments among members of the kinship network. The degree of expectations for reciprocity should be congruent with other demands on relatives. Demands from a job pose one impediment. An active social life is another, particularly if one associates with those who have less family-oriented norms. The options for those who do not share the same views on the family can be in direct conflict with the expectations from their family. Rather than a segmentation between friends and family, Lucy's social network was composed of an overlapping set of friends and relatives. Thus, the care of her parents was more easily accommodated into her social network. Moreover, there was common agreement among the participants about what they should do.

The fourth requirement is a key person who functions as a connecting link between various categories of kin and who facilitates the process by which the nuclear family is drawn into the activities of the extended family. This key person functions to keep kinship contacts operating. Lucy appears to be this individual; her beauty parlor had long been a center for sociability and a communication hub where relatives learned of illnesses or any mishaps that required assistance from each other.

Definitions of Family and Relatives: The Italian Case

The major sociological criterion in defining the nuclear family is that it is a separate residential unit composed of parents and and children (T. Parsons 1965). Like most American families, the Italian Americans predominantly live in nuclear households. Although many respondents reported having lived with parents early in marriage, by the time they had adolescent children the nuclear household was preferred almost universally. No house is seen as big enough to accommodate the extended family, particularly when it involves having two women in the kitchen. It is there that conflict can be generated and, thus, is to be avoided if at all possible. Only 13 percent of the families have a parent living in their household, and another 4 percent have another relative living with them. While the numbers of extended households comprise only 17 percent of the families, another 47 percent have relatives within walking distance in the neighborhood. Hence, although the structure is inclined to be nuclear, the family can readily incorporate members of the extended group into its functions.

The second criterion of the nuclear family is an economic independence from the kinship group. By this definition, Italians also have nuclear family systems. The cooperation among relatives in a family business enterprise is much less common than it was in the past. Second- and third-generation members who have more educational and occupational opportunities usually move into occupations that are quite divorced from the Italian community. Nevertheless, more than one-third of the families work with a relative at a family business, or more often at a large business concern.

By these definitions, the core unit for Italians is the nuclear family system. However, an examination of specific families as they have developed over three generations indicates a kinship structure that does not agree with these distinctions. How Italian Americans define family is best described through an example of the Di Nardos in Easton. Although it is larger than most families that still function as a unit, the processes of growth and development are fairly typical of the means by which socially significant relatives are identified.

Four Di Nardo brothers came from Calabria, Italy, in the early 1900s through a chain immigration where the first one assisted the next and so on. They lived together until each married and formed a household of his own, but all of these new homes were within an easy walking distance. The street names of their first homes identified the branches of the family and reference, for example, to the Lodi Street branch or the Oak Street branch is still used to place individuals in the family genealogy.

The growth of the family over seventy-two years has been carefully recorded and today includes 144 direct descendants and 78 relatives by marriage (Table 4.1). The Lodi Street branch, headed by Nicholas and Carmella, had eleven children, ten of whom married, and twenty-four grandchildren. In the third generation, seventeen had married and produced thirty-three offspring, the great-grandchildren of the immigrants. The Oak Street branch had ten children, eight of whom married and between them had fourteen children. The two younger brothers, who now comprise the Butternut and James Street branches, married sisters from the same town in Italy and had four children each, all of whom married and had fifteen and sixteen children respectively.

From the large families of immigrant brothers, which averaged 6.25

Table 4.1.

Three-generation Expansion of One Family

Branch	Second generation		Third generation		Fourth generation	
	Number	Number married	Number	Number married	Number	Number married
Lodi Street (eldest brother)	11	10	24	17	33	—
Oak Street (second brother)	10	8	14	9	9	—
Butternut Street (third brother)	4	4	16	3	2	—
James Street (fourth brother)	4	4	15	3	2	—
Total	29	26	69	32	46	—
Total descendants: 144						

children each, there is a marked decline to an average of 3.24 children in the second generation. Nevertheless, the twenty-nine members in the second generation produced sixty-nine members in the third, and they in turn have produced forty-six young children to date. Since some in the third generation have not reached adulthood, this number will increase.

While the size itself is not remarkable for European Catholics, the fact that few have moved away is indeed exceptional. Among the second generation of twenty-nine descendants of four brothers, two have died and two have moved away from the area, leaving twenty-two nuclear families and three unmarried individuals. Of the twenty-five second-generation members remaining in Easton, fourteen still live in the original area of settlement, the north side of the city. The Butternut Street and the James Street branches have always been closely linked because of brothers marrying sisters. Of their eight children and thirty-one grandchildren who live in a second residential clustering, 93 percent still live near each other and only a short drive away from the rest of the extended family.

In the third generation, where thirty-two of sixty-nine descendants are already married, nine remain in the old neighborhood while three more live in an adjacent suburb. Seven have moved out of the area, but four of these individuals are descendants of parents who had moved away. The remainder are females who live in other neighborhoods of the city, which means they are only a short ride away.

These figures indicate surprising geographic stability in both generations. It is particularly impressive in the younger generation, because most of them have gone on to college or had some technical training. While over half have not yet reached marriageable age, the trend of remaining near the family has been clearly established.

In fact, in collecting this information, my informant referred to family members moving "west," which commonly means California. In clarifying the location, however, she specified a western suburb of the city twenty minutes away from the Northside. She remarked, "Moving to Marshfield in our family is like moving out of town—it's as far away as California to most of us."

This stability persists despite the high rates of intermarriage in this family. In the second generation almost half married non-Italians, whereas slightly more than half out-married in the third generation. With the younger generation, the intermarriage rate appears to be stabilizing, but it is still somewhat less than the Italian-American out-marriage rates for the city, which was estimated at 60 percent in 1959.

Certainly, the Di Nardos meet the prerequisites of a pool of accessible relatives. However, a total of 202 individuals who are identified in Figure 1 obviously becomes unmanageable. Controlling the size of any kinship event becomes a major problem. Each generation solves this problem differently, but any significant relatives rarely extend beyond first cousins except where friendships are formed. Thus the viable kinship unit is the modified extended family (enclosed by the dotted lines in Figure 1).

From the point of view of the second generation in the Lodi Street branch, for example, intimate relatives consist of their children, their brothers and sisters, and usually their spouses and children. The pool of sociability is mainly contained within each branch. Yet all cousins, the twenty-nine descendants of the four brothers, know each other and occasionally exchange invitations for weddings and more formal gatherings. Reciprocity often goes beyond wedding gifts, funeral donations, or get well cards during an illness. For example, a physician in one branch is consulted in the event of serious illness of any family member. One cousin who owns a small manufacturing company employs several relatives in other branches. Many relatives buy their insurance from a cousin. In some cases, cousins are also close friends.

Figure 1.
Definition of Family

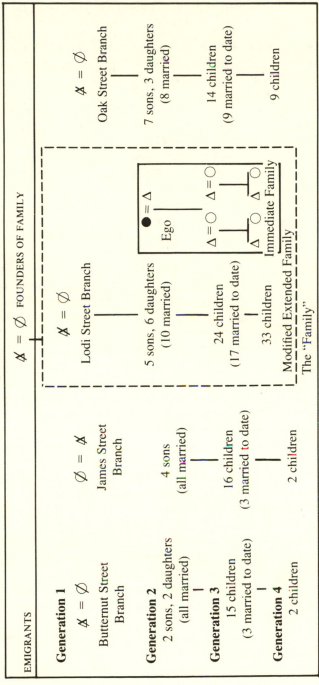

EMIGRANTS

Ꞩ = ∅ FOUNDERS OF FAMILY

Generation 1

Ꞩ = ∅
Butternut Street
Branch

∅ = Ꞩ
James Street
Branch

Ꞩ = ∅
Lodi Street Branch

Ꞩ = ∅
Oak Street Branch

Generation 2

2 sons, 2 daughters
(all married)

4 sons
(all married)

5 sons, 6 daughters
(10 married)

7 sons, 3 daughters
(8 married)

● = Δ
Ego

Generation 3

15 children
(3 married to date)

16 children
(3 married to date)

24 children
(17 married to date)

14 children
(9 married to date)

Δ = ○   Δ = ○

Δ   ○   Δ
Immediate Family

Generation 4

2 children

2 children

33 children

9 children

Modified Extended Family
The "Family"

Key: Δ male   ○ female   = married   ∅ deceased

Descendants: 144

Spouses of descendants: 58

Total number: 202

However, except where close friendships are formed, these relation-ships outside the branch are not uniformly carried over into kinship so-ciability among their children. Hence, members of the third generation in their twenties or thirties must be told who many relatives are in the re-ceiving line of their wedding. They would not recognize all second and third cousins if they met them in the street. Whereas they all share the sense of family and recognize its positive values, the personnel in the wider group have little social or psychological significance unless they are activated for ceremonial or symbolic purposes, or unless friendships form on the basis of personal choice.

All members identified in Figure 1 are the family in the most general sense. It is a collective of over two hundred individuals who descend from the four Di Nardo brothers. These relationships stem from ties of blood; these individuals are usually called relatives. Close friendships with a relative form only on an optional basis. Rather than an obligatory set of expectations, personal preferences and situational needs regulate the timing and content of social contacts. This situation is particu-larly applicable to the third generation, some of whom actually formed friendships at school with distant members of the family. The point is that these friendships might have developed irrespective of the kin-ship link.

Aside from an annual reunion, which is described in the next chapter, there are few opportunities for the large majority of second and third cousins in the four branches to congregate except for contacts based on personal preferences. The only exception is a death in the family when all the second generation and many of their offspring attend the wake. When one of the first members of the second generation died, the wake was described as the biggest in the memory of the funeral home. Lines of those waiting to convey their respects were so long that they wound around the street outside. The funeral procession the next day was said to have ninety-eight cars, an unusually large number in these days of less elaborate observances of deaths.

First cousins in the second generation are usually included at wed-dings of each other's offspring, although their children are not always invited unless they are in the same branch or unless they are personally acquainted with the bride and groom. This limitation is necessary be-cause there are so many within each branch who must be invited. In-vited guests bring a gift, the expense of which is usually based on the closeness of the relationship to the parent, not to the bride and groom. Hence, reciprocation for the gift at a later date is borne by the parents, not the recipient of the gift. It is the remnants of the family ties of the second-generation cousins that continue across the four branches.

Although the kinship system includes all four branches, each branch forms a more socially significant group of relatives who are in frequent interaction. A high level of social interaction and reciprocity takes place among its members. This group is identified as the *extended* family. As Figure 1 illustrates by the dotted lines, it is comprised of the immigrant parents (now deceased), their children (now in middle or old age), the grandchildren (whose ages range from early childhood to adulthood of twenties and thirties), and the great-grandchildren (still in early childhood). The sizes of these branches vary depending upon the original size of the sibling group and the stage of the family cycle. For example, the children of the younger immigrant brothers are only in middle age and have very few grandchildren, while some of the children of the eldest brothers are grandparents many times over.

In any case, the size of any one of these branches also becomes unmanageable for social gatherings, even if they are limited to individual branches. Those marrying into the family usually come from the area and have families of their own. While the extended family of each branch is an important unit and most members are well known to each other, it becomes necessary to limit one's focus to an even smaller group of people. This group is the *immediate* family which is composed of one's parents and siblings and their families (the members within the small box in Figure 1). This unit, usually termed by sociologists as the *modified extended* family, is the most viable and functional kinship unit in today's society (Litwak 1965; Sussman and Burchinal 1962). Unlike the unit typifying American Society, however, the form and the content of most Italians' modified extended families vary considerably from the average because of the expansive nature of most collateral relationships that cast a wide net over many members.

The Expansive Nature of Italian Kinship Systems

The expansion of any kinship system lies in the development of collateral relationships as units of social solidarity. When siblings maintain patterns of mutual aid and high sociability beyond the usual normative expectations, the relationship assumes both a social and a psychological significance that, in turn, can be transmitted to one's children. As young children, cousins become well acquainted because their parents meet frequently. If they all live close by, friendships formed in these early years can persist throughout their lives. When this situation exists, parents do not have to be present to activate the kinship bond. The elaboration of collateral relationships is one possible explanation of why many Italian families have been able to maintain a higher level of kinship solidarity than is evident for the society at large.

Brothers and sisters form very cohesive bonds in Italian families (Johnson 1982). Many women are like Mrs. Messina, who said, "I've talked to my sisters every day of my married life." One husband commented with resignation, "My wife is always crying over her sister's problems. But what can I do? I can't break it up. It's part of the family." One man described his close relationship with his sister. He often played the organ while she sang. When she died at the age of fifty, he reported, "I was broken-hearted. It was so depressing, I had to sell the organ." Brothers on occasion are so close that their relationship is competitive to the marital relationship. One source of this close bond was traced to the immigrant setting. "We are so close, I think, because Mom was too busy to spend much time with us. We had to fend for ourselves." Mr. Favolo, who recently retired, found a similar situation:

> *My wife is closer to her sister than she is to me. I want her to love her sister, but she overdoes it. She's at her sister's house more than she's home. I get lonely—she should give me more time. These two girls lived poorly as children. They suffered a lot together. I think that's why they're so close.*

In many families, it is difficult to contain kinship relationships to the immediate family, even if individuals attempt to do so. The major source of the problem in containment lies in the high degree of sibling solidarity evident among older Italians which reaches out to encompass younger members and draws them into the network of kinship activities. To illustrate, a fiftieth-anniversary party was planned for the Angellottis. The hosts were their son and his wife who originally invited his parents—as guests of honor—as well as their children and spouses and their five surviving siblings and their spouses, approximately twenty people. Then one niece, his sister's daughter, asked to attend because she was the host's godchild. Since one member of the younger generation was included, the son concluded that it was necessary to invite all of the adult nieces and nephews and their spouses. Fortunately, he was prosperous and willingly footed the bill. In doing so, he provided one of the numerous occasions for first cousins to socialize.

Frequent contact of this sort persists down through generations, as the young adults in the third generation often form their own basis of solidarity based on mutual interests. Cousin groups are common; they socialize both formally at special occasions and informally in the exchange of dinners and other social affairs. One home bureau club was also formed and made up entirely of female cousins and wives of male cousins. Another cousin club had its own bowling team. Certain events might be identified as a time for age-similar functions. Collateral rather than vertical or cross-generational personnel might be invited to a christening party, just as siblings might originally be selected for the anniversary party.

For example, a christening in the Lepone family was originally planned for the immediate family. Parents and siblings and their spouses and children made a guest list of sixteen people. By tradition, both the godparents of the new parents and godparents of the baby were invited. Also, there were favorite cousins they wished to include as friends. If these cousins were also included, their parents—the hosts' aunts and uncles—must also be invited. It was difficult to contain the number even at thirty-five guests, as the collateral bonds enveloped the vertical or generational links.

As described in the next chapter, the events used for family gatherings are numerous: funerals, weddings, christening parties, First Communion, confirmation, graduation, anniversaries, and birthdays. If the family is large and maintains active social contacts, then special occasions are frequent, sometimes weekly. Guest lists for originally small events swell: ninety-seven for a son's First Communion, eighty for an anniversary. A "small" christening for the immediate family can reach forty individuals.

Christmas, Thanksgiving, and Easter are obviously other auspicious occasions for the family. However, since these holidays pose a problem because spouses also have families nearby, some standard solutions are usually adopted. Usually celebrations where meals are served include only the immediate or modified extended family. Some nuclear families take turns going to one side one year and the other side the next; others might attend two Thanksgiving dinners and alternate between going to one side on Christmas Eve and the other side on Christmas Day. In any case, because these events are always celebrated in an extended family setting, a woman can reach middle age before she herself has the actual experience of preparing traditional foods for a holiday dinner.

The frequency of these family events leads to the conclusion, similar to Gans's (1962) on Italians in Boston, that it is difficult for a researcher to determine between social events and family events. There is an overlapping system where friends are also relatives rather than members of separate and distinguishable social units. Initially, each nuclear family remains a semiclosed system that maintains its separate residence and, in most cases, its own economic functions. Ideologically, the marital relationship is preserved as one of primary significance, but its integrity is often overshadowed by the family. In many cases, husbands and wives actually spend little leisure time alone together. Children are usually included in family gatherings unless it is a formal occasion outside the home where costs are a key factor.

Since the nuclear family is frequently drawn into wider kinship functions, the family as a private and solitary unit is not always visible. Visits and telephone calls among family members are continuous events over the course of an average day. Family help patterns are sufficiently well developed that babysitting and other services provide an extensive number of contacts. Furthermore, a drop-in visit to a parent frequently means one will also see visiting aunts and uncles. Finally, since many friends are also members of the family, the social life of the nuclear family is not as segmented between the family, relatives, and friends as is usually found.

However blurred the levels of family interaction become, the modified extended family, or what respondents call the immediate family, is the first order of expansion in Italian families and most other kinship systems in this country. Parents and siblings are one's immediate family and the first loyalty is due them. In many families we interviewed, this unit is the primary kinship unit, while a more extended group assumes little social significance. However, in families where sibling relationships are well developed as a basis for solidarity, a wider network of relatives inevitably is included through the parental link. Ultimately, this lays the framework for cousin solidarity, relationships that can persist after the deaths of the parents' generation.

Contact and Mutual Aid among Relatives

An earlier chapter described a series of primary relationships that was created by the Italian immigrants to buffer their adaptation to a foreign environment. The *paesani* (townspeople) and the *compari* (godparents) functioned as fictive kin until families were formed. Today, families have expanded to the extent that 90 percent of the Italians interviewed said they have at least thirty relatives, most of whom are in the area (defined as within one hour's drive). They identified significantly more relatives (<.004) than the Protestants, and these relatives are significantly more likely to live nearby (<.007). In fact, 65 percent of the families have relatives within walking distance. Thus, rates of geographic mobility are low among Italians, a factor that has created a large pool of available kin.

Since the Protestant control group also was drawn from a geographically stable population, they too have relatives in the vicinity. However, the degree to which these relatives are socially significant differs considerably from non-Italians. Italians are much more likely to choose relatives over friends as a basis for social interaction (<.008).

When parents are alive, their home is most often the focus for kinship gatherings. Sons and daughters drop by frequently during the week and after church on Sundays when there is often a large meal at the parents' house. Frequent contact with parents generally means contact with siblings, and often aunts and uncles who also have well-established visiting patterns: "I see my brother at my mother's," or "My aunt is always around when I stop by." It is interesting to note that the Italian Americans are almost twice as likely as the Protestants to see a parent daily, or at least several times a week. If personal contact is not possible, frequent telephone contacts are made, sometimes several times a day. The Protestants, on the other hand, reported more telephone contacts than visits.

Given the high involvement of the elderly in the lives of their children, particularly those children who married within the group, it is of interest to know what effect the parent's death has upon the solidarity of the kinship group. In all groups, there is no significant difference between those who have parents living or deceased and whether they are likely to spend a large portion of their time with relatives. Apparently, this investment in the kinship group does not change dramatically when the parents die. Visiting among families who have long been immersed in kin activities is not usually affected by the parent's death. The presence of the parents, in itself, does not perpetuate sibling solidarity.

There were few only children in immigrant families, so today almost all respondents have at least one brother or sister. In fact, the mean number of siblings for each Italian Americans is 3.3. Although most of the Protestants also have siblings in the area (mean 2.3), differences in sibling contact are enormous.

Table 4.2.

Nuclear Families' Contact with Relatives (by percentage)

Relatives contacted	In-married Italians, n = 74	Out-married Italians, n = 98	Protestant non-Italians, n = 56
Parents			
Daily	55	38	23
Weekly	37	43	48
Monthly or less	8	19	29
Siblings			
Daily	63	32	12
Weekly	25	41	34
Monthly or less	12	27	53
Other relatives			
Daily	10	4	13
Weekly	26	16	8
Monthly	18	27	17

As reported in Table 4.2, an Italian woman is five times as likely to see a sibling daily. Whereas only one in ten sees a sibling monthly or less, over half of the Protestants have such a record. The intermarried families fall somewhere in between, again indicating how intermarriage acts to change the Italian family organization. As is the case in most contemporary kinship systems, men are less likely to be as involved as are their wives. However, as reported in Table 3.1, Italian men are much more likely to see a sibling daily than are Protestant men, indicating that they are more kinship-oriented than most men.

Other relatives are less important in the families studied. In the in-married families, aunts, uncles, and cousins are seen at least weekly in one-third of the families. In contrast, these relationships were rarely reported as important in the Protestant families, so it was difficult to get extensive information. The more distant relatives are "wedding and funeral" contacts who do not assume significance upon other occasions for most Protestants and approximately for one-half of the Italian Americans. (However, as noted in the next chapter, these contacts might be underreported.)

An examination of the measures of contact reflect the propensity for Italian Americans to concentrate their time and energy on family matters. It is a rare family that is not embedded in a system composed of spouse and children, parents, brothers and sisters, and their children. This system means frequent telephone calls and visits; and weekends, particularly Sundays, are devoted to some family social affair. In fact, these relatives were referred to as friends: one chooses to see them frequently out of preference, because it is an enjoyable form of sociability.

Social contact among relatives usually means an active system of exchange. Help from a relative in finding jobs and achieving promotions is one prominent means of transferring mutual aid to the work role. For example, the frequency of reports of numerous family members working at one large industrial concern prompted us to explore this pattern further. In one extended family, ten members work for this company. Relatives functioned as intermediaries to advertise job openings and even provide an introduction to a foreman. Sponsorship in unions or introduction to friends who have job leads are common practices and eventually lead to a clustering of relatives at the work place.

The use of kinship assistance can serve other purposes. For example, a man had worked as a professional for a nationwide company for five years. Although he was successful, the job had several disadvantages. He had to travel extensively, a factor which alone would not have initiated a change. The real problem, as he saw it, was that good promotions could only come with transfers to larger branches in other cities. Both he and his wife had close ties to their families, which neither wanted to sever by having to move away. He chose to join a local firm where he could use the same skills. This firm's office was in a building owned by his second cousin who provided an introduction to the manager of the firm. It is difficult to determine, as the story unfolds, whether universalistic criteria played the major role in the job decision or whether it was an informal connection through a kinship link. Nevertheless, the family ties themselves influenced an important career change, a situation that came up time and again in the course of the interviews.

When a family has a business, the utilization of kinship personnel is even more extensive. If it is successful, the sons and even sons-in-law are expected to join the business. If it is a small business, such as a neighborhood grocery store, the resources become overly taxed. The Turturas had such a grocery and meat market. Over the years, the immigrant parents bought property around the store, so that by the time their children were adults, two sons and one son-in-law were able to work for the store and live rent-free with all the food they could eat. After all, these benefits were deducted, however, the establishment was not large enough to pay much else. The wives became discontented with the neighborhood, which was deteriorating, and, as children were born, they began to need spendable income. Several left the store for other jobs and also moved to newer neighborhoods. One son took his first job outside the family business when he was forty-one and, as the wife described it, it was the first time they had a regular income. Paradoxically, this was also the first time they had financial problems for they now had to pay for all the living expenses previously taken care of by the parents.

Working with family members can pose other kinds of problems. Mr. Lobisco worked for two cousins who own a successful construction company. As the business grew and prospered, he took on more and more duties, many of them menial chores. Since he never received a raise, he finally quit in anger. The reactions were heated among his close relatives, who rose to his defense. His two brothers went to the offending cousins and complained. "You have overworked him so much that he had to quit," they said. "You are leaving him and his family unprotected, a man without a job at the age of fifty-one—with nine years to go for a pension. You have taken advantage of our branch of the family." These complaints were of no avail, however, for Mr. Lobisco felt his cousins had been so heartless that he refused to take his job back even when they finally relented and made him a better offer.

One can only conclude that most families are independent economically from the extended family. However, in looking more closely at the situation of many families, one finds that the financial standing of the nuclear family is frequently improved through the informal assistance of relatives either by contacts, jobs, or patronage of family businesses. By strict definition, Italians live in nuclear families and tend to segregate their economic roles from the family roles. Yet for all practical purposes, the extended family plays an important role in daily life. Relatives are often the focal point for sociability, the source of much assistance, and in some cases facilitators to improve the financial standing of the nuclear family.

Highs and Lows in Kinship Solidarity

The Caglias illustrate a typical Italian-American family that is embedded in its extended family; they had one of the highest scores on kinship contact. Both Mr. and Mrs. Caglia are the children of immigrants and are in their late forties. Mr. Caglia is a foreman in a local industry, while Mrs. Caglia is a housewife. They have four children, two of whom have graduated from college.

When I arrived at the appointed time, no one answered the doorbell. Since cars were in the driveway, I went to the rear door leading to the kitchen. The doorbell had not been heard because of noise in the kitchen where Mrs. Caglia's elderly father, her sister, her two nieces, and their four children were having lunch. Babies were crying in the midst of much laughter and talking. Delicious-looking cold cuts, bread, and fruit were on the table. She led me into the living room leaving the others to finish their lunch. However, all were in and out and contributed some information during the interview. Her teen-age daughter and young son also joined us when they got home from school.

Mrs. Caglia described her social life as limited. She said she had very few friends. Since there were ten people in the house over the three hours, it was clear that she was referring to nonrelatives. Of relatives, she had many, and many of them clearly were close friends. She and her husband together had five siblings and nine aunts and uncles. Of these fourteen primary relatives, only one lived outside the local community. Her daily contacts usually included one sister, her father, her husband's sister, and her mother-in-law. Other siblings and aunts and uncles were seen almost weekly. Cousins were seen several times a month.

That day's lunch was described as resulting from the gloomy weather. Every Monday, her sister brings their father to Mrs. Caglia's for lunch. On the day of the interview, Tuesday, both sisters had decided it would be good to cheer up their father by repeating the routine. When her sister's married daughters found out, they also wanted to come "to have some fun."

Informal aid and sociability such as this took place spontaneously all the time. More formally, all graduations, birthdays, and christenings were recognized by dinners where at least fifty to sixty attend. For her daughter's college graduation, Mrs. Caglia had seventy guests for a picnic dinner. Gifts are exchanged on these occasions, although extensive gift-giving for Christmas has been abandoned.

Her ninety-one-year-old father was described as being very independent. Although he lived next door to her sister, he cooked his own meals and had only recently stopped baking his own bread. All his children had invited him to live with them, but he said his independence was the only thing that kept him going.

When asked about the source of her obligation to her father, Mrs. Caglia replied:

*We've always had a close family. We were taught the importance
of needing each other. We cry a lot; we're very sentimental. I regret this sometimes—that we're so involved with each other to
the extent that we exclude many other interests. Yet I see the children doing the same thing, so they must find it appealing.*

Upon graduation from college, their son did move away to take the only
good job he could find:

*He was very homesick. He lived at home during college so he was
unprepared for it. We were both upset about the move, but since
he had a good education, he had to use it. Fortunately, with the
help of my brother-in-law, he was able to find a suitable job here,
so he moved back.*

This family illustrates the close interdependence of a relatively large
group of relatives which transcends mere sociability. There is a strong
matrilineal focus with the solidarity of sisters maintaining a high level
of sociability. At the time of the interview, they were concentrating
much interest on a father who after years of authoritarian rule was now
relatively unproblematical in old age. Even with his eventual death, it is
most likely that high contact will continue, for the sibling solidarity has
expanded to include the youngest generations.

The fact that the dynamics of this solidarity were explained in terms
of sentimental ties is also quite representative of Italian families. When
the luncheon guests left, all eight of them kissed the respondent. When
asked what the best way is to show a mother's love, Mrs. Caglia responded, "to convey feelings." The words "love" and "heart" were frequently used.

In contrast to highly interdependent families such as the Caglias,
those Italian families who had little kinship contact had varied circumstances. However, three-quarters of them were in the working class.
Some had experienced divorce and early deaths of parents in their
childhood. There were several cases where dire economic circumstances prevented interaction with relatives. For example, the husband
of one of these families had such an erratic work history that they
could no longer afford either a car or a telephone. This series of re-
verses caused many moves, so by the time of the interview they had
been long removed from an Italian neighborhood. Without transportation or communication, contact was difficult. In other words, they had
joined the lower-lower class, a position which in their case was well

outside the boundaries of the ethnic group. The parents of both husband and wife had been divorced, so both had experienced some family instability in their own childhood.

This example illustrates the insurmountable difficulties that marginal
economic status imposes. For reciprocity to operate, some assets are
necessary even if one must receive more than one can give in return.
In this family, these minimal assets were absent. There were five children to support on the erratic wages of the husband. The wife worked
nights cleaning offices in order to augment the income. Consequently,
there was little energy or time left to give after the survival of the family was secured. Middle-class families do possess these assets. In
a group such as Italians, where middle-class women usually do not
work, the wives are relatively free from economic responsibilities
which enables them to establish patterns of reciprocity with parents
and relatives.

The Female-Linked Kinship Bond

Most studies of American kinship describe the importance of females
in maintaining kinship solidarity (Troll 1971). While the American
kinship system is usually described as bilateral at least normatively,
studies of contact and aid indicate that it is the females' activities that
give the system a matrilateral emphasis. In active kinship systems, the
mother-daughter bond is the central relationship over the life span, but
it has been noted that this bond intensifies as a daughter marries and
replicates her mother's role (Bott 1971; Gans 1962; Young and Willmott 1957). Daughters have close ties with both parents particularly as
they approach old age, as illustrated by Mrs. Caglia and her sister.
Parents are more likely to call upon a daughter over a son when they
need some assistance because of declining capacities in old age.

A kinship system that hinges upon the activities of women logically
could be affected by other demands upon the women. The high percentage of women working today is sometimes mentioned as a variable affecting the family and kinship system (Brody 1981; Treas
1977). In contrast to childbearing, which can be carried out in the context of the family, a job today does not generally take place in a family setting. Italian men have long been opposed to wives working. The
cultural ideal is a division of labor clearly segregating the economic
role from the domestic role. While recent research from historical rec-

ords indicates that many immigrant women had to seek jobs, these jobs generally were concentrated in home industries or in work places where relatives also worked (McLaughlin 1971).

Today, Italian women married to Italian men are somewhat less likely to work than women in the other groups, although the differences are not significant. Furthermore, whether or not women in these samples work depends upon their socioeconomic status; women in working-class families are more likely to work if their children are older.

An examination of correlations between a wife's work status and her family activities shows few areas of significance. If a wife is home all the time, she is somewhat more likely to have more sense of obligation to her parents and other relatives, but the amount of contact she has with these relationships is not affected.

There is considerable evidence in these interviews that, when a women works, she must rely on her family for more assistance than she would if she stayed home. Although most of the children are in high school, and thus do not need constant supervision, the role the grandmother or the aunt plays is usually impressive. In earlier years, they might have babysat, while now they act in some supervisory capacity such as checking up on children after school. Food sharing for dinner also provides valuable help to a busy working mother. In other words, if a woman has a job, her kinship supports provide some domestic and childcare assistance. It is conceivable that kinship contacts increase in such instances.

Thus, among the factors affecting kinship solidarity and the typical matrilateral emphasis, the incidence of women working is not one of them. This situation is particularly true in families that have always maintained a high level of kinship solidarity.

The Connectedness of the Social Network

When Italian Americans gather with relatives, they are associating with other Italians, individuals who place high priority on the family. Thus, in the majority of families, their social network is largely dominated by relatives as well as friends who share a common social background. Primary relationships can be lifelong. For example, many respondents recounted their childhood in a large extended family where grandparents lived in the household and aunts and uncles on the same block. English was not necessary until one entered school, but even then most of the students were Italians. Since these friendships could last into adulthood, extensive exposure to wider American values was minimal. Many of our respondents facing difficulties with an aged parent would agree with Mrs. Nicita, who said "My friends are all in the same boat. We have our own therapy group." Thus, Old World values are less often challenged.

One friendship group of twelve couples described themselves as "our little Mafia." They all had attended St. Teresa's, the national parish school, so many of the close friendships were formed in elementary school. Today, they have a regular schedule of parties. At one, skits are prepared caricaturing numerous aspects of Italian-American life. One talented amateur performer is still remembered for her skit on the Italian mother.

Nevertheless, few Italian Americans can limit their friendship group solely to their own ethnic group. Too much intermarriage has occurred to make that possible even if it were a choice. Furthermore, most respondents find it distasteful to recreate the insular "Little Italies" they remember from their childhoods. Having non-Italian friends is desirable and about 60 percent report a mixed friendship group. However, only three families (4 percent) have mostly non-Italian friends, a statistic that increases to 21 percent among intermarried families.

Voluntary associations such as clubs, parent groups at school, and religious and political groups, do not have widespread appeal among the Italian respondents. Only 25 percent are active in at least one such organization. Even fewer are active in ethnic associations, such as the Daughters of Columbus or the Sons of Italy.

One interpretation of this pattern of association stems from the nature of Italian family life. Altruism and sociocentric interests are quite evident, but philanthropy is usually confined to the family. When close friendships develop, they are likely to assume many of the features of kinship relationships. Hence, measures of participation in voluntary organizations would tap only one small and relatively insignificant feature of the social life of most of the respondents. The relatively low level of outside participation has important effects, the most likely one being the limited exposure to competing norms stemming from secondary associations. Furthermore, active participation in numerous clubs is more likely to mean a loose-knit network, for it is less likely that club membership overlaps. For example, a mother's club at school or other social clubs do not always include the same members. Finally, low participation is generally not accompanied by social isolation; it means that, with the reduction of secondary associations, more time and energy can be concentrated on the family. With this concentration on the family comes a connected network in which members can develop and maintain consensus on the norms of family life.

The effects of these close networks are more evident when one examines the degree to which they are ethnically contained (Bott 1971). For example, correlations between the ethnic composition of the network and other family variables found that the families that socialize mainly with other Italian Americans are likely to have values and behaviors characteristic of that group. Those who confined their networks to other Italians are significantly more likely to display high filial behaviors ($r = .2571, < .02$). Likewise, ethnic contacts also are associated with traditional childrearing practices ($r = .3918, < .02$). These friendships with other Italians most likely result in a normative consensus on preferred family patterns which reinforces traditional practices.

The networks dominated by relatives are also associated with high filial behaviors ($r = .2852, < .007$) and more traditional patterns of raising children ($r = .1961, < .05$). Obviously, a high degree of association among kin means that one is also absorbed with others in one's ethnic group, which in turn tends to reinforce values on relationships to one's parents and to relatives. Finally, these factors working together exert some pressure on individuals as to the valued way to raise children. In all likelihood, it would be difficult to use permissive childrearing techniques if one is continually surrounded by family and friends who hold different values. In particular, if children are likely to be included in adult social functions, they are pressured to conform to the strictures of traditional ways.

Sentiments and Emotions

No discussion on the Italian-American family is complete without some discussion of the manner in which emotions and sentiment color the daily life of the family. Rudolph Vicoli (1974), in a review of the contemporary Italian-American family, identified this area as one of its major distinguishing features. A fluctuating emotional climate exists with expressions of love briefly erupting into anger and hostility and, upon the cessation of conflict, few resentments are observable. Thus, conflict is a regular feature of family life, but it is usually con-

fined to periodic outbursts and does not usually cause open and permanent ruptures. The interview material indicates that both positive and
negative sentiments are permissible or even encouraged among family
members. The respondents were rarely neutral when it came to family matters.

In fact, emotional neutrality to them was generally interpreted as an
American characteristic and one that denoted noninvolvement or even
the absence of affection. For example, non-Italian relatives by marriage
were often singled out as different from others because they were distant
and unemotional. "He acts like a stranger, even after all these years
married to my sister." Or some non-Italian affinal relatives are seen as
treating relatives as friends, meaning absence of emotions, which can
be an offense in Italian families. "He is aloof and cold," said one respondent. Another called her brother-in-law "Mr. Non-Personality" because he does not relate to others on an emotional basis.

The emotional bond is reaffirmed by frequent kissing. "It's kissy-
kissy all the time. We're not afraid to express our feelings." One important politician described how he differs from his non-Italian colleagues.
"If my father walked into a room, even if I were meeting with the gover-
nor, I would get up and kiss him." One Irish woman who married into
an Italian family and adopted many of its ways recounted, "When I see
my sister's children, they call me their kissing aunt. Here's Aunt Ann,
she's going to kiss us."

There was general agreement among the respondents that the Italian
family is closer than other groups because as Italians they are warmer
and have more heart and feeling for each other. In commenting upon
family, the affective and emotional elements far outweighed pragmatic
instrumental concerns. For example, one respondent described the intensity of feeling created by the emotional bond as she got off a plane in
Italy to meet her mother's relatives for the first time. "We all said after-
wards that our blood started to boil, our hearts beat faster." Another reported, "We cry a lot. I guess we're too sentimental."

Hence, neutrality in regard to family is an American characteristic
when contrasted to the Italian way of relating to one another. In many
respects, interviews with Protestant respondents confirm these judgments. In general, one has one's own life to lead. One Protestant woman's response was typical: "I teach my sons to be independent—to think
for themselves. We aren't always running to each other with our problems. Our lives are our own to lead as we please as long as we are
happy." Another confirmed this judgment. "I like my family and my

husband's too, but I don't feel an obligation. I feel the same way doing
something for friends." Or, "No one expects a great deal from others in
our family. We wouldn't be devastated if we had no family around."

Lastly, for the Protestants, marriage is what counts, not family.
"Once you're married, you are on your own. It's tough enough leading
your own life; you can't be that involved with relatives."

The view of the Protestants can be contrasted to that of the Italians
who consider the bond between relatives as sometimes burdensome but
always a source of security. Mutual responsibility and potential for sacrifice also were considered key factors. This affiliation was expressed
as, "What you want for others you want for yourself. There is less distinction between the two, because that's the way you are brought up.
You just wouldn't put your family down." In this ideology, sacrifice in
the name of family creates a security so that "one never has to face a crisis alone." Another phrase used to describe this strong bond was "We
stick together like glue."

Love, respect, self-sacrifice, and mutual responsibility essentially
summarized the diffuse sentiments most respondents expressed in regard to their families. The intensity of these sentiments among some respondents was such that nonrelatives were invariably excluded. "A family is all you really have. You can have friends, but the family is really
all you have." Only the family can meet these diffuse needs for related-
ness. "You can have five million friends, but they're not worth anything
if you don't have relatives to love and care for you."

Although neutrality in discussing family is virtually unheard of
among Italian respondents, they did not continually glorify their families. In fact, criticism of the family also signified an expression of feelings, and thus was not condemned. These criticisms often are a source
of humor and comic relief, where one can poke fun at practices in which
all are deeply involved. Such humor probably functions as an escape
valve, to let off steam at times when family responsibilities become
too burdensome.

Thus, idealism in regard to family matters is qualified by numerous
reservations. For one thing, the sheer number of people creates problems for some. "It's overpowering—all the people, the noise and the
confusion." An even more frequent complaint is that the family stifles
growth to the extent that one can not develop as an individual. "We
would have done more with our lives if we hadn't been so involved with
family." "One cannot lead his own life, because he must always think
of others first." Or, "The sense of family can be carried too far

—parents smother children with love, so they can't lead lives of their own." Sometimes the expectations can be too much: "If you don't go to a fourth cousin's wedding, you're in trouble."

Although emotions of love and warmth are highly valued, that too has its negative side. When one is bound to others, then one by necessity is involved in the daily trials and tribulations of numerous individuals. Consequently, "their problems become your problems." Crises of various proportions were frequently observed. The interviewers can document this fact by the many times the telephone rang during interviews and heated discussions took place. One respondent summarized the problem as such: "With so many who are so close, you have to carry a big load. You get heartbroken awful fast." Another described a neighbor who was without family ties as a truly happy person, because she was not caught up with many relatives and daily concerns of illness, marital problems, or the balancing of the emotional needs of many personalities.

Thus, the positive features are often weighed against the negative. While the expression of emotions is viewed postively, it is also recognized that one can easily lose a sense of objectivity. "We should be more rational—instead, we're all feelings."

While these conceptions of good family life—love and warmth, security, and the expression of emotions—are the most commonly mentioned features of the Italian family, each one was hedged with a consideration of the disadvantages. These comments can be categorized into paired oppositions. Love and warmth of Italians in contrast to coldness and aloofness of others essentially describes the conflict between mind and heart. Likewise, the advantages or disadvantages of security can be described as the problem of resolving the dilemma of freedom or independence versus interdependence. Lastly, the expression of emotions describes the opposition between rationality and emotionality.

In a later chapter, the conception of a good family life held by elderly Italian Americans is summarized rather simply in four elements: good food, a clean house, respect, and affection. While the middle-aged respondents would espouse some agreement with each of these categories, they do not accept the old-fashioned way in its entirety. For the second- and third-generation respondents, the old-fashioned way is colored by a great deal of ambivalence even though most heartily endorse the value that family is of supreme importance and the most central unit of life.

The resulting ideology of the families is a study of opposites, often in basic contradiction. As these opposites are examined and filtered through the respondents' normative system, the paradoxes are recognized and accepted. Choices are usually made that give precedence to one without totally suppressing the other. When some behaviors were at odds with family values, these were justified on the basis of emotions as long as it was only a temporary infraction.

For example, respect is a catch-all concept usually used to explain the positive features of the family: "Italian families work well because there is respect." However valued, respect does not mean one must suffer silently in the face of some injustice. One can even challenge a parent and freely ventilate feelings. Yet the respect is not seen as being diluted, because the parent understands it is merely a show of emotions which does not change the quality of the relationship.

A second theme was that of forgiveness. Despite clearly defined values on family obligations, the Italians generally did not reject another family member because of an infraction. They would complain and argue with the deviant member and hope for the desired result; however, if that failed, they usually accepted him as he was and lived with the consequences. For example, Mrs. Nappa's brother had been in trouble with the police and had never completely reformed. Yet he was never rejected for he was not seen as being to blame. He was excused because, as she reported, "He has always had bad friends."

In other words, Italians are pragmatic when dealing with the personalities of individuals. Bad behaviors were usually traced to some uncontrollable emotional force or to bad influences in the social environments, both of which were viewed as beyond the family's ability to control.

Consequently, this expression of what is initially viewed as absolute values, such as respect, sacrifice, and devotion to the family, actually are juxtaposed with their opposites. One can hold idealized conceptions of family at the same time realistic concerns are weighed. Hence, there is a hedge against acting upon these values; an out is provided if idealistic goals cannot be fulfilled. The result of this pragmatic orientation essentially means that family expectations are generally met because there is a sliding scale of expectations where individuals must strive to meet family goals. If an individual fails, there is foregiveness, and the individual is accepted as he or she is. Any blame to be assigned is traced to the uncontrollable forces of emotions or to the immutable elements of the environment.

In any case, many of the daily activities of the average family do not take place within the privacy of the nuclear household. Instead the family, although nuclear in structure, is relatively public to the purview, advice, and sometimes interference of a host of relatives. Neither independence and self-direction for the individual nor privacy and intimacy in a nuclear unit are likely to develop, because individuals are encircled by relatives who generally have a consensus on values of family life.

Chapter 5
Celebrating the Family Cycle

Patricia Quinn Pirro and Colleen Leahy Johnson

This chapter extends the analysis of kinship to include a description of the many special occasions when relatives congregate. In the course of the interviews, it was often reported that cousins or aunts and uncles were seen only on special occasions. It was difficult to secure more specific information on the frequency of contact and it appeared that the time of the year the interview took place determined the frequency reported. Upon further examination, it was found that "special occasions" meant ritualized religious and life-cycle events. Because the numbers of socially significant relatives were large, these occasions were frequent.

In the cyclical passage of time, family centeredness is continually reinforced through different types of periodic rituals and celebrations. First, life-cycle events are ritualized by the formal sacraments of the Catholic church: baptism (*battesimo*), First or Holy Communion (*comunione*), confirmation (*conferma*), wedding (*sposalizio*), and the funeral (*funerale*). Second, secular life-passage rites such as birthdays, graduations, and wedding anniversaries are usually recognized by a kinship group. Third, holidays such as Thanksgiving, Christmas, Easter, and New Year's are focal points of sociability. Fourth, some families have devised an organizational structure to oversee activities such as reunions, family club meetings, or even bowling teams. While only some families have reunions, virtually all celebrate the calendrical and life-cycle events by including numerous relatives outside the nuclear family.

Nutrimento

Throughout all these rituals, parties, and commemorations, the common thread is always the same: food, known to Italians as *nutrimento*.

Food, rather than alcohol, is the focal point of festivities when family members have parties. Strongly spiced entrees, rich desserts, and potent homemade wine are usually present. This close connection between food and family life, according to Gambino (1974:24), stems from the symbolic importance of food and the likening of family meals as "daily communions."

Historically, the plight of the family hinged upon uncontrollable events such as wars, invasions, and political repression. According to Cronin(1970), behind the safe walls of their homes, the Italians could at least have control over their food supply. In fact, plumpness was a status symbol in southern Italy for it indicated a family head had succeeded in his primary role even in the face of other failures.

While setting a good table today is a source of status for most Italian women, the contemporary woman has some ambivalence about that point of honor and the equally important goal of retaining a now fashionably thin figure. Long plagued by stereotypes of Italian women who turn to fat by at least the age of forty, the average woman finds herself continually on diets to attempt to reach both cultural ideals: provider of ample meals and one who also has to control the weight gain typical of middle age.

Daily meals are usually set aside as a time for sociability within the nuclear family. Children are required to be home for meals at the designated time so the family can eat together. If father arrives home from work at five o'clock, dinner will be served shortly thereafter. If he arrives as late as seven o'clock, the children are usually required to wait for their meal even if it means missing out on their other activities. Many times wives glanced anxiously at the clock if interviews lasted late into the afternoon, for it meant dinner would be delayed.

The respondents often cited eating patterns as an indicator of ethnicity. "If someone doesn't eat pasta twice a week and on Sunday, he's not Italian." "Families become American when they stop serving lasagna with the Thanksgiving turkey." "A household which does not have at least two pots simmering on the stove does not have an Italian wife." "Wherever you find two Italians, you find food." Italian men who marry non-Italians are frequently described as thin and hungry looking, and their mothers and aunts express concern over their diet.

The provision of food lies with the Italian father, but the dispensing of food is the mother's domain; the quality and quantity of the food reflect on the quality of her maternal nurturance. She uses food not only for daily sustenance but also as preventive medicine. For example, chicken soup has the same curative power among Italian mothers as among Jewish ones. Its preparation is almost ritual in nature and is considered a highly prized talent. A good chicken soup, like other key foods, reflects her talents as a wife and mother.

This close association between food and mothering results in some predictable problems, according to an Italian pediatrician in Easton who related an incident that is fairly representative of his Italian clientele. A young Italian-American mother brought in her three-month-old baby for his monthly check-up and immunizations. The infant weighed in at eighteen pounds, a five-pound gain over the second month and only a few pounds less than the average baby weighs at one year. During the examination, the young mother's repeated complaint was, "This baby doesn't eat!" To her, the fatter the baby, the healthier. The size of the baby was also an index of the successful maintenance of her maternal and wifely responsibilities. The expression *"mange, mange"* or "eat, eat," was on the lips of many immigrant mothers and is still heard today.

Food is also a common medium of gift exchange. For example, buying gifts for Mrs. Martini's mother-in-law was a tedious chore. Not knowing what to buy her for her birthday, Mrs. Martini presented her with a gallon of olive oil. "She was delighted," Mrs. Martini reported, "because it's so expensive these days. She won't cook with anything else."

Gifts of food can also serve as an apology for some oversight. Forgetting an aunt's anniversary, for example, can be forgiven by baking her a cake. Marital squabbles are sometimes resolved with food. In order to make amends, one husband surprised his wife with a gift-wrapped gallon of the best imported olive oil. The wife's response was, "I thought he was supposed to bring me candy or flowers. Well, at least he knows it's something I can use. After all, it costs almost $10.00."

By some reports, food also has been used in combating depression. When most individuals feel depressed, their energy level declines, they cannot work, they retreat from others, they have difficulty sleeping, or they may increase their consumption of alcohol. For Italian Americans, alcohol has never been a major source of combatting emotional lows or, for that matter, a focal point of sociability. Camille Paglia (1976) has observed in her ethnic background that the great restorative powers of food make depressiveness alien to Italian character:

*I believe our ability to take great pleasure in parties and cele-
brations and to find spiritual restoration in the almost ritualistic
preparation and consumption of food is one of our great
strengths. . . . When under pressure, I, for example, will seek
out some rare delicacy—the spicier, the better. As a consequence, I am immediately cheerful again. Unfortunately, the
disadvantage of this method is a tendency to gain weight.*

In the celebrations described in the following, food is an important ingredient and its preparation perpetuates long-established traditions.

Battesimo

Even before a baby is born, Italian-American parents begin thinking
about who will baptize the baby. "It's an honor to baptize a baby. The
baby becomes a special person to you," according to one respondent.
By church guidelines, the role of godparent is one of religious responsibility; the godparent is responsible for the baby's religious guidance
and rearing in case of the death of the parents. Most godparents would
agree that they see themselves responsible for the actual rearing of the
child if the parents were deceased and if there were no other immediate relatives to assume the parenting role. This formal responsibility,
however, is overshadowed by important ongoing social functions. The
custom creates kinship relationships out of non-kin relations and it further cements the existing bond among relatives.

A rigid set of rules for the selection of a godparent is not recorded.
However, there is high probability that the choice will come from the
following categories: relatives such as a sibling of a parent, a sibling
of the baby, a close aunt or uncle, or a cousin. Among nonrelatives,
likely candidates are the best man or maid of honor at the parents'
wedding, or old school friends of the parents. Immigrants who had
few relatives in this country usually chose a *paesano* out of necessity,
but today parents tend to choose relatives. Whoever is chosen is
treated with respect and deference by both the parents and the child.

The *battesimo* is the ceremony that combines church doctrine, family ideology, and some vestiges of old superstition. Up until the ceremony the *bambino* carries some of the burden of original sin, so the
ceremony is performed as soon after the birth as possible. First-generation Italians believed that every time an infant smiled before he was

baptized, he was smiling at the devil. If the baby showed any signs of illness before he was baptized, it was the devil's doing. Thus, the ceremony itself was seen as causing observable difference in the behavior of the baptized infant. A fussy baby might suddenly sleep peacefully through the night. Even though young parents no longer find much appeal in these folk beliefs today, they take special care not to expose their infant to any danger before baptism.

By custom, the godparents "dress" the baby for baptism by furnishing the clothing the infant wears the day of the ceremony. If the family already has a special outfit used for all christenings, the godparent might buy a white blanket, baptismal bib, fancy booties, or little silk shoes. It is not unusual to provide a bracelet, necklace, or ring adorned with a religious medal to ward off the evil eye (*malocchio*). This tradition echoes the godparents' responsibility to the child. They are not only guardians in the eyes of God, but in the realm of the real world of economic support, if necessary.

Parties are usually held after the morning or early-afternoon ceremony. They can range in size from the immediate family to a host of relatives and friends. Parties may last into the evening, and a few have been known to continue for three days. It is a safe assumption that the mother of the baby and perhaps her mother and mother-in-law have been busy preparing the food several days in advance.

From this day on, reciprocity vitalizes the bond between the godparents and the godchild as both now have a special responsibility to each other. Gifts are exchanged for birthdays and Christmas, and godparents are honored on Mother's Day and Father's Day along with one's parents. Informal exchanges of aid, support, and sociability are also part of the relationship.

The seriousness with which the godparent role is taken varies according to the individual, but mutual responsibilities are both social and religious. For example, Mr. Montini was the godfather of his sister's son. Being a strict Roman Catholic, he took his job seriously. As the boy grew, Mr. Montini always treated his godson as someone a bit more special than his other nephews. When his godson recently got married in a Protestant church, Mr. Montini's grumbling was apparent to everyone. He announced that he had to leave the reception to attend mass, although there were several masses he could attend the following day. He did not return to the reception. After days passed and no words were exchanged, his wedding gift was returned to him.

Mr. and Mrs. Sardella were happy to baptize the infant daughter of their close friends, the Vitos. Shortly before her second birthday, the little girl died. Each year on her birthday and on the anniversary of her death, they place a bouquet of roses on her grave.

Mrs. Rossi was on her deathbed. It was just a matter of time before she was expected to die. Being from a poor immigrant family, the Rossis did not know how they could pay for the funeral they thought their mother deserved. Her godchild was aware of the situation and offered to help. As a sign of love and respect, she sewed the dress in which Mrs. Rossi was buried.

Comunione

After a period of catechism the Roman Catholic child at the age of seven is prepared to receive his or her first Holy Communion. It is a special occasion in any Catholic group, but to the Italian Catholic it becomes analogous to elevated family membership. The First Communion signifies that the child has become a bona fide member of the Holy Family.

Family and friends flock to the church to witness this sacrament. On one such event, Saint Teresa's Church was filled to capacity. Relatives started arriving over an hour before the mass to secure aisle seats for the best view. Cameras of all sizes and shapes, flashcubes, and movie lights were ready to record the event for posterity. Anxious relatives were chattering in Italian, English, and broken English. Grandmothers smiled and babies cried. At last the singing children filed in procession into the church.

Boys were dressed smartly in suits of all variations, and all wore identical white ribbon armbands. The girls resembled miniature brides with their white dresses and veils. Although the nuns tried to provide the girls with identical veils, they had to make exceptions, as always, for those girls who wished to wear veils made or worn by relatives. A few of the veils were handmade by relatives in Italy and sent to the girl to be worn on this special occasion. Such attire can be viewed as part of the socialization process that represents and reinforces the ideal of virginity and foreshadows the marriage ceremony as the ideal family bond (A. Parsons 1969).

After the ceremony, everyone from the family circle is invited to a party to celebrate, and some families even rent halls to accommodate large numbers. At some big parties, the food is very lavish, and gifts, usually money or religious items, may be given. On the next day at school, children in the second grade at Saint Teresa's school have been known to compare amounts of their net profits from each of their individual parties. One boy proudly announced his total acquisition of four hundred dollars.

Conferma

After special religious instruction, twelve- or thirteen-year-olds are admitted to full church membership. Again, the social functions overshadow the religious ones. At this time, an additional godparent of the same sex is chosen as sponsor. Although the parents may influence the choice, it is the adolescent's responsibility to choose a *comare* or *compare* with whom he or she is already close. The sponsor is often a young adult who also serves as close friend and confidant.

Like the communion, the church ceremony is followed by a party. Gifts of money or religious items are given once again, and the godparent traditionally gives the child a watch. This occasion sets into motion the same type of reciprocity found between the baptismal godparent and godchild, but since the godparent at the time of confirmation is closer in age, the choice usually functions to strengthen collateral relationships.

A godmother might also be a confidante to a young person. Mrs. Nardello was concerned about her goddaughter-niece. At the age of sixteen, the girl was having a conflict with her parents which deteriorated to the point where she threatened to quit school and run away. Mrs. Nardello felt compelled to intervene so she took the girl into her own home where she remained for almost ten months. "I couldn't just sit by and let that girl ruin her life. She just needed a vacation from her parents."

Sposalizio

The wedding ceremony transcends the recognition of union between man and wife because it functions to bring together the friends and relatives of both families. Although judged by some as conspicuous consumption, the elaborate wedding and reception are meant to underscore the establishment of this new relationship between two families.

A wedding is a gala event, particularly if it involves a "nice Italian boy and girl."

Prenuptial festivities begin early. The bride is honored by showers where friends and relatives give household gifts and money. Stag parties are staged for the groom by his male friends and relatives. Since few parties include both sexes, these traditions reinforce conceptions of separate sex roles with the female's centered in the home and the male's outside.

The wedding celebration is so important in some families that when a daughter is born, the father anticipates the eventual party by saving money. (A son, on the other hand, prompts a savings account for his education.) Families have been known to go into debt to provide a fitting wedding for their daughter. In order to avoid high costs nowadays, however, a few families are breaking the tradition of having the bride's family alone bear the expense. In order to provide a really sumptuous feast, they enlist the help of the groom's family, if they are Italian. When a son marries a non-Italian, the stand-up affair without a banquet provided by the bride's parents is usually noted with disapproval. Some Italian families host a large dinner for their own relatives after the "American affair."

An old-fashioned Italian wedding means an all-day celebration. We were told of a wedding that began with a high mass at 10 A.M., after which drinks were served to approximately one thousand people. At one o'clock, there was a dinner for two hundred family members and close friends. After a short respite for the family, over one thousand people returned in the evening when pizza and other Italian foods were served, and guests were provided with an open bar and an orchestra for dancing well into the early hours of the morning.

The expense and demands of these old-fashioned weddings are causing many families to turn to smaller affairs of four to five hundred people. To cut costs, children outside the immediate family are excluded. Guests sit down to dinner at tables of eight or ten which are festooned with colorful place cards, individually wrapped cookies, and other souvenirs. Many courses of food are served along with wine and other liquors.

Seating arrangements must be carefully planned for they reflect the hierarchy of family and friends. Those closest to the bride and groom are placed near the head table. When the bride and groom are both Italian, attempts are made to mingle their family and friends, so that new bonds of solidarity are formed. Scrupulous hosts also consult with other relatives on seating preferences, particularly if there is a rift in the family; hosts avoid seating relatives together who might be squabbling. The outcomes, of course, are noted by the other guests.

Gifts are so generous that they can function as initial economic support for the new couple. These gifts often form an economic tie between the bride and groom and their families and relatives as they initiate new patterns of reciprocity. Gifts also signify an investment in the new union and its future stability as well as a recognition of the expanded family group.

Funerale

A death is a great social loss and it brings an immediate response from everyone. It means sending food and flowers, giving money, congregating at the home of the deceased, and, of course, eating. The emotional outpourings can be profuse, and the activities around a funeral provide especially distinct examples of the difference between the Italian and the American way of ritualizing life events. For the Italian, it means three to four days of wake, both in the home and the funeral parlor, and a large meal after the funeral. An "American" wake means a shorter one, and, in some cases, abandonment of the meal after the funeral. While traditions appear to be changing as many families begin to adopt features of the American wake, Italian funerals remain more elaborate than are generally found today.

All important life events must center on the home, and funerals are no exception. In the old days, Italian funeral homes did not exist. Undertaking was a thriving business, but undertakers principally handled only the ritual preparation of the body; the other functions remained in the hands of the family. Since wakes were held at home and funerals at church, they could operate out of small establishments, sometimes even embalming in the home, where the individual usually died. In the home, the family kept a twenty-four-hour vigil over the deceased. Out of respect, all other activity ceased, a restriction which brought the traditions of "feeding the family."

The earliest undertaking establishments in Easton had both men and women as embalmers. Today, these many small businesses have disappeared, leaving two large, prosperous Italian funeral homes. Families select between them according to which funeral director knows their own regional customs and social activities centering around the wake.

Like other life events, among the first response to death is food, which is brought in by friends and distant relatives. Interview questions about what goes on after a death in the family frequently brought the reply of "cooking mostly." "Italians feel food will solve any problem, so I send lasagna." One woman described her reaction as such:

I shop at a German market. Whenever I get a stewing chicken, the butcher asks, "who died?" We feel that death leaves you cold and you need chicken soup to warm you up. The family needs plenty of food, for closest relatives go sit with them for three days of wake. Then a meal is served after the funeral.

Sometimes the culinary response begins even before death. Naturally, food is brought in when a member of the family is ill so others do not have to cook, but these offerings are more moderate than funeral food. In one case, a young Italian woman was critically ill in the hospital. "Her parents and aunts and uncles were beside themselves. All congregated daily at their home and to fill the time they began cooking. Fortunately, she recovered, and no one minded freezing 170 veal cutlets."

Food is abundant during the days of the wake. After the funeral, a large meal ideally should be served in the home. In a few cases, meals are held in restaurants, but this act often brings disapproval. Even having a meal catered at home causes some criticism, for it means the family does not have a tradition of helping each other, or, worse yet, they have no one available. It also means the American way of doing things. In order to preserve tradition, one family avoided having a wake in the home of the deceased parent's son because he had a non-Italian wife. "She never got into the Italian way." "Getting into the Italian way" means providing a profuse array of tasty dishes. one respondent remembering this even in his childhood concluded, "Death never scares me. It has always seemed like a big neighborhood social."

Whether the wake is in the family home or the funeral parlor, the open casket is strategically placed, where mourners can file by, pausing to kneel and say a prayer. Some occasionally touch the corpse. Male relatives stand near the casket, while the women are seated along the wall. The room is full of flowers; some floral wreaths or chairs given by the family cost up to two hundred dollars.

Today, friends are less likely to give flowers and more likely to give money and mass cards. Since a "good funeral" costs over $2,500, one concludes the family can use the extra cash. The wife of a wealthy businessman might still have four rooms filled with flowers, but a poor widow receives fewer flowers and more money to carry on with afterwards. Such assistance is necessary, for many times a family pays more for a funeral than they can readily afford. This display represents the respect for the dead one, an expense most are not willing to forego.

All family and friends are expected to participate. Distant relatives and associates also attend out of respect for the family even if they are not personally close to the deceased. Hard feelings often occur when those who are expected fail to appear. The arrangement of relatives at the wake, the funeral, and the funeral procession represents a hierarchy of blood relations, and thus those most closely related are placed first regardless of their social or emotional bond to the deceased.

The funeral procession to the cemetery is another symbol of the status of the family. There is great pride in the "bigness" of the event which is usually stated by the numbers of cars in the procession. For an active leader with a large family and many social ties, the procession numbers over 150 cars. Relatives also note who stands by as the procession goes down the streets of the Northside. During the immigrant days, a truly complete funeral had an empty limousine near the head of the procession representing the bereaved relatives in Italy who could not be present.

Although there is a tendency today to cut down on the elaborateness of the *funerale,* it remains very much a family and community event. Its ritual recognition far exceeds current American practices of deemphasizing death. Family and friends still acknowledge the need for the mourning process in the company of loved ones in order to accommodate to the loss. Abundant tears and moaning are still recognized as the proper expression of grief. To give up these customs would mean to many an improper expression of respect for the deceased. In fact, where the loss is great, such as in the death of a child, expressions of grief continue for years. Frequently, classified ads in the obituary sections of the paper carry a picture of the deceased and a word to the beloved on the anniversary of the death.

Other Life Events and Their Rituals

Passage through school is also marked by family celebrations. While smaller family parties are held at graduation from elementary school when only members of the immediate family are invited, high school and college graduations merit a more elaborate event. If the family can afford it and have a larger group to entertain, a restaurant may be used. One family honored their son's high school graduation with a buffet dinner and open bar at a restaurant. Of the 130 invited, 80 were relatives. The guests gave money which the son saved for college expenses. The costs of the dinner were split between the boy's parents and two bachelor brothers of his mother. It is not uncommon to hold June graduation parties at home for seventy to eighty members, particularly since the warm weather allows use of the yard for overflow guests. The mother and other female relatives cook for days ahead. In fact, it was more difficult to schedule our interviews in June than any other month because of the abundance of graduation parties. Unlike weddings, where food is supplied by the caterers, graduation means the mother and other female relatives must cook an elaborate array of food.

Birthdays are honored mainly by the immediate family, and gifts are given only by guests invited to the party. Children's birthdays include parents, siblings, grandparents, and favorite aunts and uncles. These are among the smallest of traditional celebrations. After childhood, there is less formal recognition except when an individual gets on in years. A large party might be held for an elderly parent which probably indirectly expresses the concern that the individual might not be around much longer.

Wedding anniversaries are honored at the milestones of twenty-five and fifty years when a large group of relatives and friends are invited to a dinner. These celebrations are held either at home or, if the budget permits, at a restaurant. However, in an average year, other anniversaries, like birthdays, are usually marked by small dinners with the nuclear family and selected relatives.

There is great flexibility among families in how they observe these annual events. In some cases, gatherings do not differ greatly from a weekly get-together except for the inclusion of a special cake. Whatever the family custom, opportunities to celebrate always ritualize an individual's relationship to the family or, in the case of graduation, on progression into adulthood where one's relationship to the family must undergo some changes. Notably, there were no reports of retirement parties, for that segment of life—the occupation—is clearly separate from the family, so changes in status do not affect continuity in family roles.

Holiday Celebrations

The holidays of Easter, Christmas, Thanksgiving, and New Year's Eve and Day guarantee further contact among family members. Since each family has two sets of relatives, time must be carefully allotted so neither side is slighted. As one's own children marry, the expansion of the family creates a space problem and further division of loyalties, so flexibility is important. For the most part, meals only include the immediate family: parents, offspring, their spouses, and children. Unmarried or childless aunts and uncles who might otherwise be alone are also invited. Although meals are usually shared on holidays among immediate families, visiting also takes place at some point over the Christmas holiday so everyone can pay his or her respects to a favorite aunt or godmother. At these holiday meals, one can always expect to find the Thanksgiving lasagna, the Christmas stuffed squid, the Easter ravioli, and the birthday rum cake.

Sometimes if a parent's health is failing, great efforts are made to have all children and grandchildren present at Christmas. In one case, a daughter lived five hundred miles away. She was pregnant, and her doctor did not want her to fly. Her brother drove to fetch her so she would be there for her father's last Christmas.

Family Clubs

In some families there are more formal organizations that serve integrative functions. Clubs are more often found where the family size is too large for informal mechanisms to work well. In these cases, someone must assume the responsibility of keeping lines of communication open. For example, Mrs. Grassi is one of twelve second-generation offspring of immigrant parents. Her mother is still alive and lives within an hour's drive of nine of her children. Three children have moved away, but they too remain active in the communication network. A sister who lives in Florida frequently visits and stays for long periods, because her son has bought a house three doors away from the Grassis'. All the brothers and sisters are married, and, of these, only two have married a non-Italian. One is now divorced and the other, a brother, has a wife who is described as "rather aloof and not one for entertaining. She tries to keep him away from our parties, but we just ignore her. My brother comes anyway." Mrs. Grassi goes on to explain how family ties are maintained:

> *Now with everyone's children and grandchildren around, there could be seventy or eighty people coming to our parties. We had to get more organized, so we started a club. My eldest brother is the president, and we have a secretary and a sergeant at arms. I have a toll-free telephone at work, so I can settle a lot of business on it.*
>
> *We collect two dollars a month from everyone. This pays for a summer picnic and a dinner at a restaurant the night before Christmas Eve. Since Mother sold her large house, no one has a place large enough to entertain everyone. The club also pays for masses and rosaries for my father and sees that flowers are placed on his grave.*
>
> *We also had a birthday party for my mother on her eighty-first birthday. It was also held at a restaurant. Her thirty or so grandchildren all came. They made a scrapbook for her with many family pictures and other mementos. My brother made a speech and President Ford sent a telegram. Each grandchild and great-grandchild gave her a rose.*

Descendants of the four Di Nardo brothers described in chapter 4 and illustrated in Figure 1 include over two hundred relatives, most of whom still live near their original family homes. For the cyclical life-passage events, it is far too large a group to include everyone. For example, at weddings, young children of first and second cousins must be omitted. The bride and groom in the third generation might not even recognize a second cousin who comes through the reception line. Thus, an annual family reunion is one of the few events that includes everyone.

The Di Nardo reunion has been held almost every summer since 1938. Probably initially it served the same functions as the Grassis' family club. Today, however, the numbers of relatives attending is over 200, many of whom are unacquainted. Thus, its functions have become a more symbolic representation of family than a mechanism for maintaining social contact.

Early in the summer, members are notified of the reunion. The last notice was entitled, "It's a Great Day for All in the Family." It announces the park where it will be held, the dinner to be served and its cost, and the games and other festivities scheduled. The planning committee includes representatives of each branch, the descendants of each of the four immigrant brothers. The second generation, the four brothers' children, are now in their fifties and sixties. They agreed that it is time to pass on the responsibilities for planning to the third generation so continuity will be well maintained.

One of the activities of the reunion, the making of the family quilt, must begin early in the year. Women in each branch design and make squares of cloth which are incorporated into a big quilt. Each square represents some activity or interest of the family and provides a concrete symbol of family. The quilt is raffled off, often bringing in as much as $200. Proceeds remaining after all costs of the reunion are paid are either donated to charity or given to a family member in need of money.

For many who attend the reunion, particularly in the third generation, "family" in this larger sense is one form of identification linking oneself to the past and to a social heredity. Being a member of the family in the most general sense means that a parent or grandparent was one of the four brothers who came to this country and began a large family. The reunion and its related activities assure that the family history is preserved and that it is transmitted to each new generation. The link is both sentimental and historical. It is sentimental in the sense that family memberships can be used, if and when one chooses, to provide a source of identity that does not necessarily have functional significance in daily life. It is historical in the sense that there is a feeling of connection through one's parents and grandparents and ultimately to the country of origin.

Summary

These ritual celebrations fulfill important integrative functions. First, they are both ethnically based and family centered. Since they provide occasions for sociability, they also reflect a firm base for solidarity. Second, because the celebrations themselves have a tendency to expand and envelop many relatives, links are maintained that might otherwise wither if the events were not recognized. Third, since many specific customs stem from southern Italy, these occasions provide an important source of identity, not only with one's family but also with one's origins. In this capacity, they symbolize a link to one's past and a recognition of one's present affiliation as a member of an Italian-American family.

One should note in passing that there are means available to pressure individuals to conform. Those who are forgetful or resistant to handling responsibilities centering on these events soon learn the importance of their slights. A favorite niece who goes out with friends rather than paying her respects at her aunt's anniversary party gets the "cold treatment" from all of her aunts and uncles. Rather than verbal sanctions, hurt feelings are expressed through a withdrawal of warmth. Yet amends can easily be made by increasing one's attentiveness to family matters, usually by belatedly sending food.

These family events are termed special occasions and are recognized as such. However, it must be remembered that in large families special occasions can occur almost weekly. In this sense, their ritual recognition formalizes the relationships among kin and assures that sociability is maintained.

Chapter 6
Cultural Ideals and the Reality of Marriage

Jessica Field Cohen and Colleen Leahy Johnson

In the description to this point, much emphasis has been placed on the blood ties of the average Italian American. However, the nuclear family is the core unit to Italians as it is to most Americans, and its character is determined in a large part by the marital relationship. This chapter describes marriages between Italians and examines how this dyadic relationship fits into the wider system of allegiances to parents and other relatives. It will also analyze how traditional definitions of sex roles have been modified in contemporary marriages.

There is no doubt that American marriages in general have undergone great changes in recent decades, a situation from which Italian Americans certainly cannot remain immune (Fullerton 1977). For example, there has been a shift from segregated roles to arrangements where husbands take over some domestic functions, and wives the economic and political functions. Second, most women no longer have to suffer silently at the hands of male authority since they generally have more power today and participate more actively in making decisions concerning the family. Third, the cultural ideal of contemporary marriage is laden with conceptions on romantic love, companionship, and emotional support. In contrast, to modern marriages and their important emotional functions, traditional marriages are usually characterized by sex role differentiation and more emphasis on instrumental rather than emotional functions.

Research in the past twenty-five years indicates that there are several factors associated with the persistence of more traditional marriages. Social class position, for example, is prominently associated with marital forms, with blue-collar families retaining more segregated, hierarchical marriages and placing less emphasis on romantic and emotional concerns (Komarovsky 1962; Rubin 1977; Young and

Willmott 1957). Another important determinant, at least theoretically, is the character of a family's social network (Bott 1971). Husbands and wives who participate in a closely knit social network of relatives and friends of longstanding generally have more segregated gender roles. This situation, where many of the couple's emotional needs are satisfied by kinship relationships rather than by a spouse, is more often found in the working class.

The Italian-American respondents more often fit into both of these categories associated with traditionalism. Over half of the families are in the working class, and the majority are embedded in a social network where relatives play an important role in the activities of the nuclear family. Furthermore, the culture of southern Italy probably placed more emphasis on traditional role arrangements than is found among other ethnic groups in this country. Although these factors predict a marital role system at odds with the current ideals, a comparison in chapter 3 of in-married and out-married Italians and the Protestant control group found that social class, rather than ethnic background, is associated with the performance of marital roles. The analysis used a composite measure of the major dimensions of marriages, which include patterns of communication, emotional interdependence, power distribution, frequency of shared activities, and the degree of role segregation. Comparing groups on each of these dimensions, Italians differ from the comparison groups only on the degree of role segregation. Since this difference is of considerable statistical magnitude ($x^2 = 33.0389$, $< .00001$), while other dimensions were quite similar between groups at the appropriate class level, I conclude that Italians have far more segregated roles irrespective of their social position.

Overall, these findings suggest that Italians have marriages in which communication, emotional interdependence, power distribution, and shared activities are associated with either middle-class or working-class status. The major dimension, which is perhaps of ethnic origin, is their segregated roles in which the wife dominates in domestic affairs and the husband in the family's relationship with the outside world. Thus, while many of today's cultural ideals on marriage have been adopted by our respondents, the definitions of what husbands and wives actually do remain quite traditional in following the gender-linked performance of family roles.

These attitudes are prominent among both middle-class and working-class Italians. Women are as likely as men to concur with traditional arrangements, as one woman's comment illustrates:

I don't agree or feel that a woman should set herself up as an independent, self-sufficient person. She is not capable of doing that. She should do what she was designed for . . . be a wife and a mother first. Woman was put on earth to be man's wife and the mother of his children.

Antecedents to Marital Roles

The marital behavior of Italians in this sample have their roots in the family system of southern Italy, where the roles of husband and wife were rigidly prescribed. As noted in chapter 3, the family was usually described as patriarchal or father-dominated, but in reality was mother-centered (Moss and Thomson 1959). The male head of the family, the *capa della famiglia,* was at least nominally considered to be the supreme authority over wife, children, unmarried sisters, and younger brothers. He was respected, feared, and revered.

The male's role was instrumental, chiefly that of breadwinner, and from this position he derived most of his prestige and authority. His functioning within the family revolved around the dual roles of upholding the family honor and making a living. The Italian man, in his role as provider, was seen also as the protector, especially of women (A. Parsons 1969). The protection of women, which was important for the preservation of the *onore della famiglia,* or family honor, was coupled with a high degree of jealousy and very little public affection shown to women (Gambino 1974).

While male domination was a central feature in the family structure, wives were not totally subservient and indeed had their own important roles within the family (Covello 1972). They were seen as the center of the family, devoted to childrearing, caring for the house, and providing emotional support for the family. Older Italians referred to the Italian wife's existence as *vita miserable* with all the cooking and cleaning she had to do, but they also concluded that she was supreme in the home. As the bearer of the culture, she was responsible for training children in their gender roles and in instilling proper moral values. Often referred to as the heart of the family, she symbolized warmth, nurturance, and love. Anne Parsons (1969) indicates that the woman's image has been so adulated that in Italy it is linked to the

Madonna. Some observers term Italian culture one of "motherolotry" because of the special status she maintains in her children's lives.

Sex role training began early so young girls had few experiences that weren't home- and family-centered. While her brothers were allowed much freedom to work and socialize outside the home, a girl was sheltered and protected. Family honor hinged upon her chastity, and it was the responsibility of her father and brothers to protect it through careful chaperonage.

Immigration to the United States didn't radically alter the division of labor, the patterns of male authority, or of female home-centeredness (Gambino 1974). The immigrant father stood above other family members and was the ultimate enforcer of social control. His status was so elevated that he was often feared as much as he was respected, both by his wife and children. His role of protector of the family went beyond the usual economic responsibilities to include a scrupulous supervision of female family members. For younger girls, dating, of course, was forbidden, and even going out with female friends was not usually allowed (Ware 1935). Older brothers were equally as vigilant as the father in these duties, because, as numerous respondents remarked, a "young woman out alone could mean a baby out of wedlock."

Since women primarily were responsible for raising children, the exclusion of women from contacts and experiences outside the family was an effective mechanism by which Old World patterns of family solidarity and family honor were preserved. Grace Scalzo at the age of forty-five described her life growing up in the Italian section of Easton where her sex role training began early.

> *My duty was to come home after school and take care of the house. I didn't have time to play in the streets. Being a girl, I had a role in life that was different from that of my brothers. I had to walk the straight and narrow. The reins were so tight, especially since I had an older brother. It was like I had two father images. That demanded so much of you. They had put me on a pedestal. I had to be good. I was raised to be a young lady, not a little girl or a teenager, so my life was so limited.*

Another respondent indicated that strong policies of chaperonage were evident as recently as twenty years ago in her young adulthood. She lived at home until her marriage in her late twenties and was still strictly watched until her wedding day.

We had rented an upstairs apartment in my aunt's house. Before the marriage, my mother wouldn't let me go up and help my husband fix up our apartment without a chaperone.

Females were to be preserved for marriage, an all-important life event. They were raised to be family-centered and to observe the sex differences carefully in their future marital role, a role that left little room for conceptions of equality or romantic love. Upon marriage a female was instructed on her new order of priorities which was frequently stated as "When you are single, your first loyalty is to your parents. When you are a mother, your first loyalty is to your children, then your husband, and then your parents." While such a clear statement of loyalties was sometimes difficult to carry out in practice, this transfer of loyalties to a husband was repeatedly stressed. Equally as specific was the mandate of marital endurance; the marriage vows were to be permanent.

Thus, the cultural antecedents of Italian-American marriages that remain discernable today center upon the segregation of roles where, nominally, husbands have ultimate authority, but in actuality wives exercise a great deal of power in the home. Since home and family are so important, the wife's role is equally prestigious. Her training for this important role comes from years of protection and supervision by her male relatives, and from close collaboration with her mother at home. Upon marriage, her husband replaces her relatives as her protector, but as long as she confines herself to domestic matters, she has considerable power and security. Furthermore, there is continuity between her adolescent activities and her adult role.

The Marital Dyad and Its Competition

Marriage as a union between two families is an old-fashioned dictum that receives scant lip service today in the United States. For Italian Americans or any other population that is family-centered, such considerations cannot be totally ignored, for the marriage does not cause a sharp break with the family of origin. Parents and other relatives are not usually relegated to a less important status upon marriage, and their continuous involvement colors the relationship between husband and wife.

The mother, we have seen, is of great symbolic importance and

practically, of course, a source of emotional sustenance and need fulfillment. Her influence does not end on the wedding day; in fact, many
of the respondents point out that their mother and mother-in-law continue silently to rule their marriages. Even many years later, their
influence is taken for granted.

Consequently, the husband-wife dyad is in active competition with
the husband-mother and wife-mother dyads. The marriage is also con-
tending with new alliances in the sex-linked relationship with their
children. Anne Parsons (1969) has provided a rich psychological analysis of these relationships in southern Italy which are little altered
upon adulthood and marriage. On the whole, much of her work can
apply to Italian Americans as well.

The emotion and affection in the mother-son dyad in particular colors the marital relationship, much to the dissatisfaction of some of the
wives interviewed. In many cases, the mother continues her influence,
through active competition with her daughter-in-law, in providing
food and services to her son. The unspoken conclusion is, "Your wife
will never be able to do it as well as your mother can." Husbands are
not aloof to such attentiveness and sometimes expect the same behavior from their wives. As one woman reported, "He tried to mold me to
be like his mother—a waitress, waiting on him hand and foot." Such
situations in some cases can stimulate active competition for a man's
affection. One college-educated Italian woman recounted how, after
years of conflict, she had successfully managed this task:

> I had to fight my mother-in-law for my husband. I told her, "If
> you give me a husband, then I will give you back your son, but
> don't fight me for him." I finally had to throw my wedding ring
> at her to show her I meant it. I told her to make the decision. It
> was a terrible scene, but I had to cut the cord.

Another wife concluded,

> Italian mothers will baby a son until he's fifty if a wife doesn't
> step in.

The husband in alliance with his mother may subtly try to influence
everything from the food that is cooked to the decoration of the home
and the care of the children. Yet most of the respondents had coped
with the influence of the mother-in-law in a realistic fashion. As one
respondent summed up a discussion on this subject: "You have to understand that when your husband's mother is Italian, that's how it is.

If you are Italian you understand it and can put up with it." Occasionally wives referred to the necessity of tolerating a demanding mother-in-law because of her generosity—the gift of her son.

The relationship between the woman and her own mother is also an important factor in the marriages of many Italian Americans. It was aptly described by one respondent who said, "In every marriage there are three people, the husband, the wife, and the wife's mother." In many ways, the wife's mother is as powerful as the husband's mother is in the marriage. The difference, however, lies in the fact that her influence is in the domestic arena and is not in direct competition with her son-in-law's roles. Consequently, few Italian men complain openly about their mother-in-law.

Prior to the marriage, mothers and daughters share many interests because of their common investment in home-centered activities. As noted above the average daughter was protected and somewhat limited in her freedom. Generally the woman's role is extolled, so she anticipates stepping into the role of wife and mother with few reservations. Upon marriage, when she replicates her mother's role, her status is almost equal to her mother's. The close relationship between mother and daughter is a reciprocal one, with an equal give and take. As one respondent indicated in discussing her relationship with her mother: "I am the only daughter and there is no one else for her. Mothers seem to depend on daughters a great deal." Another respondent said simply, "My mother and I have a different type of relationship. I am not only her daughter, I am a close friend."

The mother-daughter tie is reinforced by the segregated roles within the marriage, so many wives turn to their mothers rather than their husbands to discuss their problems. The mother and daughter can also form a coalition, which enables the daughter to deal with her husband's close bond to his mother. However, an Italian mother would never encourage anyone, particularly a daughter, to disturb this bond; instead she would assist her daughter in accommodating the demands of her mother-in-law. For example, one respondent described her mother's role in strengthening the bond between her husband and his mother:

> My mother will remind me to call my mother-in-law. She says, "It's up to you and your husband to look after her. Remember she gave you her son."

Mothers of both husbands and wives in the Italian family seem to reinforce the role segregation through their behaviors. It should not be surprising, therefore, that the patterns found in the marriages of Italian-American men and women remain more segregated than the marriages of the non-Italian respondents. As in other areas of family life, a number of individuals readily respond to preserving traditional family ways.

While members of the family of origin play an active and often competing role in the course of a marriage, the norms are clear that the marriage should be the major priority.

My first responsibility is to my husband. That's the best way, so things don't get in a dither. If children see unity between mother and father, the rest follows.

One respondent reported how some mothers often instruct their children on these priorities:

I tell my children, "I love every one of you, but you will leave me. If I don't treat my man right, he won't love me when I'm old."

Marriages are sacred, as one elderly respondent described. Over the nineteen years she had been widowed she had many chances to remarry but rejected them because, she stated, "I have only one God and only one husband." She then turned to more practical reasons, "Anyway, widowers these days are only looking for a maid."

Both middle-aged and elderly female respondents indicated that the husband should always come first and that parents should neither interfere nor be considered more important than the spouse. However, the anecdotal and interview data indicate that wives can not always put their husbands first, so the transfer of loyalties and responsibilities is often a fiction rather than a fact. A more realistic analysis of the order of priorities is described by one middle-class, college-educated woman, who said:

We were brought up that the family is everything. The family unit is isolated from everything else. Your flesh and blood come first—everyone is considered important, but you were really given the feeling that if it wasn't flesh and blood, it wasn't that important. Even now, I think that my parents would believe that I should consider my brother more important to me than my husband.

In the early years of marriage, the dominance of the mother or the mother-in-law over her son or daughter is prominent. As that issue becomes resolved or is eliminated by the death of the mother, the influence of one's family of orientation by no means ceases.

Questions on priorities between husband and children were difficult for many women to answer, but the behaviors of the women indicate that young children typically come first, relegating the husband to second place. Later, as the needs and demands of elderly parents increase, they take priority over the spouse. Upon their death, a favorite sister or brother may replace a parent as closest confidant. Thus, marriages of Italian Americans are affected by a lifetime of competing relationships and priorities. However, few of our respondents rejected family ties as did the Scivettis who finally moved away from their families:

> *I finally realized that we disagreed more when we were around them—they caused friction between us. It was suffocating our relationship.*

Parents have been known to cling to their offspring. If a son moves even a short distance, it can seem a long journey to some Italian parents. The Albros have lived next door to their son and his family for twenty years. Now, to their distress, he is moving to a nicer house. Although his new home is only eight blocks away, Mrs. Albro complains:

> *I like to see him get ahead, but they shouldn't have to move. We've put our house on the market, for we don't want to live here after they leave.*

Husbands and Wives

From the perspective of academic researchers, who usually espouse the contemporary ideals of equality, companionship, and emotional reciprocity in marriage, these patterns might point to low marital adjustment. Descriptions of the traditional marriages can appear to be vestiges of a long-ago time, so interpretations are often negative and described as "worlds of pain" (Rubin 1977) or the "trained incapacity to share" (Komarovsky 1962). Upon closer examination of the data, however, one can see that marriages do not have to be modern and companionate to be labeled adjusted. The marriages of most Italian respondents were stable, the level of conflict was not extraordinary, and the majority were quite satisfied with their present lot.

Mrs. Aragoni is a good example of a type of satisfaction that is at odds with contemporary conceptions of marriage. She described a husband who would disturb the sensibilities of most modernists. He dominated most decisions, he doled out money to her paternalistically, and expected perfection from her in her domestic role. She related that on their twenty-fifth anniversary he got drunk with his friends after a golf game and did not get home in time for a dinner celebration. After a long, objective description of these behaviors, she added, "I make him sound like a louse, He really isn't. He's a good husband."

The ideal that husband and wife must communicate intensely about every concern is not uniformly endorsed by Italian men and women. More often than not some problems are better left undiscussed. "I don't talk about my activities, for that would bore him," a wife might say. A husband, on the other hand, concluded that, "I shouldn't bring my worries home—the family should be protected from all that." Problems at work, then, are not always a proper topic for discussion. Neither are those vaguely defined problems stemming from minor depressions or "feeling blue." Husbands conclude that their wives are overreacting or being too emotional. For a man to share an emotional problem with his wife also is inappropriate, for it is incongruent with norms of male superiority.

To many, these issues are not concerned with the family and are better discussed with someone else. Important problems with children or other family members are the appropriate ones for husbands and wives to discuss, for they are family matters requiring a joint decision. Only 26 percent of our female Italian respondents took their emotional problems to their husbands. They saw no reason to question these practices: "That's just the way it is." Mrs. Viano echoed statements made by many of the respondents in the sample when asked to whom they would turn with their problems:

> *I take them to my sister or my husband's aunt. My husband doesn't understand my feelings. I can talk to them better. It's no big deal. It's just the way it is. If I'm upset and go to him, he overreacts and it makes me more upset.*

Whether by default or intention, there are numerous relatives to whom a husband or wife can go, such as a parent or aunt or collateral relative like a sister, sister-in-law, or cousin. Women particularly go to their female kin for advice. Sisters were often referred to as "my best friend" who replaced the husband as a major source of emotional support and companionship.

Power Issues

The divergence between the cultural ideal and the reality of marriage becomes quite obscure when one turns to power issues between husbands and wives. Italians discuss their marriages largely in terms of power, but the findings are inconsistent. Italians do not differ significantly from Protestants in the distribution of power. However, Italian women tend to have more power in economic decisions because many husbands turn over their entire pay checks to them to run the home. Women also dominate in discussions on childrearing and in planning the family's social activities.

Frequent reference to their Italian background and their parents' marriages, however, stressed a long tradition of male dominance. Italian men were sometimes referred to as tyrants, or dictators, but Italian women were also seen as domineering. One point of general agreement, however, is that Italian women have more power today than their mothers or grandmothers had in the past.

The elderly respondents themselves have opposing views on the way things were and the way they should be today. Elderly women generally view the changes toward equality with approval. "A woman can say what's on her mind today. In my time, we would have been beaten up for that." "Wives are not being pushed around today—that's a good thing," or "Husbands are helping their wives more. My husband wouldn't lower himself." "*Schiavissimo Italiano* is what we had in the past—that means the husband could declare himself boss and women were dragged all over. I like the equality better today."

Elderly men, on the other hand, note current changes with dismay. "Women today are the bosses—how can a man feel good about going home after a hard day's work?" "Husbands should be head of the house, but today, it is on a fifty-fifty basis," or "Women's lib is going too far. A man can't say a thing or his wife will run off and get a divorce."

Whereas there is some disagreement ideologically on questions of dominance in marriage, the question of power is resolved fairly simply within Italian homes by rigidly defining the roles and areas of responsibility and authority. The distribution of power by role segregation has not changed a great deal from the roles of the southern Italian *contadino* family or the first-generation Italian immigrant family. The

issue of power from the female's perspective is summed up by one respondent who cogently indicated: "The Italian woman might be the
boss in the home, but her power ends at the door."

The male's point of view differs only slightly. Many of the males
interviewed commented that the Italian woman is typically seen as
domineering but only with respect to the affairs of the home. Italian
men felt that when it comes to authority within the home, the men are
the underdogs in this society. One man laughingly described the
power situation in his home, "I am the boss, but my boss is my wife."

There is general agreement, however, among both males and females that the spheres of influence and power are clearly delineated
and accepted. The "domineering" Italian woman recognizes that any
dominance she may have over her husband does not extend beyond the
confines of her home. Her domain includes the household, childrearing, and kinship duties and it is within this sphere that she is powerful.
At the same time, she respects her husband's role as breadwinner and
typically defers to him as head of the family because of this role.

The acceptance of this power distribution by its segregation into
separate realms is one aspect of marriage that distinguishes the Italian-
American relationships from others. This well-specified delineation of
roles and responsibilities for each spouse probably minimizes marital
conflict because one knows the mandates well and can predict the
costs if he or she should act to the contrary. The "separate but equal"
status of marital roles, which functions both normatively and in reality, may be more workable than that of more modern marriages in
which norms of equality are incongruent with actual power distribution. An Italian wife, in contrast, has few illusions about marital
roles being interchangeable. One wife's view of the women's movement is relevant:

> I think that women have lost more power by doing what they are
> doing [asking for equality]. I think that women had more power
> before. As long as she didn't let her husband know it, I think she
> had more power.

Whatever complaints arise regarding one's spouse, Italian Americans usually have a commitment to live by their earlier decision.
There was a frequent theme that it is fate or destiny, "what life has
given me." One respondent describes her philosophy of marriage and
points out how the inevitable acceptance of a situation facilitates marital stability:

You marry a man for better or worse. My mother would bawl me out if I complained about my husband, but I was lucky. He was good to me, he gave me his entire pay check. I've known cases where the husband and wife would disagree and never talk to each other or sleep together for the next twenty-five years. For religious reasons, or pride, they did not separate or divorce.

The fatalistic attitude toward marriage is interpreted as a strength that binds the family unit together. This attitude is exemplified in quotation after quotation from the interviews. One women said it best: "Marriages were made in heaven, so now you have to live with it." Even when free choice in marital selection is reported, marriage is seen as irrevocable; "I've made my own bed, now I have to lie in it."

Men do have more routes of escape from an unsatisfactory marriage since much of their time is spent outside the home. They are not as dependent on their wives socially and emotionally and in this sense they do have more power (Emerson 1962). They have their own parents, siblings, and peer group to provide solace, and these ties probably buttress male dominance. While women also have their mothers and sisters as sources of support, they still are confined, even if they work, to the primary responsibility of maintaining the home and raising the children. Discontent with marriage and its male authority has fewer outlets, so women have to work with existing resources.

One means wives can use is a subversion of male authority through deception. This pattern is explained by one respondent who said with a twinkle in her eye:

My husband still believes that as the man he has to be the head of the family, but all I have to do is say that he is the head and that satisfies him.

If a husband tries to replicate the old-fashioned role, forbidding his daughter to date, for example, a wife can be forced to use deceit by keeping her activities a secret from him. He is told his daughter is going to the library or to a movie with her sister when she is out with a boy. Thus, few wives silently suffer an unreasonable husband. These means of skirting his authority incidentally wins approval from her female relatives. Indirectly, these subversive techniques also increase her power in the home and at the same time expand the social distance between a man and his family, thus reinforcing the role segregation between husbands and wives.

However, most Italian men would agree with one comment, "If you have a happy wife, you have a happy home." They attempt within reason to achieve this goal through the socially accepted means of the Italian community: let wives rule the house, the men rule the outside world.

Summary

Contemporary observers of family life would certainly view Italian marriages as quite old-fashioned and incongruent with the changing roles of women. Italian marriages differ from the comparison groups in the greater segregation of marital roles. Male dominance is espoused, female domesticity is prided, and marriages "should" accommodate to the demands of a wider family circle. Where husbands and wives do not relate with each other in a way defined by current mandates for emotional support and romantic love, to outsiders it is deviant, but to insiders it might be judged as, "It's just the way it is—it's no big deal."

Certainly Italian marriages are changing. As noted in chapter 3, social class is more of a determinant of marital roles than ethnic background, so with increased social mobility, the marital patterns reported here would be modified. Certainly Italian women today are more equal to men than their mothers were. Most Italian mothers want their daughters to have more freedom than they themselves had. Yet few want the increasing equality of women to threaten family life, so changes most likely will be congruent with other changes taking place in the family.

Chapter 7
Intermarriage: The Other Side of the Coin

To this point, statistical tests have consistently indicated that intermarriage causes considerable change in Italian family life. Each partner brings to the marriage his or her own perspective based on past experiences and cultural meanings. When these perspectives differ, conflicts inevitably arise. While many Italians who married other Italians recognized and complained about the constraints imposed by such an enveloping family life, most were quite content with it and felt little need to change the patterns of relating with the extended family. Such was not the case with intermarriage where divergent cultural backgrounds were thrown into clearer relief in the intimacy of marriage. Few dimensions of the family were taken for granted; all customs and values were usually lucidly examined, candidly discussed, and often heatedly debated. Where husbands and wives had not been able to resolve their differences, conflict more readily was brought out into the open. For the researcher, these cultural differences provide a rich source of insights into the configuration of the Italian family.

Italians who marry out of the group tend to choose mates of similar social background. There is little difference between them and their non-Italian spouses in their parents' socioeconomic status or their own educational and occupational achievement. Most non-Italian spouses were Catholic, of whom the largest proportion were of Irish origin. Table 1.2 shows that the in-married and out-married families do not differ widely in their mean ages, the mean age of their children, the length of residence in their house, or the length of their marriages. The out-married families did tend to have more children, which reflects the presence of three families with Irish wives who each had eight or ten children.

Despite these similarities in demographic characteristics, the out-married families differed significantly from the in-marrieds in five dimensions of the family (see Table 7.1):

Table 7.1.

Differences between In-married and Out-married Families

	In-married Italians, n = 74	Out-married Italians, n = 98	Statistical significance
Network connectedness	9.01	7.86	t = 4.37, <.0001
Kinship solidarity	41.20	35.82	t = 4.54, <.0001
Marital roles[a]	13.06	11.82	t = 2.07, <.04
Childrearing[b]	28.07	26.15	t = 2.73, <.007
Filial behaviors	24.82	22.93	t = 2.90, <.004

[a]Score measures traditional versus companionate factors of roles in power distribution, emotional interdependence, and the degree of role segregation.
[b]This measure is a composite of traditional versus developmental approaches to childrearing in discipline, supervision, and nurturance.

1. With intermarriage, the network is less dominated by relatives and other Italians. There is also less inclination to include children and elderly parents in adult activities.
2. Childrearing patterns vary from the more traditional forms described for the in-married families. In the out-married families discipline techniques are more permissive, supervision is relaxed, and maternal attentiveness declines.
3. The marital relationship of the out-marrieds is significantly less segregated and less hierarchical as it comes to resemble the companionship model of the Protestant control group.
4. Kinship solidarity decreases with intermarriage as contact and mutual aid declines.
5. With intermarriage, filial behaviors decrease in one respect; responsibilities to parents decline in number. (It should be noted here, however, that the values on filial obligations of the Italian spouses in the out-marriages do not differ greatly from their in-married counterparts. See chapters 9 and 11.)

Given the high rate of intermarriage, these differences suggest future changes in the family. However, when gender of the Italian is

Table 7.2.

Differences in Italian Wives by Intermarriage

	In-married Italian wives, n = 74	Out-married Italian wives, n = 53	Statistical significance
Network connectedness	9.01	8.00	t = 3.32, <.001
Kinship solidarity	41.20	34.68	t = 4.80, <.0001
Marital roles[a]	13.06	11.74	not significant
Childrearing[b]	28.07	26.24	t = 2.34, <.02
Filial behaviors	24.82	23.53	not significant

[a]Traditional versus companionate factors.
[b]Traditional versus developmental techniques.

controlled and the two groups of Italian women are compared (the in-married and the out-married), the changes with intermarriages are more selective (Table 7.2).

As with comparisons of the entire sample, the out-married Italian women have social networks that are less likely to include relatives and other Italians. The older and younger generations are less likely to be included in social activities. Kinship involvement is less for out-married Italian women, and they are also less likely to use traditional childrearing practices.

Despite these changes when Italian women marry out, there are also important similarities. These women have marriages similar to Italian women married to Italian men, a finding which again suggests that social class status rather than ethnicity determines the form of marriage. Also, for Italian women, intermarriage does not necessarily change the relationship these women have with their parents. Their filial behaviors do not differ significantly from their counterparts in in-married families. This variable will be discussed in greater detail in a later chapter, but here I suggest that, despite other changes in the family, filial behaviors are less likely to change for Italian women who intermarry. The same also applies to Italian men who intermarry.

Cultural Differences

Cultural differences are prominent in these families. Differing values on family practices can be one source of potential conflict. However, even when there is basic agreement between husbands and wives on most issues, more mundane matters can provoke antagonism. For example, matters such as Italian customs and rituals can become a source of derision by a non-Italian spouse who has different views. In one interview, Mrs. Tonini, an Irish wife, reported no major problems in her relationship with her Italian husband, yet she was extremely critical of many Italian ways.

On funerals, which Italians see as a time of ritual and mutual support, Mrs. Tonini has much to criticize:

Italians mourn more—the open casket, all the flowers, the hundreds of people. Yet it is so ironic. When my mother-in-law died, the women in her church club came to my husband to pay her back dues before they could say the rosary. Then you have to hire all those limousines—she never even rode in one when she was alive. At the same time, all those attending discuss how much it all costs.

On mourning in general, she questions what Italians would call empathy, "My mother-in-law was a crepe hanger—always lamenting bad things." On the church-going habits of Italians who consider themselves to be good Catholics, she has this to say:

Italians only go to church when they have something nice to wear. I've known some who will go to a church in another neighborhood if they can't be nicely dressed. They just don't seem to be sincere about religion. They have a big party for a child's first communion and then not go to church for the rest of the year.

She was also critical of the celebrations of children's birthdays:

Italians have a strange way of being thrifty and extravagant at the same time. I've seen my neighbor divide a stick of gum three ways to give to her children and turn around and give the most expensive birthday parties for them. At these kinds of parties, all the adults are invited, and they have their fun while the child is ignored.

In her litany of complaints, Mrs. Tonini uses a bantering, sarcastic style. It seems apparent that she is adapting to cultural conflict by projection in order to deflect her criticism from her husband to ethnic traits relatively immune from the day-to-day activities of the family. She had few complaints about her husband as an individual. Mr. Tonini himself was more analytical and somewhat resigned. When asked about the advantages of the Italian-American family, he responded:

> *There are advantages, but the minute you marry outside, they become disadvantages. You just can't explain another culture to a person—even your wife. If you were raised strict, you can't suddenly become lenient with children. In Italian culture, the husband does the decision-making. My father did, but now I have trouble getting my point across. I try to teach the children obedience. There's more peace and quiet when the father is stern, but it just doesn't work.*

> *We're as different as night and day. My wife's parents were permissive. They wanted the children to enjoy being children. When I, like my parents, want to teach them responsibility, then she gets mad.*

Despite discrepancies between the husband's and wife's views, there is no evidence of serious family problems in terms of how effectively the family functions. Both seemed resigned to the incongruent cultural backgrounds and have incorporated their differences into a joking relationship which has deflected anger or hostility. While there are large areas on which they have agreed to disagree, their marriage is confined to a low level of conflict.

Not all cultural conflicts can be as satisfactorily resolved by the mechanism of projection or joking. Near the end of the research, an article appeared in the local paper which described our project and some of the findings. In response, I received an anonymous letter that described a situation not unlike those reported by others who married into Italian families.

> *In your article on Italians, you very appropriately called inter-marriages out-marriages. . . . The non-Italian is very definitely the out-law. . . . From the day I married my husband twenty years ago we catered to my mother-in-law's ways. Contact with the children was indeed high. We didn't dare have it otherwise.*

We didn't visit them because we really felt we wanted to. We just were afraid not to. Let us miss one week and we heard about it for months. We had to do what she expected, plan our holidays completely around her.

Everything has just been too one-sided. No one is ever sicker, no one works harder, no one is kinder than my mother-in-law. Even if it were true, we just plain get sick of hearing about it. My husband feels freer to ask my parents or anyone in my family for help than his own. He knows he is not going to get a perpetual sermon about it. So who feels left out because her children or grandchildren aren't running over or calling every day? My mother-in-law.

I feel that I do work hard, have pride in my home and children, try to be a good mother to my children (a fact that I've often thought my in-laws should appreciate since they are their grandchildren and their son can rarely stay home enough to even realize he is a father of five). I have trouble respecting them as strong healthy adults who have nothing to do all day but sit around and cry that their children don't visit often enough. Don't they realize that we have the same amount of work, plus some, that they had when they were raising their children?

Italian mothers-in-law get along better if the daughter-in-law expects nothing and is forever grateful for her mother-in-law giving her son to her. We've never forgotten a birthday (I might add she has never given me a birthday gift, which I don't mind), anniversary, Mother's Day, etc., but let me get something new and I have to hear remarks like "If my son hadn't married you, all this would be mine." Statements such as that, and there have been many, certainly have done nothing to help our relationship.

I could go on and on for several more pages, but I think you must have a pretty good idea of the other side of the picture, from my point at least, Dr. Johnson. After more heartaches and disagreements than I care to mention with my husband over his mother, not to mention the black eyes, I just don't bother any more. My mother-in-law nags my husband no end; he in turn would take it out on me. I got to the point where I couldn't take it any more. I'm much happier without them and I don't have to wonder what I did wrong any more. I know nothing would ever be enough.

   I will not sign this. . . . I have three daughters and I can truly say that I hope they never have to cope with an Italian mother-in-law as I know them. I'm sure there are plenty of lovely Italian women who do not fall into this stereotype, but I have many friends who are the non-Italian in "out-marriages" who would never do it again.

It is difficult to determine the prevalence of such indictments of the Italian-American family by non-Italian in-laws. Obviously, a husband and wife will have some conflict if they differ markedly on values, but so also might a spouse who comes from the same ethnic background, for the range within groups is also large. However, marrying into an Italian family means one is establishing a potentially close relationship with numerous relatives, a situation for which many non-Italians are unprepared. Individuals who select a non-Italian mate, and who do not want to face this unhappy woman's problems, can avoid them by separating the nuclear family from the Italian relatives. For Italians, however, such a solution is not always easily accomplished or even considered.

Patterns of Adaptation to Cultural Differences

While there is no statistical evidence that finds significantly higher conflict in intermarried families, the qualitative data from the interviews abound with reports of cultural differences. Such differences are potential sources of conflict in childrearing practices, kinship allegiances, and filial responsibilities. Most of the conflict reported centered on the distribution of power in marriage, the latitude permissible in enforcing conformity in childrearing, and the extent of reciprocity optimal in extended family relationships. At the practical level, non-Italian wives pointed to the dilemmas they faced: "How can a wife raised to be independent from family ties accommodate to the high demands of the Italian mother-in-law?" "How can an assertive woman adapt to an authoritarian husband?" And, "Why does a husband object to children being raised as free spirits?"

In order to identify how intermarried families adapted to these conflicts, three individuals who played no role in the interviewing read the ninety-eight out-married interviews and singled out those where conflict was found to be associated with cultural differences. This technique resulted in culling out forty-one interviews or 42 percent of the sample. In the resolution of these difficulties, attempts were made to establish rules on the extent of involvement with each spouse's family of orientation. In some cases, the conflicts had been resolved years ago and the respondents used retrospective accounts. In other families, it had never been successfully resolved, so conflict continued to arise as a regular feature of family life.

The adaptive strategies involved one of three types of reorganization of the nuclear family's relationship to the kinship group: (1) a unilateral focus in which both husband and wife concentrated time, energy, and loyalties to one side of the family; (2) a segregated focus in which they divided their loyalties and each focused on his or her own family of orientation and had little to do with the spouse's family; or (3) a nucleated focus in which the couple deemphasized both families of orientation and confined their time, energy, and loyalties to the family of procreation. Where these structural alignments of the family weren't adaptive, conflict went unresolved. In this category, there was a small group where conflict seemed to have less to do with cultural differences than with the personalities of individuals. In other families, ethnicity was used as a strategy for defense against the conflict. For example, some respondents like Mrs. Tonini did not blame their spouses or themselves as individuals but rather pointed to the ethnic background as a source of the problem, "What can you expect from someone who has been raised in such a family?"

Unilateral Focus

There is a common saying among Italians that when intermarrige takes place, the Italian family wins out of hand. In other words, those marrying into the family become Italianized, so that they come to accept the Italian way. Of the forty-one families, sixteen chose one extended family system on which to concentrate their loyalties. Of these, eleven chose the Italian side. In some cases, no conscious choice was necessary, for the non-Italian spouse's family was not a viable option because there were few available relatives with whom to relate. Some non-Italian spouses we interviewed came from families in which there had been early deaths, divorces, or a long history of family problems, so that marriage into an Italian family was a refuge and a source of security.

Most often, the wife determines the kinship involvement. Since women are the key persons in maintaining kinship solidarity, it is not surprising that 69 percent of all in-married Italian families are matrifocal in orientation. Upon examination of the group of Italian women married to non-Italians, we find that this emphasis increases to 87 percent of the families. Therefore, the pull of the Italian family is impressive, particularly if the wife is Italian. In many cases, a husband with other views must stand by helplessly as he is swept into an all-embracing family system.

The Schmidts are an example of the continued struggle between an Italian wife and her German husband. Both are high-school graduates and work in white-collar occupations. The Schmidts are of mixed background, both in religion and in ethnicity. She claims her German husband "hates Italians and hates Catholics." Although she says she "looks to God for strength," the family is not active in any church, even though the children were baptized as Catholics. Their religious difference is only symptomatic of the vast gaps separating this couple. In regard to social activities, each goes his or her separate way. She enjoys socializing, but he is a "loner." Mr. Schmidt likes carpentry, a hobby which eventually became a second job. When they are home together, "there is always TV. My family watches too much of it," Mrs. Schmidt reports.

The real source of conflict, however, concerns her investment in her own family, an allegiance which, Mrs. Schmidt recognizes, stirs up jealousy in her husband:

> We could never have my parents live with us. My husband would strongly object. He resents my father. He is even jealous of my talking to him on the telephone. There is real animosity there. If my parents were here, he would go out all the time. I don't know why my husband has never felt a part of my family, even though he has little to do with his own family [a widowed mother who lives with his brother]. My parents never interfere—they're easy to get along with.

Mrs. Schmidt continually refers to her father and the many interests they share. During her repeated visits to her parents, she and her father garden together and leave the household interests to her mother.

In addition to marital disagreements on social activities and allegiance to parents, this couple also had the usual disagreements about money. He accuses her of taking those problems and many others too lightly, while she accuses him of being too serious.

Although their basic conflict stems from her undivided loyalty to her father, another difficulty centers on their divergent views on disciplining children. They had two teenagers who were having difficulty at home, at school, and with the law. Like most Italian women, Mrs. Schmidt expects the father to be the source of final authority in the family.

> *I depended upon my husband to discipline the children. It's supposed to be the man who is head of the house and he should make the decisions. He thought it was my responsibility. I guess I should have been more firm, but it was always, "Wait until your father gets home." So my son and daughter always fought constantly, they made poor grades, they refused to help me around the house. I've had a tough time. My daughter first ran away at fourteen. My son was in trouble with the law at sixteen. We had to go to court several times.*

With these problems, the family on occasion had sought counselling, but according to Mrs. Schmidt her husband resisted continuing it, so she ended up taking tranquilizers and hoping for the best.

> *I also jump from job to job. It's a form of therapy that gets me out of the house. I just wish we could sit down and talk things over, but my husband doesn't have the patience for that. I do believe it's improving, however, now that the children are almost on their own.*

A reconstruction of the family history can point to the role cultural differences have played in this family. Differences in religion and ethnicity, of course, do not always lead to troubles of the magnitude described here. However, different expectations and preferences for the ways one spends leisure time initially can drive a wedge in the marriage. Segregated activities, as described here, can lead to a division of loyalties, such as the way Mrs. Schmidt substitutes her father for her husband to satisfy her emotional needs. Mr. Schmidt's resulting jealousy and resentment causes more conflict, and these factors lead to a breakdown of communication and a weak parental coalition in childrearing. Different views in matters of discipline and parental supervision obviously do not always lead to delinquency in teenagers, but in this family it is apparent that family resources could not be mustered to intervene.

The pull of the Italian family was undoubtedly one source of marital conflict. Mr. Schmidt appeared to be defenseless and could offer no alternatives to the immersion of his nuclear family into the activities of his wife's relatives. He was isolated from his own family of orientation and not readily accepted into his wife's. His family of origin did not have the resources to offer him an alternative, leaving him more isolated than was usual for this sample.

Generally, in families that are drawn to the Italian side, non-Italian in-laws are readily accepted as long as they accommodate to Italian ways. If they are seen as warm, affectionate, hospitable, and conscious of their family duties, there is little apparent difference in how they are treated in comparison to Italian in-laws.

In some cases, a genuine Italianization takes place. For example, the Secretis, a middle-class family with an Irish-English wife, settled any ethnic conflicts early, mainly because her family was some distance away. She describes herself as having become Italian over the years because she is in daily contact with her in-laws and is quite dependent upon the assistance they extend, enabling her to work full-time. She proudly reports that her father-in-law calls her "my Irish-English wop." She has rejected her own background and could not imagine having the daily reciprocal interaction with her father that she has established with her in-laws.

> I can only take so much of my father. He has such a pessimistic attitude and he's so cheap. I'd go nuts if he lived with us. He is so anti-progress and doesn't like change. It drives him crazy when he sees the money we spend. When he's here, he turns off lights and turns down the furnace. And we eat differently. He doesn't like tomato sauce. I've learned to use it on everything.

Although she spoke very fondly of her in-laws, she reported some conflict that occurred earlier in the marriage.

> We lived with them for nine months. We could have continued the arrangement, but my mother-in-law and I fought all the time. I know her better now and instead of arguing, we kid each other. If she is widowed, I'd want her to come with us.

At the time of the interview, she described her mother-in-law as "wonderful." Over the years, her mother-in-law came to fill the role of

her own mother who had been dead for some time. Mrs. Secreti said
her mother-in-law is uncritical of her housekeeping habits, generous in
the expensive gifts she gives them, and very helpful in babysitting.
Her mother-in-law even selected the godparents for her children, and
"they are the best ever." Contact with the in-laws involves daily phone
calls and visits three or four times a week. Mrs. Secreti also joined
several of her mother-in-law's clubs, which were comprised of Italian
women only.

Other non-Italian men and women have adopted the Italian family
as their own through a conscious personal preference. For example,
Mrs. Misita came from a disorganized family. Her father was an alco-
holic, her parents were divorced, and her mother had remarried twice.
She described her satisfaction:

> *The Italian family was just what I was looking for. Kids and
> home are important. I knew if I married an Italian man, it would
> be different. Now I even think Italian.*

Others accepted their absorption into the Italian family with resignation, "When you marry an Italian, you marry the whole family." A
wife of German background was proud of her acceptance into her husband's family:

> *I feel that now I'm Italian myself. If I can't talk with my hands, I
> can't talk. I don't think I have any American ways left. I cook
> completely Italian. We run our house the Italian way—the
> man is the head. I tell him my feelings. I even yell and scream
> the Italian way, but he has the last word. My old friends I now
> view as "American." They're different. The only people I see
> are Italian.*

An Italian husband described his wife:

> *I had to break her into our ways. She was shy and overwhelmed
> by showing emotions. At first she was reluctant to show affection
> as we do. Now she is very involved with my family. She says
> we've made her a good Italian. Also she appreciates the close-
> ness. When she needs help from her own parents, they are never
> there, but mine are.*

Those families with a unilateral focus that have rejected the Italian
family in order to concentrate their loyalties on the other side are
few in number. There were four such families in our sample, three of

which made that choice out of necessity because the Italian relatives did not live in the area. In the one case where there was an option, the nuclear family focused on the wife's Irish relatives. Both husband and wife attributed this choice to the large size of the husband's Italian family. He was one of ten siblings, the majority of whom are sisters. These females had formed a solidary unit that, in the wife's opinion, had excluded them.

When this priority was established, it most often became a total commitment, an "all or nothing." Few families were able to apportion their time equally between Italian relatives and others. Either a couple accepted the Italian family without reservation, or they devised another option that resulted in less contact with Italian relatives.

Segregation of Loyalties

In some intermarriages, husbands and wives could not arrive at a concensus on how their loyalties would be distributed. As a result, in 15 percent of the families, there was a segregation of loyalties, where the husbands and wives separately invested their allegiances in their own families to the exclusion of their spouse's family.

The need to establish priorities between affinal and consanguineal relatives is a common problem when both families are in proximity. Unlike other cultures, the American kinship system is bilateral with both sides having equal rights. However, when both husband and wife come from families that have high expectations of loyalty and commitment, a potential for conflict is likely unless rules are clearly specified. The Italian-American family has a normative ordering of priorities which is well understood in in-married families and which clarifies the situation somewhat by spelling out solutions to potential problems. It is taken for granted, for example, that all offspring, irrespective of sex, should extend service and love to parents. In the event that competing loyalties present a dilemma, the wife's family normatively should receive priorities, for the family interests so often center on the affective domain which is the responsibility of women. Hence, extended family solidarity often rests upon the solidarity of sisters.

After some years of marriage, most families interviewed had long ago established their patterns of solidarity and decided how to spend holidays or determined visiting patterns. In some intermarried families, however, a division of loyalties persisted throughout the marriage. For example, the Agnos family has an Italian wife and a Greek husband, both of whom are offspring of large, solidary immigrant families. She described her mother-in-law as a possessive woman who was constantly interfering in their lives and who expected her son to devote much time to her. The problem became accentuated upon the long-delayed birth of the Agnos's first child two years before the interview. She describes the solution to the long-term friction.

Last year, the situation with my mother-in-law finally came to a head. She can be a very nasty person and is very possessive. We had always given her an allowance, part of which came from money I earned. With the baby, we needed the money. Since my husband is the nice guy in the family, she took advantage of him. I got fed up and decided things would be better if I didn't see her or speak to her any more. My husband finally agreed. He still sees her and everybody all the time.

Apparently, choosing this option caused no great conflict in the marriage. The husband established token visiting patterns with her family, and although the wife did not see her mother-in-law, she did see her husband's sisters several times a month. The Agnoses were in basic agreement on most values regarding family and childrearing. Both of them placed a high valuation on traditional family patterns. Even though their activities became increasingly segregated to the point of attending different churches, they did not report great conflict.

Other marriages that segregate their loyalties to their family of orientation have opted for this pattern because of basic differences in values. Mrs. Toscano is a high-spirited, attractive, Irish woman who holds a managerial position. She and her Italian husband, a college graduate, appear to disagree on almost everything, although there has never been any consideration of divorce or separation. One major source of disagreement lies in the parenting of three teenage daughters. Mrs. Toscano refers to them as her "little Mafia," a stereotypic reference that is usually distasteful to most Italians. She refers to the fact that they are so close they exclude her from their confidences. Mr. Toscano, in her opinion, is far too strict and supervisory over them.

He does nothing on weekends but hover over all of us. He feels the girls are going wild, when they are really typical adolescents. He has a short fuse and is not easy-going like me or my mother.

Mrs. Toscano is fiercely independent and attempts to train her daughters for a life of achievement and independence, a source of considerable value conflict with her husband who feels that females must be watched and protected. These disagreements extend not only to childrearing but also to money, decision-making, family obligations, and her career commitment.

Both the Toscanos have elderly parents who need some attention and service, she explains.

> However, my mother demands little. She is easy-going and non-complaining. I feel I should see her more, but she understands how busy I am. My mother-in-law is very different; she expects so much. If he doesn't call daily, she lures my husband over to her house with her cooking. He goes constantly, but I don't have the time.

Neither husband nor wife complain about the arrangements they have worked out. Each one fulfills obligations to his or her own family without involving the other. Such an arrangement obviously acts to reduce the number of problems that might ensue from contradictory conceptions of how families should operate. However, it does not alleviate the basic disagreements on childrearing.

The Nucleated Family

Fourteen families, or 35 percent of those where ethnic differences had posed a conflict, chose the nuclear family form, where loyalties to both families of orientation were minimized. Although one might assume that the potential for conflict would also be reduced, such is not always the case. Six of these families experience continued conflict over some issues of family life. Two more have joined Pentacostal religions where their churches provide quasi-family supports. It would seem that the nuclear option is a viable alternative for an Italian American who marries outside the group only when there are supports that replace the long-accustomed solidarity of the Italian family system.

Factors associated with withdrawal from both branches of the family stem from several sources. The first and most common one is the dominance of one spouse who rejects extended family ties. In these cases, the wives were not Italian. For example, one Polish-American wife held strong ideas on the precedence of the marital relationship over kinship bonds. She had long been critical of the demands her husband's parents made on them and had increasingly resisted conforming. Her husband, whatever his preferences, was defenseless, for he was not assertive and somewhat deaf. In an interview, he described himself as shy and isolated.

A second pattern stems from a dominant partner who feels superior to the Italian family and is able to assert his or her preferences for the priority of the nuclear family over the objections of an unwilling spouse. Two wives married to Italians, for example, described themselves as educationally superior to their Italian in-laws and insisted on a concentration on the nuclear family. The resulting nucleated family in these cases, however, did not result in a strengthened marriage as a substitute for the customary kinship supports.

In contrast, the third pattern of nucleation centered on the development of a strong marital relationship through a consensus of both partners. These families were middle class, and the Italian spouses had more assimilated parents. Usually, decisions were made early in the marriage to minimize activities with the extended family, and the couple concentrated their efforts on each other and their children instead. In two cases, the families had lived away from relatives for some years early in the marriage so that the nuclear pattern had already been established.

As noted earlier, kinship loyalties are weaker in intermarried families. With high rates of intermarriage today, a more nucleated pattern most likely will be dominant in the future. It would seem, however, that the severing of family ties by individuals who were embedded in them during their childhood can raise some adaptive problems in adulthood, unless the marriage can substitute for some of the accustomed supports.

Coping with Ethnic Differences

There are many difficulties arising from intermarriage, particularly among the less assimilated first and second generations in this country. The realistic obstacle of language differences, for example, often impeded communication with new in-laws, irrespective of the dissimilar values. In fact, early opposition to a mixed marriage often centered on the language problem. A German-Irish wife described a common situation upon her engagement to an Italian man:

His family was opposed. I wasn't Italian and I wasn't even Catholic. But to plan the marriage, we had to get both sets of parents together and we needed an interpreter. It was like a three-ring circus—his family on one side, mine on the other, and the interpreter in between.

Once I gave Tony back his ring. I told him he had to leave the Italian in him behind. He lived in America now. He told me I had to live like a human being—meaning the Italian way. It took years to get all this settled.

Even when the language problem was surmounted, other obstacles had to be faced. Some described a wedding where one side of the family refused to attend. Or, even when Italian in-laws accepted a non-Italian daughter-in-law, they would habitually describe her as different. "My mother-in-law's sister gave me a wedding shower. I was introduced as 'She's American, not Italian, but she's nice.'"

One Italian woman who has had to adjust to a non-Italian sister-in-law describes more general problems:

Intermarriage makes for complications. Both sides have their own way of doing things. It's like having strangers in our midst. We are willing to bend a bit, but not completely. So there's conflict in everything—money, gift-giving, and entertaining.

The marriage mix complicates everything. We have the energy to help each other a lot. When I lend a helping hand to my sister-in-law, she thinks I'm telling her what to do. If I don't help, she thinks I don't care.

Another Italian woman also described the difficulties she had in understanding her Protestant in-laws:

They expect nothing. They are so detached in their relationship. I find it unusual. They talk—well, like they are friends, not family. We just took a vacation with them, so it's fresh in my mind. They don't tell each other what to do. If Italians don't like something, they tell you. It shows they care. My in-laws go overboard to prevent me from responding to them.

In addition to the language barrier and different values and customs stemming directly from the immigrant background, it should be pointed out that these mixed marriages were formed by individuals who grew up in the pre-war years, when prejudice against Italians was a daily occurence. Hence, the derogatory views and stereotypes were sometimes carried over into the marriage. By the time we interviewed these individuals some years later, negative views were still vented. Ironically, however, these stereotypes often served to defuse tense marital situations. Rather than being directed toward the spouse, negative comments were displaced onto his or her family of origin or the ethnic group in general. This mode of handling marital problems deflects the conflict from day-to-day interaction between husband and wife. According to non-Italians, Italians have the following characteristics:

- They are obsessed with money. All talk revolves around how well off others are. They are gossipy.
- They are old fashioned. They come out of the dark ages.
- Italian men (or women) are too domineering.
- Italians are too emotional—they overreact to everything. They cry a lot.
- My mother always warned me about Italian men. She was frightened of them.
- Italians tend to dwell on things too deeply—they make mountains out of molehills.

Since these complaints are directed at an ethnic category, rather than at the spouse as an individual, and in fact are often a source of jokes shared by the in-group, they are not necessarily an impediment to marital adjustment. One of the most common sources of complaints, however, which did cause problems, centered on interference from Italian relatives. Although some of these problems were past and had long since been resolved, a low level of conflict frequently persisted:

- Italians are too possessive. My brother-in-law can't distinguish the status of brother from husband so he feels he can monopolize my husband.
- My in-laws always want to help us, but then they never let us forget it.
- The families are completely different. I had a completely different life—I could do things on my own. This family has to do everything together. Even when my husband had to go into the hospital

for an emergency, they didn't even call me at work. It was a big commotion, and I wasn't even part of it. My husband forgets that when we married, he had to place me first over his family.

- Our marriage began with daily visiting back and forth with his family. I put my foot down early. It had to stop.

Some non-Italian spouses go so far as to doubt the sincerity of the concern and involvement of their relatives. Some non-Italians described their own family sentiments as sincere and their spouse's as "duty-bound" or forced. Hence, one's own kind is easy-going and relaxed and the in-laws are "up-tight." A Polish woman discussed this point with her husband during an interview:

> *How can I say this politely? Italians always talk about close-ness, yet they do less about it than my Polish side who doesn't talk about it.*

The husband jokingly responded, "You mean we're all words and less action. You are all action and not words." While this interchange was in the best of spirits, other non-Italians are more critical, calling their in-laws hypocritical. "My husband's family speaks about respect all the time. Then they talk behind their parents' back. I think it's fear, not respect."

Other non-Italian wives complain about the extra work that is involved when one marries into an Italian family and has to live up to relatives' expectations. "My husband was warned by his mother when he married me that I was an American and he would get skinny from my cooking." A German wife describes her distant relationship with her sisters-in-law as stemming from their single-minded absorption with domestic life:

> *They are only concerned with children and cooking. I find that boring. There are always many pots simmering on the stove. Life for Italians is eating. When a five-year-old nephew stayed here, he said, "I know what's different about this house. There's nothing cooking on the stove."*

> *Every get-together has to be a big celebration. They aren't content with coffee and cake, so it's a lot of work. My cleaning is never right. Italian women are obsessed with cleanliness. If she could, my mother-in-law would wash the walls and take them out to hang in the sun.*

Another respondent said archly, "My mother-in-law is so clean you can eat off her toilet seat."

Among the many problems reported of varying magnitude, probably the most common centered on the discrepancies in the expressions of emotions. Non-Italian spouses viewed the Italian family environment as "emotionally charged," and had problems with the atmosphere. As reported by non-Italians:

- I can't stand the noise and confusion.
- I get disoriented when I'm with his family. It's a big, booming, noisy confusion.
- I never cried so much until I joined this big emotional family.
- The way that family talks is unreal. They yell and scream at each other. Everyone talks at once. Then the next minute everything goes on as usual.
- I can't get used to them talking about everything. Even when something comes up with my parents which they don't even discuss with me, my husband's family will dwell on it for hours.

Those who cannot accommodate to the ways of their spouse's family generally experience a gradual withdrawal from their in-laws. By the time they were interviewed, they had come to see themselves as "outcasts" or "black sheep." Whether the withdrawal was mutual or unilateral, these non-Italians experienced a sense of rejection. "They only want to see Italians and only family, I'm neither of these to them."

While criticisms generally outnumber praises, most non-Italian respondents pointed to the support capacities of the close family system. Many singled out the male's responsibility to family, and his stability, as positive features. Others praised the strictness in childrearing. Finally, respondents of other immigrant groups who moved here recently from countries other than Italy singled out the common problems faced by all immigrant groups in adjusting to this country and struggling to reach the middle class.

Italian Americans who married out, with some exceptions, have parallel opinions on their spouses' families:

- They don't show affection.
- They aren't open and candid.
- They are so wrapped up in themselves, you can't approach them.

- We don't see the in-laws. They're not family people.
- They aren't hospitable. You're lucky to get a cup of coffee out of them.
- They're cold, they show no emotion.
- My mother-in-law couldn't care less what goes on with us.

In a few cases, Italians married outside the group because they joined their spouses in their objections to Italian-American family values. Family interdependence was called "meddling," or the individuals involved were "busybodies." Italian husbands are not viewed as potentially conscientious husbands or fathers; they are tyrants.

In any case, where values and customary behaviors in families differ markedly, what appear to be advantages to one spouse can easily seem like disadvantages to the other. Unless the intermarriage was prompted by a desire for options different from one's family of orientation, these problems have to be resolved if conflict is to be minimized. In contemporary marriages, the types of conflict described here are reduced by establishing a physical and emotional distance from one's original family. The sample did not choose this route; all were living in the community where they married fifteen to twenty-five years ago, so both partners had numerous relatives nearby. This evidence suggests that Italian Americans are most likely to remain near their original homes after marriage, even if they marry non-Italians. Remaining in the home town after marriage for Italians, however, means remaining immersed in the family. Since these marriages have stayed intact, we can assume there has been some success in coping with cultural differences.

From the perspective of the older Italian Americans, however, intermarriage does affect their status. The comparison between the in-married and out-married families as a whole reveals that both contact and aid to parents decrease in numbers when one's spouse is not Italian, even though the strength of the filial values is much the same. The elderly who have daughters rather than sons who married outside the group do fare somewhat better in the attention they receive.

Nevertheless, the out-marriage rate was high between 1948 and 1960 (48 to 59 percent) and is probably higher today. This situation will most likely affect older Italians in the future. An examination of group differences indicates that, with out-marriage, the influence of the extended family diminishes. As a result, new values and lifestyles are introduced which weaken the normatively based ethnic boundary around the nuclear family. Thus, such a dedication to older parents as described in an earlier chapter will most likely diminish as the younger generation of Italians reach middle age.

Chapter 8
The Elderly and the Old-fashioned Way

Over half of the Italians over sixty-five years of age in this sample were born in Italy, and most arrived in America in childhood or early adult years. Those born in the United States were born to recent immigrants. A large majority spent their lives in the "Little Italies" without extensive exposure to American society. To them, their world was divided into the Italians and the Americans (or "Merigans" as imitated by their children.) Most would agree with one Italian father's advice: "Trust family first, relatives second, Sicilians third, and after that, forget it." (Ianni and Reuss-Ianni 1975). Except for *paesani*, few allegiances in their early years were outside of the family and its extensions. Both consanguineal and fictive relatives provide the immigrants with economic, social, and psychological support within the ethnic community.

The older Italians' conception of family is explicitly traditional. They usually described the family in its ideal form as the "old-fashioned way." To them, the family is the only unit of real importance in life, and they single-mindedly extoll the virtues of its traditional forms. The old-fashioned way mandates that all members should make sacrifices for the family honor, respect all of its members, and reject any outside influences that might dilute family allegiances. Generally, they conclude that even with economic security and social mobility in America, the family remains one's only defense against a difficult and often hostile outside world.

Although they are no longer subject to erratic forces of nature or the exploitation of the church or landowners as they or their parents experienced in Italy, older Italians generally view non-family influences as undesirable and even threatening. They perceive the major threats to the family today as coming from American culture and its potential capacity to dilute family allegiances. Thus, constant vigilance is required. In order to convey their concerns to their children and grandchildren, these respondents repeatedly extol the past and complain about the present dangers inherent in the American way of life. The list is long. The greatest complaints involve increasing affluence and materialism which in their eyes have eroded the values of thrift, hard work, and generosity to others. One respondent lamented, "In Italy, there was only misery, but people helped each other. Here, the streets are paved with gold, but people are only out for themselves. Now we have everything but peace of mind." To them, money is linked to selfishness, laziness, and increasing independence from the family. "The younger generation is so busy chasing the dollar, they don't have time for the family. With money, everyone thinks only of themselves. When people had nothing, there was more respect for each other." Older respondents also worry that money has weakened family ties by enabling parents to go out and socialize with friends instead of spending time at home with children. One elderly man feels that the material successes of his children and grandchildren cause disharmony in the family:

> In the past, Italians shared their last piece of bread. There was always room for a visitor—another place at the table and a place to sleep. That was when no one had a dime. Now there is jealousy over who is eating or dressing better.

The social change since World War II has been most difficult for the elderly to understand and accept. Neighborhoods have changed as prosperity stimulates moves to the suburbs. "Chasing the dollar" distracts people from family loyalties; and worse yet, people watch television rather than visit one another. The final assaults came in the late 1960s when women began to reject their traditional roles, children began to choose other options over family, and chastity for women lost its value. To the elderly, the early years of poverty and subjugation were usually viewed as preferable to the foibles of contemporary American life.

Usually the foundations of a good family life inherent in the old-fashioned way were stated in quite simple terms: home ownership, good food, the instilling of respect, and the display of affection. The directives by which these should be achieved were repeatedly discussed and held up to their children and grandchildren as major goals in life.

The first, home ownership, signifies the values of hard work and frugality; in fact, it is seen as a major source of contentment in old age. One respondent, a retired railroad worker, put it this way:

Italian Americans are frugal, thrifty people who worked hard all their lives. They always strived to have a home of their own and some security in their old age. With this achievement, I feel content. . . . Some people are not content. . . . I reply—you have a home, you have worked hard all your life, and now you are enjoying it.

This high valuation on the home has persisted long after children have departed; 77 percent of the respondents over sixty-five own their own homes. These homes are invariably well maintained and spotlessly clean. Unlike other older people, few Italian Americans want to move to more modern, labor-saving apartments unless financial problems require a change. Often, the house is changed with the stage in the family cycle: first, it is a large home suitable to raising a family, next it is converted into apartments to make a multiple-unit dwelling for adult and married children, and, finally, in old age, the apartments are rented out to provide extra income upon retirement. The high percentage of elderly who remain in the homes they had occupied most of their married life documents its importance, and respondents frequently describe sacrifices they make to keep the home. One woman separated from her husband in order to stay in the old family home when he insisted on moving to Florida. Another couple refused to sell their home even though they needed money. "Our home is the trophy of life, the symbol of all we worked for."

The second component, good food, also signifies a successful family. It is a focal point of family sociability. It attests to the earning power of the father and the domestic skills of the mother. The importance of food to Italian Americans, as discussed in chapter 5, is expressed by lavish meals shared with the family. To the elderly, it is a concrete manifestation of hospitality and generosity among family and relatives.

Less tangible than a clean home and good food, but no less important, are values of respect and affection. In the research, respect was the word used most frequently as a vague reference to describe the family at its best and most successful. It defines the proper mode of behavior for successful family relationships. In regard to the parent-child relationship, the term connotes a hierarchy where egalitarian norms are not accepted. The parents, especially the father, should be in a superior position from which they demand obedience from the children. These clearly demarcated roles call for parents to be parents; they should not act like brothers, sisters, or friends to their children.

Affection, the fourth component, is linked to the nebulous qualities of heart, warmth, emotionality, and love. Like respect, affection is a key component of successful families. Central to this success is a mother who is all-forgiving, compassionate, and self-sacrificing. One woman said, "Italians are all heart. They do more for you. They feel sorry for you. We all worry a lot about each other. If anything goes wrong, we go to pieces." An analysis of the interviews suggests that affective bonds among Italians are seen as the result of instilling respect. According to this ideology, if respect is instilled in children and emphasized over the years, then one's rewards will eventually come in the form of affection.

The values built around these components of good family life—a clean home, good food, respect, and affection—are simple statements reflecting a traditional ideology that centers on family relationships. A home represents the hard work and frugality both of the father as the provider and the mother as dispenser of family benefits. Likewise good food, also a result of hard work, provides the focal point of family sociability. This conviviality and sharing must be reinforced by the perpetuation of respect, a value underpinning the family hierarchy. To Italian Americans, particularly older ones, respect must be taught by strict discipline; it does not come naturally or easily. By this logic, if respect is instilled, bonds of affection among family members will follow.

Some space has been devoted to these values and goals as expressed in the idealism of the respondents because they were so repetitively and extensively discussed in the interviews. Middle-aged respondents also confirmed that their parents' views on family life dominate many conversations; "It's like a broken record. How could we forget?" Since adult children are in such frequent contact with their parents, and often aunts and uncles, the reminders of the good life of the past are difficult to escape or forget.

The Life Situation of the Elderly

Of the sixty-six respondents who were sixty-five years or older, 42 percent were men (Table 8.1). Their average age was seventy, with

Table 8.1.
Social Characteristics of Italians, 65 Years and Older (n = 66)

By percentage			
Sex		At least one child	97
Male	42	in proximity	
Female	58		
		Household status	
Birthplace		Alone	35
Italy	56	With spouse	38
United States	44	With spouse and child	14
		With child	8
Marital status		With relative	6
Married	56		
Widowed	33	Education	
Divorced	5	None	10
Permanently single	6	8 years or less	70
		9–12 years	18
Fluency in English	75	College	2

By means	
Age	70 years
Number of children	2.6

a range from sixty-five to eighty-five years of age. Fifty-six percent were born in Italy but the majority of them emigrated before adulthood. Almost one-third were widowed, and three others were divorced or separated. One-fourth of them were not fluent in English. With the exception of four individuals, the men had retired from blue-collar positions. Even though the majority spent much of their childhood in this country, 70 percent had fewer than eight years of schooling and 10 percent could not read or write.

Resembling the population as a whole, elderly Italian Americans in Easton have a mean number of children of 2.6. Eleven percent have no living children. However, the elderly Italians, unlike others, have been relatively unaffected by geographic mobility. Only two of the respondents, for example, have no children in the city or the surrounding suburbs. In their household situation, 22 percent share the home with an offspring, while another 34 percent have a child within walking distance.

Even though this report stems from a relatively "young old" who have lived in America for many years, most continue to espouse the old-fashioned way. Given this ideology, one would expect some gap between the elderly and the younger generation. In order to measure this potential distance, the social networks of the older respondents were examined. Who do they see and how often? Can they call up allegiances to family to the extent that children are readily available to tend to their needs?

As Table 8.2 reports, the close proximity of children leads to frequent interaction; 76 percent have contact within a given twenty-four-hour period, and another 21 percent have seen children in the past week. Consequently only those who have no children and the two individuals with no children in the area are deprived of sustained contact and support.

Grandchildren are almost as important as children to most of the respondents. Three individuals had a grandchild living with them while the parents lived elsewhere. In one case, a granddaughter lived with her grandparents in order to be closer to the Catholic school connected with the national parish. In the other two, the grandchildren chose to stay in the area after their parents moved from the city. While 30 percent of these elderly see a grandchild daily, 89 percent see one at least weekly.

Table 8.2.

Social Contacts of Italians over 65 Years (by percentage, n = 66)

	Children	Grandchildren	Siblings	Other relatives	Friends
In past 24 hours	76	29	23	14	70
In past week	21	60	39	32	27
In past month	2	3	18	22	3
Yearly or less	2	7	19	32	—
Number with no relatives present	7	7	4	32[a]	—

[a]Indicates no relative other than children and siblings are present.

Unlike gerontological research which has found that normally the
grandparent role does not provide a source of life satisfaction to the elderly (Neugarten and Weinstein 1964), the Italian elderly report numerous rewards from the grandchildren. One respondent expressed a
view shared by many: "Not being around grandchildren is one step
into the graveyard. Children add variety to life." Although our respondents went to great lengths to criticize the sexual behaviour of the
young, as well as their selfishness and general permissiveness, most
reassured us that their own grandchildren had escaped the vagaries of
their generation and had maintained the family honor. In fact, while
the elderly continue to espouse traditional discipline techniques, they
are usually permissive with their grandchildren to the point that it is an
occasional source of conflict with the parents.

The relationship among elderly siblings is also more important than
is generally found (Shanas 1979). Over two-thirds have at least one
brother or sister nearby, and almost all see that sibling at least weekly.
Considering that the majority of the elderly sample were immigrants,
siblings most likely came to America together and continued to live
near each other throughout their lives.

The elderly see other relatives quite frequently as well. Sixty-three
percent report having at least five other relatives in the city, and all
said they see them at least monthly. Two-thirds see these other relatives in the area at least weekly. In fact, almost one-half still include
siblings and other relatives in activities with their children, by inviting
them to both informal gatherings and family celebrations.

In our society in general, it has been found that friends of one's
own age dominate the contacts of the elderly. As noted earlier, age
segregation and preference for age peers has been linked to higher life
satisfaction and morale (Blau 1973; Rosow 1967). Although most Italian Americans see more family and relatives than friends, friendships
comprise a frequent and important part of their social network. Seventy percent see a friend daily, while a total of 97 percent have weekly
contact with a friend (see Table 8.2). On the other hand, neighbors
are less important to the elderly Italian. Only one-third report frequent
contact with and help patterns among neighbors.

Godchildren are another important source of social contact for the
elderly. This relationship is socially significant for 69 percent of the
sample. They see godchildren frequently and exchange gifts and services. In some cases, godchildren can assume a significance equal to
one's biological children in cases where the latter are unavailable.

There are significant differences between Italian Americans in this sample and the population as a whole (Johnson 1983; Shanas 1979). Although the numbers of children and surviving siblings are roughly comparable, Italian Americans are less likely to live alone if they are widowed. Furthermore, if they are married, they are more likely to incorporate children and other relatives into the household. In regard to their children, they are more likely to live near them and to see them within a twenty-four-hour period. The same situation holds for the sibling relationship; they are more likely to see a sibling at least weekly than is the general population.

Recent studies (Shanas et al. 1968) indicate that, in the general population of elderly in this country, few are isolated from family contacts. However, Italian Americans in comparison to a national sample are even less issolated. Contacts with children, siblings, and other relatives are more frequent than is found in the population as a whole. Even the 16 percent who live alone are not isolated; only one person had no contact with a relative during the day before the interview.

Because their time is amply filled with intimate relationships, the Italian elderly usually shun organizational contacts. For example, Mrs. Motello was persuaded to go to a senior citizen lunch program and came home visibly upset. "They treat us as if we have no friends or family. If I'm lonely, I can see them. Why would I want to eat with strangers?"

These older respondents did report a decline in social involvement in comparison to their middle age; 88 percent see less of friends, 42 percent go to church less regularly, and 62 percent participate less in club activities. Rather than undergoing disengagement or a progressive withdrawal from social life, however, these elderly have generally compensated for these social losses by family involvement. The frequent contact reported suggests that as some roles are lost through widowhood, retirement, death of friends, or physical impairment the void can be filled by members of the family.

Factors Associated with the Social Situation

Although engagement in activities with family and relatives is higher for Italians than others, there is still considerable variation among the respondents. Examining variables associated with the level of interaction allows us to make several interesting conclusions.

For one thing, Italian males and females participate equally in the family networks and do not differ in their degree of isolation. For the population as a whole, the preference of men for work life over family has a cumulative effect, which by retirement can result in an inability to reenter the lives of children and other kin once time becomes available. Clearly, this pattern does not apply to Italian-American men, which suggests that their lifelong activity pattern has focused on family, and will continue in old age. Although the Italian father is often a somewhat distant authority figure in his younger years, his power and authority become eroded in old age, probably much to his own advantage in terms of his relationships within the family.

The second significant variable is that of age itself. Those over seventy-five are significantly more isolated than those between sixty-five and seventy-four years of age. These "old, old" Italians are more likely to be widowed, a factor also associated with increased social isolation. The lifelong pattern of avoiding social contacts outside the family makes it more difficult to compensate for role losses with widowhood. Forming new friendships or devising new activities in order to keep involved are alien activities. Hence, even when one remains actively involved with children, grandchildren, and siblings, there is a shrinkage in the life situation because of a decline in other contacts.

Measures of acculturation are also important variables affecting the life situation of Italian elderly. Place of birth or the designation of generation level is one variable. Although one would expect that the foreign-born would be more involved in family life because they are closer to traditional family forms, it was found that those born in this country have a more significantly active social life. They have more contact with relatives than the Italian-born, and they report a larger number of relatives in proximity. These findings reflect a more expanded kinship group with each generation. Since these relatives are also more likely to live nearby, one's circle of sociability is high.

Language usage, or the level of fluency in English, likewise indicates acculturation. It was found that those who are fluent in English have more social contact with children and kin. Thus, ease of communication with children and kin apparently stimulates the older generation's integration into family activities. This evidence suggests that a degree of acculturation facilitates family centeredness rather than causing changes toward an American model of family interaction.

Despite the fact that some degree of acculturation has a positive effect on adaptation of the elderly, there is evidence that this change might eventually entail some costs. Presumably, the parents who are in the second generation and have an English-speaking home more readily introduce their children to the larger society and encourage more contact with non-Italians. As a result, their children are more likely to marry non-Italians. As noted earlier in reports of middle-aged children, though, intermarried Italians have less contact with parents.

Not all Italian Americans escape the hazards of isolation in old age. A careful examination of the six respondents with the lowest scores in interaction reveals that the common characteristic among them is the absence of children, a situation that pertained to five of the six individuals. One woman, a retired secretary who had never married, illustrates this situation. Although she lives with her brother, she reported much to her dissatisfaction that her social contacts dropped dramatically with retirement.

Other more isolated respondents, even those with a surviving spouse, find life more circumscribed in old age. Retirement for one man decreased a large portion of the usual social relationships stemming from the work role. Arthritis diminished one respondent's mobility so that it became more difficult for him to visit friends. Failing eyesight and the subsequent loss of a driver's license limited another so that he couldn't go out daily. Another man remained in good health, but his wife was quite ill. Since there were no children to share in the responsibilities of care for this incapacitated woman, he was confined to the home.

In an ethnic group such as Italian Americans, where failures in filial obligations are negatively sanctioned, the proximity of children is probably the single most significant facilitator of family supports in old age. Since childless elderly are a minority in the ethnic neighborhood where most of their peers are surrounded by children, they do not tend to band together after their retirement to form age-based social units. Few respondents used senior citizen groups available in their neighborhoods. Since contacts with siblings also decline after age seventy-five because of attrition by death and impairment, these factors leave the childless more isolated in a community where there are few substitutes for the sociability focused on parents and children.

One force that compensates for this isolation and disengagement is the godparent relationship. Mrs. Donato is a widow, seventy-two years of age, and a retired seamstress. She began working in a clothing factory at the age of fifteen, shortly after her family moved to

Easton from Pennsylvania. She married at nineteen but, she laments, "God never blessed me with children." She worked almost continually until her retirement seven years ago. Since her own kinship group remained in Pennsylvania, her family was always more nucleated than others around her. For Mrs. Donato, real problems with depression began with the death of her husband six years ago, her mother three years ago, and her brother last year. These deaths, she reports, took a terrible toll on her, for she had lost contact with friends over the years and, with her husband's death, rarely saw his family.

What prevented her from being almost totally isolated was the proximity of two godchildren who were daughters of a friend. They were very affectionate with her, calling her "sweetie pie." One, who was unmarried, telephoned her daily and visited several times a week. The second daughter had just adopted a baby, and Mrs. Donato was sharing in the care. She felt this child's adoption was the "work of the Lord," for she had been very depressed over the recent series of deaths. To be included in a new family was a great consolation. In reciprocity, she planned to leave all she owned to her two goddaughters and, at the time of the interview, was slipping them money or buying them gifts.

Despite high rates of involvement with family for many of the respondents, there were examples of profound isolation as well. In the case of Mr. Muselli, personal factors and his long-standing inability to get along with others seemed to be the cause of what amounted to complete disengagement at the time of the interview.

In his youth, Mr. Muselli played minor league baseball and later held a series of unskilled jobs. He reported that his non-Italian wife was no help, for she was a "psychiatric case" who had been hospitalized eight to ten times. Two months before the interview, she had left him and, in his opinion, turned his children against him. "Now they won't even answer my phone calls," he said. He sees a sister who lives nearby only once or twice a year. Most of his good friends are dead, leaving only barroom friends who, according to him, "are a dime a dozen," but of no real support. The only person from whom he has received help is a neighbor who rents his garage. He reported that once the neighbor found him passed out and called his daughter and daughter-in-law, but neither was willing to come to his assistance.

Mr. Muselli feels that everything has gone wrong in his life. After a lifetime of hard work, he bemoans the absence of rewards. Even relatively unimportant things bothered him: "Everything is changing—so much new construction downtown. I can't find some of my old haunts where I used to hang out." Financially, he is less secure than most, for he still has to pay monthly mortgage payments on his house. Mr. Muselli described an average day:

> *I get up early each morning—about five or six. I do my own cooking, washing, and cleaning. I don't go out much, but I do odd jobs for neighbors for extra money. Most of my time is spent reading the newspaper and watching t.v. I must have watched more television in the last two months (since his wife left him) than in the last ten years.*

Mr. Muselli feels that if he had retired at fifty-five rather than at sixty-five, he could have enjoyed himself for a few years before everything began to go wrong. Nevertheless, the withdrawal of his family apparently was the cumulative result of long-standing relational difficulties. It is not easy to determine the nature of the event that finally led to his children's almost total lack of involvement with him at the time of the interview. Since he reported the last time he was invited by his children for Christmas dinner was several years before, one can conclude that his wife's departure was actually only one event in a long process of disengagement, a disengagement that was hastened by his general problems in interpersonal relationships.

The six respondents with the highest scores of interaction, on the other hand, were distinguished from those with the low scores by the proximity of the children and other relatives. Other than the children's proximity, these six with high scores were varied in characteristics: half were men and half were women; half had greater economic resources than the sample in general; their health ranged from excellent to one with debilitating arthritis. While their numbers of relatives were about the same as the sample in general, these highly engaged individuals had a long-enduring pattern of frequent social contact and reciprocity. Children and siblings lived nearby and were readily available to assist.

The typical day of a highly engaged sixty-eight-year-old woman can be contrasted to that of the lonely and disgruntled Mr. Muselli. Mrs. Lansini has been widowed for thirty-six years and retired for eight years as a clerk at her father-in-law's fruit stand. At the time of the interview, she worked for a few hours each day in her sister's grocery store. Although she lived alone, her daughter and family lived in an upstairs apartment, and they shared their meals with her. Her other three children were within a five-minute ride. She saw them all almost daily. Her seven grandchildren were continually dropping by.

Her eleven siblings lived in the city, and she saw most of them weekly. She spent time each day "babysitting" for a neighbor who was ill. This busy schedule changed dramatically at 6 P.M. when she locked her doors and enjoyed rest and solitude for the evening.

Mr. Corsello, a retired carpenter, said his days were completely taken up with family involvements. Since retirement, he "take[s] care of thirteen members of his family," meaning that he makes rounds from nine in the morning until nine at night, touching base with all close kin. When he mentioned the possibility of a son leaving the area, he described how he would handle it:

> There's no reason why I won't see him. As long as I have two legs, two arms, and two eyes. With two legs, I can go to him. With two eyes I can see him. If I ain't got eyes, I can feel him, so I know he's there.

All these examples indicate that while long-standing supports can be utilized in old age, it is improbable that they can be suddenly developed when the need arises. Instead, the long tradition of help patterns, which have been an important source of support throughout the life cycle, is important. Shanas (1968) comes to a similar conclusion: "Once weakened, family relationships are difficult to renew or repair; they need to be regularly reinforced—like conditioned reflexes."

In summary, Italian men and women participate equally in family activities; there are few lonely men who are cast aside from female-dominated family activities. Although both men and women participate in fewer social activities in old age, such withdrawal is not noticeable in family life. Only a few see a day or two go by without contact with a son or daughter, a brother or sister, a godchild, or a friend. Like the elderly in general, however, illness and advanced old age stimulate some withdrawal just as the intermarriage of children does. The Italian-American elderly who can stem this tide are more acculturated in their relationships with their children and make concessions to the New World ways.

Expectations and Reality

These objective reports on contact indicate that, in comparison to the population in general, these Italians are more integrated into the extended family, and their expectations for children and relatives are generally met. On the whole, they are not lonely and abandoned, as measured at least by the level of social contact. While they might view social change and new family forms as alarming, few reported that these emerging lifestyles had touched their lives. Yet it is clear that these respondents have made concessions to American culture. When asked what they expected from their children, only one respondent hoped for total care and support from her children. Another 46 percent expected some kind of help, but only in the event that illness or poverty prevented them from caring for themselves. Nineteen percent expected only companionship; being able to see their children frequently would satisfy their only needs. Finally, a surprising 34 percent stated that they expected nothing from their children.

Seventy-eight percent of the respondents not currently living with an offspring said they would not consider such an alternative. To most of our respondents, the ideal situation was to maintain one's own home near one's children, but not to be in the same household.

> *You don't feel the same when you're not in your own home. A mother does so much for her children, but she can't be happy living with them. Then she can't say anything without offending. I love my kids—I raised three wonderful ones. I don't have to live with them—I can get on the phone and let them know what I want.*

In other words, there is a conscious attempt to maintain some independence from children. Cohler and Grunebaum (1981) report similar findings among four somewhat younger Italian mothers. In fact, they suggest that these mothers socialized their daughters to be dependent and then became dissatisfied by their daughters' dependence upon them as adults. By old age, however, most Italians reassure themselves that their independent stance will not prevent a future dependence on children if the need arises.

Irrespective of the widespread desire to live apart from children, most elderly Italians desire dutiful children. Parental sacrifice is one device that ensures the proper care and respect in one's old age (Pearlin 1970). Expectations of rewards for the years of selfless struggle is one means by which filial behaviors are assured. However, few respondents explicitly expressed the idea that sacrifice should be used as a social control device or as a source of reward due from their children, although the idea was implicit in many discussions.

> *We don't expect a thing. My children were just raised to have the good sense to help when something is needed. But what they*

do for us they do because of love and respect for us. They know
we worked hard all our lives to give them the best we could.

In other words, when the children have internalized the values of respect and affection, elderly parents can afford to become staunch de-
fenders of their own independence. Like most elderly in this country,
these respondents repeatedly espouse the value of independence and
have an almost phobic fear of becoming a burden to their families.
The desire to live independently signifies their autonomy, even though
most elderly are dependent upon their children for at least some of
their social needs. A son who comes for lunch each day or a daughter
who stops by each afternoon satisfies social needs without detracting
from one's sense of independence.

For example, Mrs. Russo was describing her daughter's frequent
visits when the daughter appeared and listened to the remainder of the
interview. When I asked if she would like to live with her offspring,
she emphatically said no. The daughter interrupted and told me how
she wanted to build a room onto her house to accomodate her parents.
However, Mrs. Russo was adamant about her desire for independence.
It would seem that the expression of such values might not be strictly
a genuine desire for independence, but rather a fail-safe technique
to protect one's self-esteem and avoid disappointment if support from
one's children does not materialize. Such covert techniques were possibly used in this interchange. Mrs. Russo could espouse her desire for
independence, knowing with some assurance that when her resources
failed, she could assume a dependant role that would be readily accepted by her daughter.

As noted above, the measures of acculturation, generation level, and
language usage are important factors affecting the life space of the
elderly Italian Americans. The more acculturated have significantly
more social interaction. Apparently in changing their values to be
more compatible with American culture, these elderly have lessened
the potential gap with their children. One respondent described the
process as "bending a little," which means making concessions to
new values and behaviors, however much they are at odds with the
old-fashioned way. If younger members of the family do not show
the proper respect, the elderly disapprove, but they usually place the
blame on an outside force in society, a fate-like kind of force that
no one can control. In their eyes, materialism, permissiveness, and
selfishness meet one at every turn and intrude daily into the home

through television. One must learn to live with it, accept it, and remind the younger generation of its dangers. Obviously, the absence of such explicit expectations can minimize conflict and assure them a continued position in the family.

Such commendable behaviors, however, do not rule out expectations operating at the covert level. Instead of explicit expectations—"You are duty-bound to take care of me"—implicit expectations are a logical result of lifelong socialization patterns that have been geared to produce filial offspring. If sons or daughters forget their responsibilities, mothers were frequently reported to use such techniques as tears or sighs of despair rather than accusations of neglect. Elderly parents have also been known to dwell upon examples of friends who were "abandoned" by their children. "Look at them—they can't even take care of their own parents." "What did she do to raise such ungrateful children?" Many respondents asked rhetorically, "How is it that one mother can raise eight [or ten or twelve] children and they can't take care of one mother?" Another comment frequently heard over a lifetime is, "A child is your cane in old age." Tears could flow when one was recounting the abuses of ungrateful children. Furthermore, many frequently described the years of struggle and sacrifice devoted to raising children. This behavior leaves little doubt in the children's minds as to where their allegiances belong.

Nevertheless, it is evident that those who do relax the traditional value system do so to their own advantage in terms of the maintenance of family solidarity. Those who are unwilling to make concessions are more likely to face decreased social interaction in old age as their children and grandchildren by-pass the old-fashioned way for a more adaptive orientation to American society.

Hence, uneasy compromises must be made with the American culture of their children and their grandchildren. Even those who realistically assure themselves that their children have resisted many of the temptations of contemporary society still express great concern over the influences of the outside world. The outside forces that erode the old-fashioned way, particularly those which cast off the individual "to sink or swim on his own," are seen as particularly threatening. Some doubts are expressed over the family's continuing capacity to resist these effects. Essentially, they see the handwriting on the wall; if the barriers around the family are relaxed and the old-fashioned way discarded, their own status will change dramatically.

Conclusion

These extensive descriptions and statistical findings indicate that the status of the Italian Americans in old age is one of continuity rather than discontinuity. Although they are more dependent in old age in terms of their social and psychological needs, and more disengaged from the work role and roles connected with formal and informal associations, they are firmly entrenched in an extended family system. Although they have major worries about the passing of traditional family practices, such changes have not yet led to family changes that result in their exclusion from the lives of their children.

In this situation, continuity rather than discontinuity in parental roles is a key factor in maintaining the high status of the old. For elderly women, motherhood and attendant domestic roles change in intensity, but do not lose their centrality. As grandmothers, their nurturing functions continue. For the men, usually patriarchical immigrants, the loss of the work role has not noticeably affected their central role in the family. Instead, the absence of the work role permits greater family involvement. An elderly Italian-American man with pensions or social security, and perhaps an apartment to rent upstairs, can easily provide for his wife and have enough resources remaining to give something to his children and grandchildren. If he is healthy, he continues to work for his family in some capacity such as gardening, carpentry, or odd jobs which make him feel important and useful. Over the life cycle, the Italian family has relatively flexible boundaries around the various age levels. As parenting roles continue well into the adult life of their children, parenting more readily blurs into grandparenting without sharp breaks and discontinuities.

These data suggest that the transition into the roles of old age is facilitated as long as the chief roles, as in earlier stages of life, remain centered on family. Lifelong socialization patterns are marked by continuity in family roles, although retirement and widowhood have caused social losses. The majority of the elderly Italian Americans do not enter a roleless situation, as described elsewhere (Blau 1973), for family roles continue to be central.

Most elderly are included in the activities of their children's nuclear families and, in this capacity, can continue to exert some influence through extolling the virtues of traditionalism. These reminders repeatedly reinforce values centering on the affective and controlling elements in the family, namely love and respect. Even if the elderly are viewed as old-fashioned and out of step with contemporary times, most children remain filial and attentive. Likewise, their grandchildren are there to observe and take part in the intergenerational relations. At least in regard to ethnic norms of family life, it seems likely that these norms extolling the family will continue for some generations, given the continuance of other social factors, Specifically, as long as inter-marriage is not extensive and as long as rates of geographic mobility remain low, the elderly can retain their status and their security.

Chapter 9
Adapting to Elderly Parents

The description of the family position of older Americans in Easton seems to harken back to another era incongruent with contemporary society. The question arises, how do middle-aged Italians adapt the old-fashioned way to their own lives? Clearly, if they do not completely reject the old-fashioned way, and few do, they must make some accommodations to the values of their parents. This chapter describes how the 109 middle-aged Italian respondents interpret and act upon the expectations of the elderly. One example will illustrate how some accommodations are made.

Mrs. Maggio, who is fifty-two years old, lives with her husband and one daughter in a two-family home on the Northside. Her parents live two blocks away, and, of her five sisters in the city, one lives in the other apartment in the Maggios' home. As the eldest, Mrs. Maggio concluded that the major obligations to her parents lay with her:

> *My younger sisters have learned more American ways. They argue with Dad and say, "No, Dad, that's not the way it is." He'd say, "Yes, it is." It would go on all day. In the same situation, I'd just say okay and avoid any discussion.*

In one important way, Mrs. Maggio differs from most Italian women in their fifties: she had gone to college and she might have gone on to graduate school if the old-fashioned way had not intervened. She had never planned on a higher education, but during high school her academic abilities were recognized and encouraged. Teachers arranged a scholarship for her at the local university. Her father was suspicious of this plan, but after days of persuasion, he finally relented. In her senior year, she was offered a graduate fellowship to continue her studies in New York City, but that was simply too much for her father to accept. She explained:

> *A single Italian girl just couldn't leave her home. I enlisted my uncle's help, and he loaned my father his car, so he could take me there and look it over. Since it had taken so long to get my*

father to budge that far, the dormitory was full. My father didn't like the looks of the alternate rooms which were perfectly respectable and chaperoned. He wouldn't let me stay, but as a consolation, we want to Boston to visit some relatives from Calabria. There I met my husband who had just come from Italy. Our fathers were paesani.

After a supervised courtship during which the young couple were rarely alone, they settled down to married life in an apartment in her parents' home. Over the next fourteen years, she had three children and also worked in her father's store. As she looked back, these years were difficult for her:

Parents tended to dictate and criticize and expect you to live up to their standards. They were very critical of our spending money. When my daughters were babies, my father would pound the ceiling if they cried out and, if it went on, he'd send mother up.

At the time of the interview, Mrs. Maggio was including her elderly parents in everything she did. She took time off from work to take care of her mother when she was sick. She loaned them money once which had been saved for her children's college education. She and her husband used a vacation to paint her parents' house. When asked about the order of her priorities, she replied:

My first loyalty should be to my husband and children even though it usually seems to be to my parents.

I don't expect this from my married daughters. We had to make too many sacrifices. My parents have been selfish in not letting go. Our daughters see what we do. We encourage them to show respect, but we also point out their mistakes. It's hard for me to be close to my father—I can only kiss him if he is sick. There's too much distance, yet I am still too attached. It's hard for me to stand on my own two feet.

My only expectation for my daughters is that they honor us by living a good life. They should only be obligated to us if we are sick or couldn't take care of ourselves. In that case, if they want me, I want to live with them. Otherwise, I want them to live nearby. If they moved away, the world would crash in around me.

Mrs. Maggio resembled many women we interviewed. She lived near her parents. She had spent her lifetime under their solicitous concern and authority, and as they grew old, she felt she was returning a debt. Still, she wanted to relax the traditional parental obligations somewhat, so her children would have a few more options. She also concedes that her daughters, like her younger sisters, are more American. "They wouldn't put up with all I've been through with my parents." However she did not go as far as to reject the notion that her children should come to have some responsibility for her, even to the point of inviting her to live with them under certain conditions.

Motivation

The strong bond between elderly parents and their middle-aged children was amply demonstrated in most interviews with middle-aged Italian Americans, and it has provided clear contrast to the non-Italians we interviewed. However, the processes that create and perpetuate this bond are not usually a subject for conscious reflection and analysis. A third-generation psychologist responded to my queries in much the same manner as a respondent with an eighth-grade education, "I don't know—it's difficult to describe. It's like an unwritten law. That's the way it's supposed to be—a tie that can't be broken. Other things might change, but not that." A combination of motives ranged from duty and repayment to love, but the actual feelings for the parent generally were vaguely linked to the way one was raised, a special feeling absorbed throughout life.

The norms of the subculture have elevated the family to a position of central importance and established a hierarchy with the parents at the acme. In their superior position, norms dictate that parents should receive respect, gratitude, and love. Parents are elevated also on the basis of past sacrifices. There are few variations from the view that the elders should reap rewards in old age for having had a single-minded dedication to parenthood during difficult times.

Obviously, the concept of sacrifice can be a device for parents to exert control over their children (Pearlin 1970). One of our respondents describes how it operates:

Years ago, bologna only cost a nickel, but father only made a nickel. Sometimes he made nothing. I see how they raised a family so well with nothing. You respect them for it.

His remark was echoed by many other respondents:

- Father wasn't a drunk; mother wasn't a tramp. Many parents were in those days. We respected them because they were so good.
- Mother always said Italian women were born with a needle in their hands. She used that needle by working long hours in a dress factory to put us through school. How could I not respect them and lead a good life when I saw her working sixteen hours a day?
- I'm obligated to my parents for all they did for us. My father wouldn't even take a bus to work. He'd walk to save some money for us.
- My mother and father always thought of the children first. We never had much, but there was always a clean home and food on the table. I admire them because they were always so giving. Now I'd like to give to them.
- After Dad died, mother worked as a seamstress. Her small wages supported all of us. She began having trouble with her eyesight and couldn't thread a needle. She refused to quit and go on welfare. Each night my brothers and I would thread 100 needles for her to take to work the next day.

This recurrent theme also centered on the ultimate parental sacrifice, that of bringing one into the world. "If it weren't for my mother, I wouldn't be here." Repayment for one's existence is only one link in a long line of sacrifices:

My mother brought us into the world and cared for us. She was only concerned with our good. She never spoiled us, but told us what was right. She always said, "Please don't disgrace me." We never did and now we lead good lives. She was an important part of our lives. How could we put her in a nursing home when she sacrificed for us?

Very few Italian Americans phrased their attentiveness to their parents in terms of duty-bound obligation. In fact, few remembered any explicit discussion of what they should do for their parents. Many objected to our use of the term "obligation," because it meant "having to do it," rather than "wanting to do it." One common description of the source of their filial behavior was the continuation of a process that was never explicitly discussed. "Italians have been programmed for it," a respondent concluded. They also reported that parental sacrifices set an example and now it is taken for granted that the repayment is in the form of filial sacrifice. At the point that her aged parents joined her household, one respondent said, "We were never told we must do that. We do it out of love, and love is beyond obligation."

While they might also mention the idea of sacrifice, a few admitted to their devotion as a means of avoiding guilt. "It's the old-fashioned way of Mama and all she's done for me." "It's easier to sleep nights knowing that I'm doing all I can." "They never ordered us to do anything, but you can see the hurt in their eyes if you don't." "My parents are so good to us that I have to hold my tongue." "How can I reject her when she cries if I don't call her every day?"

Despite these reservations, the motives of sacrifice and subsequent repayment are generally linked to diffuse feelings of love. "Love is not an obligation. What parents and children do for each other is done out of love." According to this perspective, affection is the controlling device which enforces conformity to family expectation. "Parents should never be alone. You must give love and gratitude. They are your parents—you just do it."

The emphasis on the affective domain is linked inevitably to one's ethnic identity. It is "the Italian way" to love and respect the elderly, to retain them within the family circle, and to do so out of love and gratitude rather than obligation:

- It's difficult to explain—with my mother I feel like I want to do it. I don't feel obligated, they're just family and everyone helps each other.
- It's just that we love each other a lot.

The underlying justification of love, not duty, appears to minimize the burdens, for most respondents report that their parents are pleasant and undemanding.

The conception of parents and their due among Italian Americans differs considerably from those described by non-Italians marrying into an Italian family. A recurrent theme in this group is that Italian parents are demanding and controlling and "won't let go of their children." In other words, interpretations of the parent-child bond in the Italian family stem from the cultural perspective of the observer, a perspective that is ethnically based. An Italian invariably analyzes the nature of this bond with a point of view diametrically opposed to that of an outsider who married into the family. Such incongruities have been discussed earlier, but here it will suffice to point out that what is "love and gratitude" from one point of view, becomes "burdensome obligations" from another. And a loving, undemanding mother can become an unreasonable, demanding mother-in-law.

For in-married Italians, demands from the parents or strong exhibitions of parental interference often go unnoticed because they are not defined negatively. Sometimes they can be treated humorously. During one interview, a car with two elderly women drove up, and the respondent explained:

> *Oh, oh, here come the Snoop sisters [her mother and her aunt].*
> *They come by at least once a day to check on me—to see what's*
> *going on. Are my children behaving? Is my house clean? Has*
> *anyone gotten sick?*

When her mother and sister entered, no animosity was displayed, and both joined in the discussion.

The in-married families were least likely to describe any aspect of the relationship as interference. Even if her mother comes daily into her home and advises her on how to clean the house, cook, or raise her children, the average daughter does not usually object, for she considers these efforts as a conventional and expected enactment of the female role in the later years. The active participation of mothers in the nuclear households of their daughters obviously diminishes the privacy of the nuclear family. As personal problems become public and shared by others, parents and members of the extended family can more readily influence decision-making.

Although acculturation is increasing with intermarriage and geographic mobility, the parent-child bond is the least likely of any family relationships to change. On the one hand, as noted earlier, acculturation of Americanization on the part of the parent, defined as language acquisition and American birth, is significantly associated with a more active family life for the elderly.

Such attachments to the parents, however, have prevented some offspring from marrying and having children of their own as is seen in the fact that 22 percent of the elderly have at least one unmarried offspring. Many middle-aged Italians described to us the missed opportunities for advancement which they traced to hesitancy about leaving the fold. "We probably would have made more of ourselves if our parents didn't cling to us." Both intermarried and geographically mobile Italians poignantly described psychological conflict because circumstances have removed them from intimate contact with their parents. Others, who had recently lost a parent, said they felt great loneliness because they had few other relationships, even with their spouses, that could replace the emotional supports that had been so concentrated in the parent-child bond.

The Three-Generation Household

The ultimate test for filial sons or daughters is their willingness to bring an aged parent into their home. While only 13 percent had a parent actually living with them at the time of the interview, most Italian Americans in middle age had either lived in a three-generation household at some point during their marriage or at least seriously considered this possibility. A plurality of all respondents felt that the three-generation household would be problematical, but still possible. However, those who endorsed the possibility without reservation were most often found in the in-married families.

Among the families who had a parent living with them at the time of the interview, the outcomes were varied. Some found it a comfortable situation, others had adjusted to a low level of continuous conflict, and still others, usually wives with mother-in-laws, found it so intolerable that they were barely on speaking terms. Families that completely accepted the three-generation household pointed to the advantages:

> My husband had difficulty in finding a job when he got out of the service, so we moved in with my parents until we got on our feet. With mother to watch the children, I could work. Mother always had a clean house and hot dinner waiting for us, and father took care of many of our bills. It worked out so well that we never thought of moving. When we needed more space, father built this house, large enough for all. We wouldn't have it any other way.

Mrs. Santola described how her family adapted naturally and comfortably to such a living arrangement:

> When the last Italian son marries, it is expected that he and his wife stay on with the parents. We did, but after three years, we

*bought our own house. My father-in-law said, "We must move
in with you. We don't want to be alone." Even though the new
house was only across the street, he felt the children might get
hit by a car when they came to visit. I loved my mother-in-law.
There were no problems even though she thought of the children
as hers too. She met me at the door when I came home from the
hospital and referred to them as* her *babies. She felt she had
to be there when they came home from school. She refused invitations, even when I was home, saying she couldn't leave the
children. She planned all the meals and ran the house. I
didn't mind.*

For most families, however, some adjustments have to be made.
The kitchen is a common source of potential conflict.

*When my mother-in-law moved in, we argued over cooking, so I
finally gave her the run of the kitchen. Now she feels needed,
and I have taken a part-time job.*

A respondent in a similar situation commented, "Now we're getting
fat with her cooking." Many daughters and daughters-in-law resent
the women of the older generation who refuse to retire from cooking.
Their refusal is understandable, however, given the situation of the
immigrant woman, whose centrality in family life is closely associated
with the dispensing of food. Since she uses food as a major means to
demonstrate maternal love, this function is not readily surrendered.

Tomato sauce holds a very special place in each family's diet, and
each has special recipes for preparing it. Usually one day of the week
is set aside as sauce day when a large pot can always be found simmering for hours on the stove. This sauce and the ritual of its preparation can also be a source of conflict between women of different
generations. For the older generation, the major requirement for the
sauce, or any food for that matter, is that no part of it should come
from cans. But for second-generation respondents, the ease in the use
of commercially prepared food over home canning in the summer, or
searching for fresh tomatoes, is far preferable. We heard several reports of open ruptures developing over the tomato sauce.

Other problems also arise over the division of labor within the
homes. The Franciscos had always lived with the wife's parents with a
minimum of conflict. However, Mr. Francisco had more leisure time
when he reached his late fifties and took up cooking and gardening,

interests that overlapped those of his parents-in-law. Mrs. Francisco described how difficult it was to readjust to long-time role allocations:

> *The garden was always my father's domain, but now my husband wants to work on it. He'll plant something and my father will dig it up. It's the same with cooking. Mother did all of it until recently. She made all the sauces and soup. Now that my husband is interested in cooking, he plans the menus on his way home from work. But there is always food already started on the stove—a chicken cacciatore or something. If he decides to cook something on his own, mother immediately goes upstairs. There's never any argument, but they feel they can't stay around. Now they won't eat with us if my husband is home. I'm in the middle—that's why I've had so many headaches recently.*

Over 40 percent of the in-married families either have adapted well to having their parents in their home or, if the need should arise, say they envision no problems. Another 40 percent feel that adjustments could be made. As one respondent commented, My grandmother always lived with us. I've always assumed it's the thing to do if she is widowed."

Other families simply tolerate considerable conflict and live together for years even though the disadvantages are formidable. The adjustment to conflict can take several forms, such as being repressed through avoidance techniques. For example, Mrs. Utano recounted a hospitalization she had for a serious illness. While she was gone, her mother-in-law put away all of her things and rearranged the house, seeming, at least unconsciously, to consider her dead. They have not spoken to each other since Mrs. Utano returned from the hospital, and the mother-in-law was taking most of her meals in a small kitchen off her own room. Despite this conflict, no one moved away from the situation, and Mrs. Utano said she would not expect her husband to leave his mother. Mr. Utano was also interviewed; he vaguely mentioned some problems and friction, which he attributed to the predictable and irascible behaviors of the elderly.

Other respondents with a parent in their household reported continuous conflict, sometimes persisting for years. Mrs. Firenza, an only child, has had her mother with her for ten years.

> *Mother was eighty-one when father died. I thought that she would only be around for a few years, so why shouldn't we all*

live together? My son and daughter were both in their teens and
would be leaving soon, so there would be more room. These ten
years have been misery—it's wrecked my life. She drives us
all nuts with her interference. The children are still with us
so we're cramped for space. When I complain, mother says she
has spent all of her money on us, so she can't move. My hus-
band doesn't like the arrangement, but since he's Italian he
goes along with it. We both regret the fact that we have no life
of our own. At ninety-one, mother is going strong—it will go
on for years.

At the time of the interview, Mrs. Firenza's mother was in the
hospital recovering from a fall down the stairs. She had accused her
daughter of pushing her, but she still wanted to return to her daughter's home. Although Mrs. Firenza wanted her to go to a nursing
home, her mother was abetted by an Italian doctor who agreed that the
best place for her was with her daughter.

Mrs. Firenza's mother was back home during the second interview.
She was a regal-looking woman who appeared to rule over all she sur-
veyed. She sat down ready to participate, but after being ignored for a
time, she got up and left without a word.

The varied adjustments to the three-generation household suggest a
mixed pattern about which it is not easy to generalize. Parents are to
be loved and respected, and the middle-aged children were willing to
attempt the arrangement to avoid feeling guilty. To reject the living arrangement would mean deserting a parent. Problems will be there, respondents concluded, but in most cases they can be resolved. However, since only 13 percent of the middle-aged respondents are
currently living in a three-generation household, it is apparent that it is
not the preferred arrangement for either the parent or the child.

In interviews with middle-aged respondents, a series of questions
was designed to tap the nature of the obligation to elderly parents
ideologically. Essentially the measure is a normative-attitudinal one
which describes the "should be's." Interestingly, the results show little
differences by ethnicity; all groups feel parents should be treated with
love and respect, and they should be cared for if they cannot take
care of themselves. A combination of motives was expressed in these
norms, such as duty and repayment for all they did, love and gratitude, and avoidance of guilt. Since no clear pattern emerged, one
can conclude that, at least normatively, the relationship with the

parent transcends other options. Apparently questions so broadly phrased elicit the uniform response that it would be unthinkable to reject a parent.

Indirect measures from projective stories of potentially conflicting situations with the elderly were also obtained. These responses reflect variation according to the situation. One of these stories follows:

> Suppose a family has had the wife's mother living with them for ten years. It always worked out well while the children were young, for she was a great help. Now she is less active and has become quite irritable with the teenage children's loud music and frequent visitors. Since she causes so much conflict, the husband thinks she should move out. He says his wife must choose between her mother and her children. The wife says she could never do that, for then she would be rejecting her mother. What would you do?

Responses were coded on the basis of whether one said the stability of the nuclear family should come first, or whether one accorded the parents' needs an equal priority. (Not surprisingly, no one put their parents' needs over their children's.)

The tendency to place the parents' needs on an equal footing with the nuclear family is clearly evident among Italian Americans; two-thirds chose a three-generation household in comparison to one-third of the Protestant control group. Nevertheless, this question posed several dilemmas for the respondents. First, the needs of the mother of the hypothetical woman must be balanced with those of her children, a particularly painful choice for the average Italian. Many, in fact, spoke against the husband for siding with the children, and therefore expecting his wife to make a choice between her mother and her children. Another complication was the fact that the mother had devoted some years to helping the family, making it more difficult to discard her once she is no longer useful. Long discussions were elicited, sometimes with illustrations from the respondents' personal experiences. Most favored a compromise between the needs of both sets of relationships, so that all parties could interact with a minimum of conflict. Pragmatism characterized the solutions. It shouldn't be an either-or situation." "They should sit down and talk it over." "Influence the children to be more considerate." "Build on a soundproof room." "Have her stay with her sister for a while until things settle down." In other words, compromises by both parties are preferable to being forced to choose between one's parent's and one's own nuclear family.

The Integration of the Aged

One indicator of the status of the elderly parents is the extent to which they are included in the social activities of their children's nuclear families. In general, middle-class families are typified by age-segregated social activities (Seeley, Sims, and Loosely 1956). Parents have a social circle composed of others of similar age, background, and interests. The gatherings generally take place at night when children are left at home with babysitters. As the children enter adolescence, the teen-age peer group becomes the dominant focus of their social activities.

One method to evaluate interdependent, intergenerational relationships is to examine the inclusion or exclusion of the older generation in the social activities of the children's nuclear families. Measures of this type probe the critical distinctions between fulfillment of duty-bound obligations and a genuine desire to see the parents. Such measures tap the qualitative facets of the parent-child relationship and illuminate the voluntary character of the contact between an elderly parent and his or her adult children.

Italian Americans differ significantly from other groups in this study in their inclusion of parents into the social network of the nuclear family (Table 9.1). In comparison to the intermarried families, they are

Table 9.1.
Inclusion of Parents in Nuclear Family Activities (by percentage)

	In-married Italians, n = 74	Out-married Italians, n = 98	Protestant control group, n = 56
Usually included	36	18	7
Sometimes included	51	47	41
Rarely included	13	35	52

Chi Square 30.78, df 6, p<.0001

twice as likely to include the parents, while in comparison to the Protestant non-Italians, they are five times more likely. This measure indicates that the elderly are integrated into the day-to-day activities of their children and grandchildren. In no other measure was there such a prominent difference among groups.

Not only do these respondents include their parents in many activities, they also attempt to see them frequently. As reported previously, over half see them daily, while most others see them at least several times a week. Almost all of them telephone daily. These rates are over twice as frequent as the Protestant group.

Responsibility to Parents

All respondents were questioned on the nature of their responsibilities to parents as to the types of services and the frequency with which one performed them. These responsibilities ranged from simple sociability with the active parent, to chauffeuring of the less mobile, and extensive care of the infirm parent. It was sometimes difficult to tap the wide range and intensity of these responsibilities since most respondents said they did anything they could for a parent. In most cases it arose from "the natural way" of doing things; therefore it was not a subject for conscious reflection. "It just *is* there—they're our parents. We take it for granted." "It means you never let them be alone." "You give love and gratitude." "You make sure they are never in need." "It's just the Italian way." "You just treat parents as you want to be treated in old age."

An average weekday for a middle-aged Italian woman with an elderly widowed mother would follow this pattern. Each morning and usually late afternoon, she calls her mother to see how she is. Sometimes during the day she drops by briefly, or takes her mother on errands, or to a doctor's appointment. On weekends, several meals are shared.

Like previous studies, these findings indicate the female preference for her own parents over the husband's; all women in this sample were almost twice as likely to give priority to their responsibility to their own parents rather than their husband's. Apparently, then, one of the best forms of old-age insurance is the presence not merely of children, but of daughters.

A son is not always quite as dutiful, although he tries to call his

Table 9.2.

Wives' Responsibilities to Parents
with Intermarriage (by percentage)

	Italian wives, n = 53	
	With own parents	With husband's parents
High	37	15
Medium	35	15
Low	28	70
	Non-Italian wives, n = 45	
High	30	33
Medium	27	22
Low	43	44

mother daily. Some lunch hours he will drop in for a quick meal if work demands permit. On weekends, he helps her with any heavy household chores, and, of course, he shares at least one meal. Interestingly enough, Italian men with non-Italian wives are even more dutiful than the in-married men. Furthermore, in intermarried families, the non-Italian wives have a bias toward the Italian husband's parents. As Table 9.2 indicates, she is likely to be as active with her husband's parents as with her own.

Although an Italian woman who marries out of the group decreases her contact somewhat with her own parents in comparison to a woman who marries within the group, she is like all Italian women in that she concentrates her efforts on her own parents rather than her husband's. Such a situation does not apply equally to a non-Italian woman marrying into an Italian family. In this case, the services she extends to her own parents do not differ greatly from those to her husband's parents. In fact, she is considerably more dutiful to her husband's parents than are Italian women who are married to non-Italian men.

One interpretation of this pattern comes from the popular belief that "Italianization" of a non-Italian occurs upon joining an Italian family. The family "wins out" by socializing the new member into the ways of family solidarity. However, a large number of these non-Italian women reported some conflicts in living up to the expectations of Italian in-laws. Despite finding them demanding and rigid, however, they continue to perform filial duties.

A second and more productive interpretation comes from an analysis of the gender-linked generational bond. The close ties between mothers and daughters can be traced to the continuity in domestic roles, the content of which does not change greatly over time. In contrast, changing economic conditions exert greater changes in the work roles of fathers and sons, so they are less likely to share occupational roles. Immigrant men and their sons would have even more divergent experiences.

As discussed earlier, filial values and behaviors among Italian Americans are least resistant to change with intermarriage and social mobility, irrespective of gender. Nevertheless, the protection and surveillance of young women generally results in their greater dependence on parents and a lack of autonomy from their families of orientation even with marriage. Consequently, a daughter continues to satisfy her parents' needs obediently and to a greater degree than a son, who is permitted more autonomy at adolescence. We have seen that this pattern is quite resistant to change.

The Italian son also has been socialized into a relationship of respect, but he performs few of the day-to-day services for his parents. With the sharp segregation of sex roles, he was granted greater freedom as he was growing up and was never expected to be as dutiful. However, he can be at a disadvantage later in life if his wife is not Italian and has been raised in a family with minimal expectations for filial responsibilities. If she does not feel compelled to assist her own parents or her husband's, her Italian husband then would be faced with a dilemma, for duties to parents are not fulfilled as easily without a wife readily equipped to perform them. He then has two options: he can modify his own values which underlie the expectations for filial obligation, or he can accelerate his own filial behaviors, perhaps hoping to influence his wife's behavior in the process. There is evidence that such an accelerated process takes place. An examination of correlations indicates that an out-married Italian husband is more attentive to his parents' needs than his non-Italian wife is to hers, and if she is lax, he is likely to be even more attentive ($r = -3825$, $p < .003$).

At the End of the Road

Continual contact with and devotion to parents makes their impending death a constant source of concern. The idea prevails that one must do everything one can while they're still alive, for tomorrow they might not be here. Birthdays must be celebrated, for it might be the parent's last one. One must be kind and kiss parents when they leave, for they might die in their sleep. This notion can even be used as a threat in disciplining one's own children.

My daughter uses the telephone too much. I tell her, What would happen if Gramma needed us and was trying to call. How would you feel if something happened to her and our line was busy?"

This guilt can be a powerful determinant in life decisions. "If I move away, it might shorten my mother's life by taking her grandchildren away." One woman recounted such conflicts:

Sometimes we feel guilty. Here's an example. As children, we were never allowed to go out on New Year's Eve. It was a special time for the family. This continued well into my married years. My husband finally decided it was time for us to celebrate with friends. I said no to it, because it might be my mother's or father's last year with us. My husband pointed out that I say that every year. But father did die that year. I was so thankful I stayed home.

One sibling group decided to have a special celebration for their mother on her eightieth birthday, thinking it might be her last. At ninety-one, the mother remained alive; nevertheless, they felt that death was just around the corner and that they could not let the opportunity for showing their love and appreciation slip by unnoticed. The celebration continued annually.

The recent death of a parent brought tears to the eyes of an affluent businessman:

The trouble is you don't have parents around long enough. They work hard to raise us, then they don't have time to enjoy the rewards. My mother was a beautiful woman. We took her every place with us, even on our vacations. They die too young.

These high motivations can muster considerable devotion and duty to the parent at the end of his or her life. One respondent, then in her forties, predicted what she would do on the basis of past experience:

> *My grandmother was paralyzed for three years and became blind. She had a hospital bed in our living room. Her children and grandchildren did not miss a day in visiting her. When she died, everyone was there. That's the way it's supposed to be.*
>
> *As a child, no one ever told me I had to care for my parents like that. But I saw how my mother and aunts respected my grandparents. My friends from childhood are the same way. We would do the same thing if necessary.*

This example illustrates the maximum resources a family can rally at a point of complete physical incapacity. Despite the fact that not all families today or in the past were able to cope so long and unwaveringly, the value persists today.

Even before death, the possibility that a parent might become totally dependent creates considerable anxiety, for the use of nursing homes remains condemned. All respondents were asked, "How would you feel about your parents living in a nursing home?" Responses were coded into three categories: adamant opposition, from which we inferred the respondent would never consider it; use only if parent needed extensive medical care or was without his or her senses; and agreement that these institutions would provide good care if the parent could not care for himself. Obviously, very few individuals, irrespective of ethnicity, could accept a nursing home unreservedly. Nevertheless, there are striking differences between Italians and Protestant non-Italians in their rejection of the nursing home as a last resort for the incapacitated parent. Over five times as many Italians totally reject the possibility. Whatever course one eventually must take when serious illness requires around-the-clock care, the insistence on family responsibilities over other options remains a significant characteristic of the Italian family (Table 9.3). The striking differences between Italians and Protestant non-Italians suggests radically different attitudes toward this non-familial option to the ultimate dependency of old age.

It has long been the tradition in southern Italian culture that one takes care of one's own. The propensity to maintain primary social support systems within the family or ethnic community has also been noted in this country (Williams 1938). Community sanctions operate

Table 9.3.

Attitudes toward Nursing Home Placement of Parents (by percentage)

	In-married Italians, n = 74	Out-married Italians, n = 98	Protestant control group, n = 56
Would never consider it	47	41	9
Only if in need of constant care	49	44	79
The only option if sick	4	14	13

Chi Square 30.08, df 6, p<.0001

along with strong filial values to make placement in a nursing home one of the most undesirable alternatives. A child does not abandon the parent to an alternative viewed as worse than death. Hence, as one woman commented, "Nursing home—that's a taboo—just like going on welfare; it's never even discussed." Community sanctions also operate in this respect. "If a family puts a parent in a nursing home, others will say, 'Look at that family. They can't even care for their own mother.'" Some even worry about what the relatives in Italy would think. In other words, "Nursing homes are for those who do not have a family."

Only a small minority in all samples considered a nursing home as a place where a parent could get the best care. However, a larger proportion would consider it as a last resort because of several realistic impediments. The most obvious are the space limitations in the home, or the wife's employment. Such economic conditions prevent a full-time commitment to caring for the parent. Hence, if the parent needs full-time care, a nursing home is a last resort only if no alternatives can be found. Some respondents, when faced with this difficult decision, referred to the doctor as the one who placed pressure on them to choose it. Other difficulties concerned one's inadequacy in assuming responsibility if a parent becomes senile. The greatest difficulty cited, however, was in finding a doctor who would make house calls. In the end, when all these hurdles were examined, almost one-half stated they would consider a nursing home as a last resort.

In turning to the remaining respondents, almost one-half of the sample categorically rejected this option. Those who have never faced the possibility dealt with it hypothetically. Nevertheless, their rejection of a nursing home is best described by one typical response:

> *Never! It would make me guilty if I didn't take care of them. It would break my heart and haunt me for the rest of my life. My parents sacrificed for me—I can now make the same sacrifices.*

Another respondent, an only child, attempted to care for her mother when she became ill:

> *It was a great problem. My parents were unhappy and my husband lost his privacy and had to make financial sacrifices. Finally, mother had to go to a nursing home. Now, long after she died, it is still a traumatic experience for me. People just don't understand—they reassure me that I did my best. My son says I had to also take care of my own health. Yet it gave me such terrible guilt which still hasn't gone away.*

One depressed respondent lengthily described a series of events leading to the placement of a parent in a nursing home. The eventual death of his father was attributed to the fact that he died of a broken heart."

> *In many cases, death would be preferable.*

> *When mother was ill, we were at the point of considering a nursing home. She had bone disease and was in constant pain. It worried us to see her in agony when we could do nothing about it. Then suddenly, she died of a heart attack. It was a blessing.*

In those families who reject outright the nursing home when a parent's health deteriorates, sons and daughters decide together who should be with them and when. One child, usually the daughter, uses her home, often converting the dining room into a hospital room. Her brothers and sisters, and frequently their spouses, take turns being there to sit with the dying parent, for no one should be alone during a terminal illness. Generally, at least one-half of the families attempt to provide such an exit within the home despite the numerous difficulties discussed above.

Since no families were interviewed during a period immediately preceding a parent's death, it is difficult to determine the regularities in behavior at that time. A number of respondents described conflicts among siblings following the long vigil by a dying parent. During the terminal period, the common pattern is one of distributing the responsibilities. After the death, the ledger of who succeeded and who failed in their duties sometimes adds up to unequal distribution. There were reports of conflict and sometimes a break between a brother and sister over these inequities. In the crisis period of a parent's death, it is obvious that the bond cannot always withstand the intense outpouring of energy devoted to a parent's care.

Italians, like others, do use nursing homes, but the staff at a large Catholic home in the city concluded there were fewer Italians than might be expected on the basis of their numbers in the general population. We had an opportunity to interview several who lived there. They were typically in need of constant care. For example, at eighty-seven, Mr. Vito had lived there for six years. His wife died six years before that and, soon after, his health deteriorated. He was born in Italy but had worked most of his adult life as a laborer in Easton. Over two marriages, he had eleven children, but only seven were still alive. Four lived in proximity and each visited weekly. Some of his twenty-five grandchildren visited almost as frequently. Mr. Vito described the situation that eventually caused him to move:

> Everyone works. They all have children and their own problems. If one stayed home to take care of me, they'd lose a day's pay. I did give up my apartment and lived with my son in the suburbs. I was unhapppy in the new neighborhood. I didn't know anyone. I'd walk up and down the street all day and never find anyone to talk to.

Summary

The evidence is convincing that Italian Americans are very dutiful to their elderly parents, in fact more than the others interviewed. They can mobilize considerable support without major complaints or regrets over the costs. Some might ask themselves, as one respondent did, "Why do we do it? We certainly aren't happier than others because of our martyrdom?" Nevertheless, when the ultimate decision must be made, the majority opts for family solutions over other alternatives.

Such a situation, however, is the result of several processes. For one thing, the ethnic community itself shares these filial values. For families immersed in activities with other Italians, there are repeated reminders of the unqualified good stemming from filial devotion and, of course, regular sanctions for those who are forgetful. Moreover, the elderly themselves are not above continual reminders of their long years of sacrifice. "The old days were a struggle; the odds were impossible, yet we raised you properly—that is the Italian way." Whereas they generally do not assert explicitly that they deserve some repayment from their children, the message nevertheless is clear. "No child raised properly in the Italian way would abandon a parent." This normative consensus on the Italian way pressures offspring to conform, if they are to remain in the Italian community.

Within the family, forgiveness and tolerance of individual variability likewise serve the interests of most elderly. Both the elderly and their offspring agree that expectations were not explicitly stated; it is an outcome of long-standing, intimate interaction. In one sense, parents who have sacrificed much and remain tolerant and forgiving in their children's eyes can pressure children more effectively than those who explicitly state their expectations or act unreasonably and are overly demanding. However, if these techniques fail parents can still exert control through an all-embracing love. "My mother cries when I leave," or "I can see the love in her eyes. How could I fail her?" However constraining such situations are in the lives of middle-aged children, few are willing to take other options that might exclude the parents.

Part 3
The Internal World
of the Family

Chapter 10
Socialization to Family Attachments

When questioned on the sources of attachments to the family, respondents often became puzzled and stated that they had rarely thought about it. The general conclusion was that ties to family were natural outcomes of the lifelong processes of socialization. "It's instilled over the years as part of growing up." "It's a natural feeling that comes from within." "Love of family should not be forced. It must come from the heart." In other words, family attachments are an inevitable outcome of the way one has been raised. Probings brought about more specific responses which centered upon two themes: the realm of emotions such as love, affect, and "heart"; and the realm of social control which referred to respect and its indoctrination through the strict disciplining of children. Any conflict or ambivalence in regard to family matters usually involved problems in independence and personal autonomy.

On the major functions of socialization, nurturance, discipline, and the development of autonomy and independence, Italian-American parents differed significantly from non-Italians interviewed. With their teenage children, they were more likely to extend a higher level of nurturance, to use stricter discipline techniques, and to delay or discourage independence from family. Continuities were found in some elements of these socialization practices as these parents in turn satisfied the needs of their elderly parents. This chapter and the next will map the parent-child relationship through an analysis of how middle-aged respondents enact their parental roles with their adolescent children and, in turn, act and are acted upon in their relationships with their parents. The following interpretations add to the cumulative theory building of intergenerational relationships in later life.

Nurturance, Independence Training, and Discipline

Chapter 3 reported statistically significant differences in childrearing techniques between Italian Americans and the Protestant control

184   **The Internal World of the Family**

group. Since these differences are still evident when social class is taken into consideration, the following discussion deals only with the variable of ethnicity in describing the major dimensions of childrearing.

First, on the basis of our comparisons with non-Italians, there is significance in the fact that the Italian-American mother occupies the highest point on nurturing behaviors ($x^2 = 28.9$, p $<$ .001). Included in this measure were the services mothers provided to adolescents, the degree to which they participated in other activities that competed with mothering, and the priorities they gave to the maternal role. Generally, Italian-American mothers reported that this role was their central one and had not diminished as their children entered adolescence. They concluded that with adolescents, the mother's role was as important as it had been in their children's early childhood. Their norms mandate that maternal protectiveness and attentiveness must continue. A mother should know their friends and supervise their activities. Food-related behaviors also continue to be viewed as a sign of a devoted and conscientious mother. Most Italian mothers interviewed continue to perform the role much as they did when their children were young. There are few areas of the children's lives that escape their concern.

The concept of *noncontingent love* was repeatedly discussed in terms of rules to be followed. The mother must be forgiving, as one noted, "She should remember no wrongs." Also mothers should not be excessively demanding; other than diffuse expectations for respect and sociability, they should make few overt demands or threats of withdrawal of love. Although the efficacy of physical punishment was also among their rules, it was considered a key component of expressing their love.

This noncontingent love was also observable in their discussion of goals for their children. When asked, the most common response was, "I want them to be happy." One mother, who was unusually tolerant of the serious misbehavior of her adolescent son, explained, "I have a big heart. I can't do otherwise." Another mother said, "God can forgive, so why can't I? Anyone can make a mistake." When a twelve-year-old was very demanding during an interview, her mother concluded, "She's just tired."

In addition to the profuse nurturance and the spirit of forgiveness, Italian mothers should be indispensable to their children, a rule that involves sacrifices. They provide food, many services, and continuous concern. "Children didn't ask to be born. Once you have them, you sacrifice for their welfare." By its very nature, "Being a mother is a self-sacrificing role. I take that for granted." Another mother had difficulty eating a meal at a restaurant if her fifteen-year-old son was not along. "I feel guilty about eating a steak when he eats hot dogs at home." Some mothers try to be more objective toward their children. One respondent reported, "I try to find an appropriate balance between a mother's love and being a martyr."

Nevertheless, the Italian mother is expected to be, and most mothers are, totally devoted to their children to the exclusion of most outside interests. Not surprisingly, it is difficult for some children to leave this protective, nurturing environment. (It is apparent that few adults did leave, for among the elderly we interviewed, only two individuals had no children living in the area. Moreover, only a few of the middle-aged respondents had adult children who moved away.) As one successful bachelor approaching thirty explained, "Why should I move into an apartment? My mother washes my shirts spotlessly clean. She serves me the best food. She brings me coffee in bed in the morning that is the perfect temperature. Not only that, she stirs in just the right amount of cream and sugar."

The second component of childrearing on which Italian Americans differ significantly from other groups is the *delayed independence training* of adolescent children ($x^2 = 24.241$, df. 12, $< .02$). Questions were designed to elicit behaviors and values on the degree of independence granted to adolescent children in such areas as curfews, choice of friends, and prolonged activities away from the family. Italian women supervise their children closely in most of their activities. Their justification is based upon two premises: maternal protectiveness, to prevent harm falling on her children; and social control, to prevent her children from misbehaving. One mother described her ideology on childrearing: "When I die, I must go before God and be judged on how I raised them, so I must protect and control them."

This delayed independence of adolescent children poses one of the greatest dilemmas for Italian parents today, for it clashes most directly with the values of the American youth culture. For example, late adolescents who are economically self-sufficient commonly want to rent apartments with friends. For Italian Americans, this idea is very unpalatable and was unheard of even in the recent past. The degree of tolerance of such independence invariably is sex based. For sons it is at best distasteful; for daughters it remains unthinkable. Leaving home before marriage is considered not only uneconomical, but also likely to lead to trouble. Still, the issue has been raised in many families, stirring up considerable conflict. "The only way a daughter can leave this house is in a wedding gown or a casket," one mother maintained. While most mothers absolutely forbid it for their unmarried daughters, they conclude that for their sons a short time away would cause them to realize what a nice home they had. In any case, the average mother hopes she can eventually lure her sons home with her cooking and with her love. They hope their mature children eventually will conclude that their parent's home is the center of life and that no one should want to leave its warmth and protection. Mrs. Mizzo, who has three children ranging from fifteen to twenty-five years of age, best typifies the attitude on this issue:

> *I think children should all live at home, where they are safe. We can help them with their problems. They shouldn't feel as though we are holding them here, like keeping them in jail. We are keeping them because we want them to have a good place to live. I make their meals. I help them grow. I feel that's what I can do best. I feel until they are ready to get married, why shouldn't I continue to help them grow in the right setting? Why should they be in an apartment, struggling and tripping all over their mistakes?*

Obviously, a mother's love serves important purposes, for it can perpetuate a dependency upon her. A mother who is forgiving also poses few resentments that can drive an offspring far from the family fold. The mother has an opportunity to exert far greater influence over her children than would be the case of the less tolerant or less vigilant mother. The fact that there is less emotional distance and detachment between the mother and the adolescent in itself acts to pressure children to conform because the relationship extends over a greater area of an adolescent's life than is usually found today. An Italian mother, however, does not leave matters of social conformity to such indirect means of control. Her love is also bound up with more direct means.

The *high degree of social control* utilized in childrearing is the third pattern of differentiation between Italians and others (x^2 = 21.052, df. 12, < .05). These discipline techniques, which are generally shared with the father, are sometimes referred to as traditional techniques. Discipline is directly applied to specific behaviors. It involves physical punishment, restrictions, curfews, and continuous berating. Justification is probably best summarized by this respondent: "Any mother who doesn't discipline is not showing love. If I didn't have strictness, I wouldn't have love." In other words, the best way to raise children is with "lots of love and the back of the hand."

Mothers continue to advocate strict discipline despite some familiarity with the indirect, psychological techniques advocated by current childrearing experts. These experts are generally rejected as too permissive, a characteristic that is incompatible with traditional values and unworkable in the Italian family. As one woman commented, "Dr. Spock didn't have an Italian mother." In fact, some mothers arrived at the same conclusion as recent revisionists of psychological childrearing techniques: "It makes the children feel guilty," was how one of our respondents summed up their attitude.

Among Italians, social control techniques stem from a value system that differs considerably from non-Italians. All respondents were asked, "What is the most desired personality characteristic you would like to see in your child?" Responses logically fell into categories similar to those used by Melvin Kohn (1969) and did not reflect significant ethnic differences except in two areas. Protestants were more likely to choose self-direction values, while Italian Americans placed greater emphasis on behavioral conformity. This expectation for conformity was usually equated with respect. The underlying meanings of this value were quite similar to the old-fashioned way. In the respondents' interpretations, respect connoted a hierarchy in the family that place the parents, particularly the father, in a superior position where he could enforce his will over the children and demand obedience. Thus, "parents today should be parents, not brothers and sisters." Egalitarian norms, although sometimes given lip service, are not often translated into family behaviors. Since respect within a family is linked to discipline by traditional, old-fashioned ways, physical punishment remains today as a major means of instilling respect, particularly with small children.

This directive includes duty and service to family. Respect is also equated with love, in that one cannot extend or receive love without the accompaniment of respect. Generally, *respect* is viewed as an ascribed component of family roles; it does not have to be earned. Furthermore, it has a reciprocal aspect; one respects parents in order to gain their respect in turn. Since elderly parents expect their children to be respectful to them, to set an example for their grandchildren, intergenerational relations are colored by it.

Italian Americans interpret disrespectful behaviors among children as a failure in proper parenting. To them, parents who do not enforce their superiority through strict discipline risk a serious breach in family solidarity. Family problems were often attributed to the fact that "they let their children run wild," a serious indictment among our respondents. If parents fail to enforce their values on desired family goals, it means parental neglect or, worse yet, a lack of concern and love for the child. "I spank you because I love you" was a justification mentioned often. As the middle-aged respondents described their own childhood, they sometimes recounted the discipline techniques as bordering on cruelty. Nevertheless, they interpreted their own attachment to their parents and their own children's attachments to them as stemming from respect as much as from love. As indicated by the group differences, one can conclude that the majority advocate the strict discipline techniques not unlike those they experienced as children.

If these direct discipline and indirect nurturance techniques fail to pressure children to conform to the ways of the Italian family, the respondents resorted to several other methods. One popular technique involved the use of emotions to control children. "If all else fails, I cry." A second involved subtle reminders of the repeated services a mother has provided, so that conforming to parental expectations is usually chosen by adolescents and young adults as a means of repayment.

The third technique involved evoking distance between the mother and the child through the "cold treatment" or "scoring." In contrast to the usual interaction, emotions are absent; instead, there are long silences interrupted only by little signs of hurt and anger. This technique seems to be highly effective in getting errant sons and daughters to rectify their behavior since it is such a dramatic reversal from the usual maternal behavior.

Achievement Goals

Italian values on achievement do not differ greatly from non-Italians of the same social class level. For working-class families, if money is available, college education is the appropriate goal for those with ability. Where financial resources are slim, college education for sons takes precedence over that for daughters because males eventually will have to support a family. Many respondents were observing the lower returns of a college education during the recession when the job market became tight. Hence, a respectable trade was often preferred. Although some parents directly discourage their offspring from going to college, the majority attempt to assist if a child wishes more education.

Middle-class Italian parents, like all middle-class parents, conclude that college education is the best way to get ahead today. Furthermore, they see a bright daughter as having as much right to education as her brothers. Still, most Italian parents, even in the middle class, condemn excessive parental pressure for achievement. By their norms, motivation as well as ability should come from the child, not the parent.

Italian Americans did differ on the whole from other respondents in their insistence that they select a college near home, preferably a local community college or a small Catholic college. Prestigious Ivy League universities were viewed as too remote and too expensive for their children, so that even an all-A student was usually not prompted to apply. For example, the son of one respondent ranked second in his high school class. His girlfriend, also a high achiever, was accepted to Yale and wanted him also to apply. According to the mother, the son decided against applying to this prestigious school because the application was too expensive, a conclusion with which she concurred.

Although Italians do have class-based views on higher education, they differed on the whole from non-Italians in their uneasiness in regard to how education might change their children's view of the family. For example, the Buccinas had a son at an Ivy League college. "After he had his first course in psychology, he told us we were doing everything wrong as parents. After a few such remarks in letters, we got very upset. We went there and rented a hotel room with a sitting room. We spent hours ironing out all the misunderstandings."

On the whole, the respondents would endorse Gambino's conclusion (1974) that college education and related achievement are encouraged as long as they are compatible with family goals. If they are not, Italian parents would prefer that their sons follow in the steps of their working-class fathers. This conclusion is supported by a comparison of Italian and Yankee boys in the Boston area which found that the lower achievement of Italian boys was associated not only with social class but also with values on family allegiances and geographic mobility (Ulin 1968).

Childrearing and the Family Configuration

In Italian families, parental roles are well differentiated along expressive and instrumental dimensions. The mother is more concerned than the father with the expressive functions in the family. All that is good in Italian family life and little that is bad is traced to her. For example, most respondents concluded that Italians are warmer, more sociable, more considerate of others mainly because they were raised by warm, loving mothers. One young man told us, "A mother's love is a protective love — so much so that there is tension when you are away from it. It makes you want to seek out more people." Other themes in the interviews concern a special feeling the mother creates that lies in her forgiveness of wrongdoings. Since she is forgiving, her sacrifices for her children also create a special feeling. Largely, the fact that one's mother had so much love to give assigns her a special place in her children's life. One frequently hears such comments that, "One can have 100 fathers, but only one mother," or "One can have another wife and children, but never another mother."

While the mother's role appears to have a timeless quality, respondents overwhelmingly agreed that one of the major changes in the family involves the father's role and the dilution of his authority. Although the father still occupies an elevated status and exercises final judgment on family matters, he is less likely to evoke the fear so often described of the immigrant father. Although fathers have relaxed their authoritarian stance, there remain marked differences in power and the segregation of roles along the expressive-instrumental axis (T. Parsons 1949). While parental roles today are more interchangeable, particularly as the father incorporates more expressive components, the roles are more clearly differentiated than those described in the middle-class American family. The father *should* be the authority figure just as the mother is responsible for the emotional realm, even if there is considerable interchangeability in the day-to-day family life. Furthermore, when the mother acts as a mediator, as is often the case, in order to soften paternal authority, she essentially serves to maintain psychological distance between the father and the child. Whether she blatantly skirts his authority or redoubles her extension of affection, the outcome is a parental role differentiation that is specialized along the lines of authority and control on the one hand, and affection and nurturance on the other.

The mother's key significance in the expressive component of the family has led some observers to question the extent of the patriarchy in the family, because of the frequent appearance of mothers who are seen as domineering and in competent command of activities in the home. What appears to obscure the actual centers of power is the sharp segregation of parental roles. A man's primary role of provider and protector and the woman's primary role of nurturer and food giver persist despite increasing incidence of employed mothers and greater participation of the father in childrearing and other activities within the home.

In addition to the dynamic interplay between a mother's affection and a father's control, the theme of self-sacrifice for the family pervades the descriptions of parental roles. Both mothers and fathers are preoccuppied with this need to make their children conform to family interests. Not only do they see the need to be vigilant and protective to ward off harmful outside influences, but they also attempt to provide well for the children's social and material needs through their hard work. Such dedicated parenting is often described through comparisons of themselves with other parents who are following "selfish" interests. In other words, children become well aware of such dedicated parenting. One father succinctly described the process, "I guard my family jealously. When my son left home, I was broken-hearted. I was losing a part of myself."

Many traditional family systems likewise are noted for the sharp distinction between maternal and paternal roles, as well as dedicated parenting. Nevertheless, the elevation of family in the cultural background of Italian Americans both symbolically and structurally places parents in a key position to exert influence over their children. Parents continually remind children that loyalty to family should supercede other allegiances and should never have to compete with egocentric interests. As one father describes this philosophy, "I tell my children, don't think of 'I' or 'me,' think of 'we' and 'us.'" These injunctions, when obeyed, provide a sociocentric orientation in the children where family interests receive priority.

Childrearing Ideology

The parents we interviewed were products not only of southern Italian culture but also of the social conditions in this country. Both of these background factors have molded their ideology and their childrearing practices. The depression years imposed additional hardships on the recent immigrant groups and often reversed the small advances Italian Americans had made. Without some savings or assets to cushion the unexpected, the depression more often than not wiped out any earlier gains. Consequently, family members had to expend extraordinary energy in order to provide basic subsistence for the family.

Since the nuclear family often lived with or near a network of kin, resources were combined. Grandparents were more likely to be members of the household and aunts and uncles often lived nearby in a flat in the same building or on the same block. A group of adults working long hours and sharing leisure hours with relatives of all ages generally meant there was little time to focus on the specific needs of the individual child. Children were included in every aspect of the family activities, but they were members of a collectivity of siblings and cousins where their individuality was often obscured.

Thus, the situation in our respondents' childhood led in some cases to parental distraction. Their parents were simply too busy to focus on their emotional needs, but in any case these needs were well met by a collectivity of adults responding to the needs of a collectivity of children. In such a setting, it was rare to find parental concern for self-actualization, because out of necessity parents had to focus on practical matters. These extended families also provided children with multiple role models and acted to moderate any negative parental behaviors. The child could also use avoidance techniques when parental authority became too harsh or maternal love too suffocating. These childhood experiences dominated by economic hardship most likely had some influence on the children of the 1930s who are the parents of today.

Aside from these factors related to economic conditions and the structure of the family in the childhood of our middle-aged respondents, the southern Italian ideology on childhood remains discernable in socialization practices today. Gans (1962) refers to Italians as having adult-centered households. There is an avoidance of indulgence of children simply because they are children. The mere fact of being a child does not merit special permissive treatment beyond that granted to any family member. While children are indulged in the early years, they are expected to conform to family expectations at an early age. He or she is not the center of the universe or the family, however loved and protected. A child is expected to behave, to show respect, and to assume a work role within the family at the earliest possible age. As one mother commented, No child is too young or too old to work."

The second ideological emphasis concerns a view of human nature also stemming from southern Italy that is still evident in the values of today's parents. They generally conclude that, given the fallibility of human nature, particularly evident in children, childrearing demands continual parental vigilance. While most parents do not wholeheartedly endorse the precept that human beings are naturally evil, they do conclude that "children will fall upon bad ways if they are not strictly controlled." Hence, the potential for evil is there, and it is the responsibility of the parents to prevent its expression. Evil in their interpretation can mean neglect of family, disrespect, or sexual improprieties for females. Therefore, raising children means teaching the child to conform to family expectations. This category resembles Kohn's behavioral conformity of the working class (1969) where more parental concern is directed to staying out of trouble and responding to the dictates of authority than to achieving self-direction. Predictably, parental authority is exercised more often through external controls than through appeals to conscience.

Affection and Social Control

Leonard Pearlin (1970:45) was among the first to point out the key part that expressiveness and affection play in Italian families as a regulating mechanism to win compliance in the interests of family goals:

> Italian parents, then, want love and affection between their children and themselves. But, while love might be enjoyed for its own sake, it is employed as a means to manage and control the behavior of children. Parental control, in turn, serves to discourage independence and autonomy and to cement family solidarity.

On the basis of my data, I also conclude that the affective component parallels and reinforces direct forms of social control aimed at enforcing conformity to family goals. The interplay between these factors is summarized by one mother who asked, "What kind of heart would I have if I let my children do as they pleased?" The affective and controlling components can be used interchangeably by either parent, but usually the segregation in parental roles establishes the mandate of who should do what.

For example, the Italian-American mother can resort to the sterner methods of discipline as readily as her husband even though usually it is his responsibility. Because mothers remain unconvinced by current permissive childrearing theories, they can use the "back of the hand" without fear of damaging the child's psyche. Although they can and do evoke the hierarchical system when the need for discipline arises, they often equivocate between this function and that of nurturance, particularly with adolescents. Thus, when misbehaviors demand parental action, a woman often turns to her husband who does not feel this ambivalence about his role. Many fathers were quite explicit on the authority structure, "I am the father, I'm nobody's buddy." "My son will never be an equal to me." "They must live by my rules." "I whip them and forget it." "Children have to fear someone in order to grow up properly." One mother aptly summarized the optimal parental role differentiation: "The father is the disciplinarian, the mother is the cushion the children can fall upon."

Behavioral conformity in this sense is linked to the external world of the child and the way in which his behavior is viewed by others, rather than the internal organization of the personality and child's evaluation of his or her own performance. These values of underlying discipline are probably more absolute than generally found today, and they require external rather than internal controls. Children simply must obey. Clearly, as one informant observed, "Italian Americans spank rather than use psychology."

A frequent response to questions on disciplining of adolescents was, "As long as they live in my house, they must live by my rules." In other words, as long as transgressions are readily observable, they are subject to parental control. Since young people are invariably expected to live at home under the watchful eyes of parents until marriage, there is a strong emphasis on external controls. This view is quite unlike the assumptions of many parents today that internalization of parental values takes place when the child is young, so that parental influence continues to direct the child wherever he or she might live.

Parental Roles

Just as childrearing in Italian families is accomplished through a parental role system that differentiates between the mother's and the father's role, patterns of affection and social control are also differentiated and compartmentalized. For some understanding of the outcomes of these patterns, it is useful to turn to the structural-functional approach to family roles. Until recent years, the major conceptual approach to family analysis was a delineation of parental roles by specialization of female expressive functions and male instrumental functions. Critics of this approach (Coser 1974; Slater 1961) have correctly pointed out that such a dichotomy is simplistic and overlooks the realities in the nuclear family, where the functions of both parents overlap into both expressive and instrumental categories.

The modern family of the middle class has made more changes in a process of de-differentiation than have working-class families. Both mother and father are more likely to alternate between instrumental and expressive behaviors (Slater 1961). De-differentiation probably affects the father's role in egalitarian families more than the mother's because he is no longer an aloof authority figure. Instead, he has become a more active participant in day-to-day activities and inevitably performs more expressive functions. While the mother extends her role into the realm of authority, she also has retained her dominance over expressive functions. Unlike traditional families where the mother acts as a mediator between parental authority and the emotional needs of the child, the modern family has reduced the social distance of the father and established some interchangeability of parental roles. Such a family system, Slater concludes, is more complex and perhaps confusing to the child; nevertheless, it reflects a relational pattern suitable for the fluid social structure of a technological society.

Problems arise, however, when both parents are involved in the child's emotional life, as they often are in the contemporary middle-class family. There are fewer opportunities for the child to establish some distance from either parent. Since there is also a high degree of internalization of parental values in this family type and fewer external social controls to enforce these values, the parent-child relationship has a pervasive psychological dimension, for it is based on motivating the child to *want* to do what must be done rather than enforcing parental wishes by direct means. This situation is quite unlike traditional families where external forms of social control are used and there is more psychological distance between parent and child.

Rose Coser (1974) describes the structural ambivalence stemming from this lack of differentiation of authority by pointing out that it could lead to personality absorption of the child. This process, originally described by Arnold Green (1946), conceptualizes a physical and emotional blanketing of the child, leading to an emotional dependence upon the parents, which is continually threatened by the withdrawal of love. Coser points out that when the mother is more active than the father in the authority role and is also the dispenser of affection, it is more likely to impinge upon the child's personality. Those overlapping functions are directed at internal attitudinal as well as behavioral conformity, meaning conformity is expected not only in what a child does but what he thinks. It is more difficult, then, for the child to establish some psychological autonomy from the parents' influence. Furthermore, a child is forced to deal with a common situation where conflicting expectations and behavior come from the same person. This family type, consequently, is characterized by an emotionally intense environment where only two adults, the parents, are directly involved in both the external and the internal world of the child.

Philip Slater (1961) discussed the need for children at some point to establish social distance from the parent in order to dilute the emotional intensity of the nuclear family. He observed that this mechanism, which is usually evident in the reduction in joint activities, is necessary to reduce the ambivalence created by the lack of specialization in the modern parents' roles. In traditional families, on the other hand, children are accustomed to looking to their father as the source of authority and their mother as the source of nurturance, so presumably they are less likely to be faced with a complex and confusing psychological environment resulting from one parent assuming both the affectionate and controlling role. Thus, the common trait in the traditional family pattern of segregating parental roles along the instrumental and expressive axes relieves the child of what might otherwise be an overwhelming amount of social control intertwined with affection.

Arnold Green (1946) compares Polish-American working-class families with the model American middle-class family. He suggests the latter type tends to produce neuroses in children because of personality absorption by the parents. In contrast, the victimized children of authoritarian Polish fathers can leave the family without psychological costs because personality absorption has not taken place. Personality absorption results when a parental authority figure expects attitudinal conformity, which touches upon the motivational system and the internal organization of the personality. It is described as an emotional blanketing of the child which creates a dependence upon the parents because behind it there is a continual threat of withdrawal of love.

Returning to parental roles in Italian-American families, it must be remembered that the data come from families with adolescents, so the dynamics take place at a time when issues of control and dependence are being redefined. Italian teenagers do not seem to be as prone to the personality absorption conceptualized by Green (1946) and Coser (1974), because behavioral controls are externally enforced. However, teenagers also have difficulty establishing social distance from parents not only because of the high family-centeredness, but also because the profuse affection from the mother appears to be aimed more at dependence on family than independence. Likewise, parental vigilance prevents a teenager from moving far from the family fold, so autonomy is not prominent.

In Italian-American families, parental authority is frequently exercised with no illusions of a colleague or buddy relationship. At the same time, the mother can unabashedly provide love and nurturance at a stage when children are usually expected to achieve some independence. It is not surprising that many children do not want to leave this nurturing environment. The predicted conflict and ambivalence are less evident, possibly because parental roles are more segregated and the controlling and affectual components of childrearing have been compartmentalized.

I suggest that this compartmentalization results in a division between a formal role and the less-patterned, diffuse behaviors. Regardless of which parent assumes the role of disciplinarian, he or she is following well-defined, normative expectations and enacting an approved social role. This role is defined by more absolute values on parental responsibility in Italian families than is generally found today. In enacting this role, a parent compartmentalizes the control functions from the less-patterned, nurturing functions. Probably to the child's advantage, this compartmentalization acts as a distancing mechanism where controls are distinct from the more emotionally intense area of nurturance. Thus, the problems associated with de-differentiation of parental roles is most likely reduced.

While the controlling features in parenting stem from well-defined cultural directives, the affective features are still very much an individual matter and can be shaped by the emotions that are so prominent in Italian families. Since emotions should be expressed and any inconsistencies resulting are usually tolerated, it is much easier for a parent to revert from the affective to controlling behaviors without seeming inconsistent. For example, one parent described his physical punishment of a teenage son in strong terms, while in the next breath his eyes teared when speaking of his loneliness for another son who was then in the service. In the role of parent he was required to be a disciplinarian, but as an individual he felt free to display his emotions.

It bears repeating that the discipline that enforces behavioral conformity is paralleled by high nurturance which reinforces dependence on the family. The noncontingency of maternal love means that forgiveness is implicitly forthcoming for most transgressions. Thus, despite what a parent does, most mothers would agree with the maxim "Make your home so comfortable the children won't want to leave."

It also must be remembered that the child is not viewed as a "bundle of potential" which must be carefully nourished and molded, as is the case with middle-class children, but rather as an individual who might transgress from family expectations if continual parental vigilance is not exercised. This vigilance operates in the domains of both affection and external control. Where it operates in the latter, it frequently violates the permissive childrearing norms of the Spockian era. Some of the effects, however, leave the child relatively unscathed, because the external control behaviors are generally compartmentalized from the dispensing of affection, yet in both arenas parents exert control over children. Furthermore, controls are enacted as an ascriptive aspect of the role relatively remote from the parent as an individual.

When the child responds to parental sanctions, he or she responds according to the well-defined expectations of the role of the child, rather than in idiosyncratic behaviors. The effects of parental excesses presumably do not seem to induce the type of attachment described in the concept of personality absorption. The types of controls used are direct responses to specific observable transgressions rather than more diffuse controls over the child's motivational system or other internal dimensions of the personality. Possibly, the children are not as prone to the effects of personality absorption, since the parents are less likely to be concerned with internal motivation. As a result, relationships, while highly emotional, are less likely to be tinged with guilt.

This view can help to explain a commonly described situation

where contradictory behaviors of love or anger, and conflict or har-
mony, fluctuate as part of the daily round of events. "In Italian families, you can say what you please and it will be forgiven." "We can
yell and scream at each other and there are no grudges." "I can spank
my children, but they know I love them and have their best interests at
heart."

The communication between parent and child is undoubtedly colored by the prevailing hierarchy in the family. Parents, in their superior position, are less likely to be concerned with the individuality and
uniqueness of the individual child. Psychologically intense dyads between a parent and a child are less likely to form because the hierarchical relationship is normatively regulated to exclude concern for
internal processes. In the absence of one-to-one relationships, siblings are left to themselves and when necessary can unite as a coalition
against the elevated authority figures. This situation could lay the
groundwork for the sibling solidarity that is so evident in Italian families (Johnson 1982).

Social and Psychological Interpretations

The socialization to family attachments is a complex blend of psychological and social processes. In Italian-American families these patterns of childrearing are associated with high interdependence among
its members, particularly in the diffuse ties between parent and
offspring. Sociological explanations of the patterns described here
would usually evoke a comparison of traditional versus modern or
middle-class family systems. Traditional and working-class family
forms are usually equated, because they share patterns of authority,
role segregation, and so on. While this dichotomy is useful, structural-
functional analysis, which attempts to integrate psychoanalytic theory,
is extremely insightful in introducing the psychological dynamics.

The use of psychoanalytic explanations alone with this material
would most likely stress the internalization of parental values and the
development of superego. To psychoanalysts such childrearing practices which emphasize maternal protectiveness, strict discipline, and
the delayed development of autonomy are detriments to a child's development of maturity and autonomy. However, it would seem that in
Italian families the effect of maternal protectiveness in itself is amelio-

rated by strict discipline techniques, so that the development of a nursery despot on the one hand, or a passive, dependent child on the other, is not the general rule (Levy 1943).

It is not surprising, however, that the key conflicts for schizophrenic Italian patients center on problems regarding paternal authority or a continuing dependence on the mother (A. Parsons 1969). Parsons also concludes that symptoms of schizophrenia among Italian patients follow a symbiotic pattern of undifferentiation of self from intimates rather than autism. In other words, symptoms of psychopathology reflect the prevailing family patterns of attachments.

Recent research in child development indicates that successful internalization of parental values and identification with parental role models are best achieved by the optimal mix of both affection and external control (Fisher and Greenberg 1977; Sears, Rau, and Alpert 1965). This optimal combination of affection and control in the preschool years is identified as a lever for increasing independence. In the adult-centered Italian families, these factors are associated with self-mastery as well as continued interdependence among family members, for children are expected to serve the family at an early age. Clearly the association between factors works together in a manner that does not fit the usual psychological theories of personality development.

These processes in Italian-American families are frequently categorized as traditional techniques of childrearing in contrast to developmental techniques (Duvall 1971; Kohn 1969). The latter is generally linked to middle-class status and higher achievement, but the psychological outcomes of both techniques in terms of cause and effect are both complex and inadequately understood. One difficulty is that, generally, traits are studied microscopically and in isolation. Independence training, internal versus external controls, or other maternal behaviors are associated then with levels of achievement. When these methods are used, Italian Americans do not fare well in comparison with other groups, and their delayed independence from family is linked to lower achievement motivation (Rosen 1959). A related body of research traces present-day statuses of European groups by the distance in time from feudal social structures (Schooler 1976). Authority structures inherent in these systems are judged to have a prolonged effect on values, where rigid systems deter the development of autonomy and, ultimately, achievement.

The issues of achievement were not of central concern in this research, but the degree to which attachment processes in socialization cement the intergenerational relationships were. Both issues concern problems of independence versus dependence and group versus individual interests. In this respect, we see that social explanations alone are not sufficient in clarifying the processes without consideration of the psychodynamic dimension. The psychological approach, on the other hand, when focusing on such issues as dependency, assertiveness, or achievement, is looking at individual behaviors, but rarely in the total family context. Although some theories integrate psychoanalytic explanations on the internalization of parental values with the structure and functioning of the family (T. Parsons 1958), it is not always successfully associated with outcomes. Thus, my interpretations take some liberties with both theoretical perspectives.

Granted that when data are concentrated on norms, one can find near-universal agreement on idealized conceptions of some family relationships. For example, the relationship between parent and child at all stages of life is normatively defined as a bond that transcends usual social concerns for exchange and reciprocity. Yet, in reality, there is a great deal of variation in how this role relationship is acted out both in quantitative terms—in the patterns of reciprocity and mutual support—and in qualitative terms, of the strength of the attachments formed. The data presented suggest that the Italian-American family uses socialization techniques geared to group interdependence. Components identified center on issues of dependency, social control, and profuse maternal nurturance. This indoctrination into the group, which apparently prepares an individual for priorities of family goals over individual goals, possibly creates a willingness among adults to incorporate the elderly parent into their own lives. The next chapter will attempt to bridge these two stages of the family cycle by exploring the continuities of socialization into old age.

Chapter 11
Interdependence:
The Final Adjustments

If socialization to family attachments includes an optimal blend of affection, social control, and satisfaction of dependency needs, then it is worthwhile to examine how these factors continue to operate among the middle-aged offspring and their elderly parents. Both data from this research and clinical research on family processes suggest that, for an understanding of these processes, one must look at both social and psychological material.

Previous chapters have described the cohesive bond between elderly Italian Americans and their middle-aged children. This dimension of family life is less likely to change as rates of intermarriage and social mobility increase. For example, individuals who marry non-Italians continue to perform exceptional supports to elderly parents, even though non-Italian friends and in-laws do not always reinforce these behaviors. While these social contacts with non-Italians might play some role in changing the nature of marital, parental, and kinship roles, they leave the filial role relatively untouched. Among out-married Italians, husbands and wives quite often have very different conceptions on the performance of filial duties, yet differences are rarely resolved to the exclusion of services to parents. It appears, therefore, that a social explanation, with its emphasis on norms and consensus formation, remains incomplete. There is some amplification, however, by examining psychological material.

Psychoanalysis continually reveals the effect that early family relationships have on individuals in adult life (Boszormenyi-Nagy and Spark 1973; Cath 1972). Generally, psychotherapy aims at freeing individuals from these bonds so that one can achieve an autonomous and mature adulthood. Of all family relationships, the one between parent and child is most problematic when autonomy is sought, for it is influenced by both external and internal commitments and obligations. According to Ivan Boszormenyi-Nagy and Geraldine Spark (1973), one cannot "lose" a parent, for the bond is so firmly embedded at the unconscious level. Even if desertion, death, or divorce long ago severed actual contacts with a parent, individuals have difficulty freeing themselves from these loyalties. They argue that the psychological dimensions of the relationship are usually irrevocable. All individuals face this existential reality particularly at the point in their life when commitment is called into question. Since much of this material lies at the covert level, however, it is not directly accessible through the usual methods of the social scientist.

Social research has found that with rare exceptions the commitment to parents is conceptually distinct from other family relationships (Gibson 1972; Sussman 1965). Furthermore, few offspring abandon a dependent parent outright (Shanas 1979). However, unlike the specificity of norms mandating what parents should do for young children, the norms in our society rarely define exactly what an adult child should do for an elderly parent. The legal system intervenes when parents fail to perform their duties to children, but there are no parallels in the duties to an elderly parent even when that individual is completely dependent. As a result, there is a great deal of variation in how filial duties are performed. A middle-aged son or daughter can satisfy many of his or her parent's needs or few (Johnson 1983). Supports can be provided willingly and with much affection or grudgingly with barely suppressed hostility. Motivations also vary considerably. Some say they are dutiful out of love, others to avoid guilt, and still others volunteer that it is merely a responsibility one has, a debt to repay. One determinant of these motivations stems from lifelong dimensions of the relationship. For this reason, socialization experiences at earlier stages of the family cycle have been described and analyzed in order to illuminate on these relationships.

The family processes do not change dramatically over a short time because dimensions of the parent-child relationship have been internalized by a child early in life. An individual's evaluation of his or her role might undergo changes in the press of certain life events, and some behaviors might be modified, but the more deeply embedded role structures are assumed to persist. For the researcher, these structures can be thrown into clearer relief for analysis at the transition periods that redefine relationships. Clinical studies tend to document this proposition. Elias Savitsky and Harold Sharkey (1973), in their research on family stress during illness of an elderly parent, conclude that the long-standing family processes continue during illness and may even become exaggerated. Family members reenact long-standing relational patterns learned at earlier stages in the family cycle. Continuity in role relationships, thus, is the initial premise. The stresses with the onset of parental dependency can activate the more deeply embedded dimensions of the relationship which are less obvious in normal times.

As emphasized throughout this book, the dominant characteristic of Italian families is one of high allegiance to the primary group. Within a closely knit network of family members, there is a high degree of social contact and reciprocal services. The structure is basically hierarchical with old over young and males over females. Within this structure, however, there is a great deal of latitude for sibling solidarity to develop, for the parents' very superiority and authority encourages a coalition of collateral ties to counteract it (Johnson 1982).

Italian Americans have long been accustomed to the dialectical interplay between social controls enforced by values on respect and authority on the one hand, and attachments cemented through affection and nurturance on the other. While both dimensions in themselves operate to retain family allegiances, the process is by no means conflict-free. As the respondents' comments imply, a continual antithesis operates between constriction versus freedom, group interests versus personal interests, and independence versus dependence. In examining these issues in many families studied, the inconsistencies are puzzling. One can extol respect and then yell at a parent in the next breath. Loyalties to families can receive the highest priority at the normative level yet minor squabbles might sever actual contact from time to time. Clearly, tolerance of emotionality and forgiveness for wrongdoing usually mediate between the high expectations and the reality of daily family life. I have interpreted this to mean that these factors provide a sliding scale of expectations which gives the individual considerable latitude in conforming to family expectations. In such a tolerant atmosphere, group bonds can be strengthened and burdens minimized as long as the family remains the primary center for sociability and the source of need fulfillment.

In childhood, the socialization processes, on the whole, are geared to much nurturance, strict forms of social control, and constant fulfillment of dependency needs. Furthermore, there is some segregation of these functions, so that parents can revert back and forth between informal expressive behaviors and the more formal role of disciplinarian without too much ambivalence. In all, I tend to agree with Pearlin's (1970) conclusion that the blend of affection and control are used interchangeably to serve the interests of the family and to create high solidarity.

Factors Associated with the Parent-Offspring Bond

Given the fact that Italian Americans are more likely than the non-Italians studied to respond to the needs of their elderly parents, the analytical problem centers on identifying factors in their family system that are associated with this response. Correlations were run between the scores on filial behaviors (contact, high motivation, and so on) and all other variables. Significant correlations in Italian families were then compared to the control group. While certainly no causal relationships can be established, four variables are prominently linked to the parent-child bond in Italian families (Table 11.1).

First, high scores on filial behaviors are strongly associated with maternal nurturance. Middle-aged mothers who are most attentive and protective of their children are also most likely to extend the same concern to their parents. Apparently, the affective bonds created by these maternal behaviors parallel those one has with one's parents. Mothers who play a key role in satisfying the need of adolescent children transfer these same service to parents when the occasion demands it.

Second, families that extol hierarchical values such as respect, authority, and controls over individuals are also more likely to serve their parents well in their old age. High valuation of hierarchical

Table 11.1.

Significant Correlations with Filial Behaviors: In-married Families
n = 74

Variables	Pearson's r	Statistical significance
Maternal nurturance	.3001	< .005
Hierarchical values	.201	< .003
Network connectedness	.2641	< .01
Proximity of kin	.4074	< .001

arrangements is most likely also linked to the ability to control family members and pressure them to conform to family goals.

Third, filial behaviors among Italians are correlated with a closely knit social network. Families with age-integrated and ethnic- and kinship-dominated networks are more likely to intensify their efforts to give supports to elderly parents. Obviously, the individuals in these networks are likely to share in the same values and, in the context of so much shared activity, they can reinforce and reward approved behaviors and impede the introduction of competing norms and behaviors.

In the control group of Protestants, the pattern is quite different. Their level of filial behavior is more strongly associated with the marital role structures. Respondents who had companionate marriages, where husbands and wives shared activities on a more or less equal base, were more likely to perform extensive services for the parent. I can only conclude that caregiving to elderly parents requires the cooperation and mutual support of both husband and wife in families with low kinship solidarity. This situation was more typically found in Protestant families where kinship resources are more limited and fewer relatives can be called into action. In the connected networks more often found in Italian families, dutiful offspring can call upon the support of an extended family group, so it is not always necessary for both husband and wife to collaborate.

Fourth, families with a large pool of accessible relatives were more likely to have higher scores on these filial behaviors. This finding supports the contention that care for the elderly is considerably facilitated if additional adults can be called into service.

In this book, the concept of interdependence has been used to describe a type of family integration characterized by intimacy, need satisfaction, and group allegiances. It connotes a reciprocal, ongoing quid pro quo among family members. In contrast to dependency, interdependence generally signifies gratification of needs that are not dominated by negative elements such as guilt, resentment, and excessive conflict, or by a dysfunctional passivity or helplessness of dependent members. These factors associated with interdependence between the elderly and their middle-aged offspring are found in varying degrees in the Italian-American family. The findings suggest that interdependence is associated with the patterning of affection and authority. Both dimensions appear to be necessary, for if the nurturing aspects of roles are evident without social control, or vice versa, the outcomes for many elderly are quite different.

In regard to family supports in old age, there are four possible outcomes in terms of instrumental and emotional supports extended by children when the extent of affection and control are taken into consideration. These are illustrated in Table 11.2. First, from our knowledge of traditional families, one can assume that obligatory norms are more likely to exist when social controls are present to enforce them. Although the average Italian interviewed did not conceptualize the relationship as obligatory, his or her behaviors indicated that few considered other options. Where these obligations exist with high affection, the parents would receive both instrumental and expressive supports. In this case, as Table 11.2 illustrates, the family would function as a total support system.

Second, in families with high controls but minimal affective involvement, caregiving might fulfill instrumental needs but the social and emotional supports would leave much to be desired. The parents would have an instrumental support system, because obligatory norms are possibly enforced by the system of social control. However, emotional supports would be lacking.

Third, when a high level of affection is exchanged, an emotionally satisfying relationship is likely. Affection alone, however, does not necessarily create an obligatory relationship in which the child is mandated to help. When the affective elements are dominant, the relationship is likely to be optional and the child can select what he or she

Table 11.2
A Model of Family Supports

Affective involvement	Social controls	
	High	Low
High	Total support system (instrumental and expressive supports)	Emotional support system (expressive supports, sociability; other supports optional)
Low	Instrumental support system (services and economic aid)	Minimal support system (few supports except for perfunctory mediation with formal supports)

chooses to do. She can adapt to the situation by selectively providing supports as she balances her other commitments. In this case, this is an emotional support system.

Fourth, where there is low affective involvement and few social controls, the optional character of the relationship most likely results in minimal supports to a parent. Such a situation is rarely reported, presumably because of the transcendent bond created by the socialization experiences. In any case, where both are lacking, there would be a minimal support system, and children mainly would function as mediators with the formal support system.

However, when these patterns of behavior that elaborate on both affection and social control are embedded in a tightly knit supportive family network where values are shared, the status of the elderly is ordinarily enhanced. The nurturing patterns do not stop suddenly in transition stages in middle and late adulthood. Where a system of social control also exists, the elderly parent continues to hold some power over the offspring. Any failures in meeting these expectations are also sanctioned by other members of the network who share the same views.

Responses to Dependency in Old Age

When the problem of dependency arises with elderly parents, readjustments between them and their children are required. The resources of parents generally decrease. However, Italian parents who have long held power over their children obviously face a different situation than those with less elevated status or those who have led independent lives.

For most elderly, the onset of dependency usually stems from a realistic condition: reduced income leads to economic dependence; declining biological and sensory functioning leads to physical dependence; and the reduction of social contacts due to retirement or widowhood leads to social dependence. While the causes are realistic, the behaviors themselves are frequently associated with regression or a return to childhood.

Although the diagnosis of regression has been overused in regard to the elderly (Butler and Lewis 1977), behaviors associated with it are a common feature of old age. They inevitably stem from increased helplessness associated with physical decline. Regression in a psychoanalytical sense of reversion to oral, anal, and phallic stages is not common, but some regressive changes may be adaptive techniques to counteract psychosocial losses specific to old age. Some clinicians (Berezin 1972) conclude that the acceptance of regression in the service of ego is an active ingredient for successful aging. I interpret this to mean that normal regression signifies a wish to be dependent and the need to turn to others to satisfy dependency needs for comfort and security. If potential caregivers do not frown upon dependency, it means that the dependent individual feels no personal failure or abrogation of social norms regarding loss of independence.

Interestingly enough, the usual means with which physicians deal with dependence and regression in adult patients involves two techniques: a satisfaction of dependency needs and the exercise of authority and control as a lever to impel the patient to independence. Talcott Parsons (1953) analyzes the processes activated by health professionals during illness which tend to augment the low resources most families have for caring for dependent members. The physician can be an appropriate substitute for the family. He or she is tolerant of the dependency, yet, like an authoritarian parent, can use controls to place the patient in a position of having to get well.

Psychiatrists treating older patients have utilized parentlike behavior to deal with childlike behaviors in their patients. By equating the patient's dependency with childlike behavior and extending support and gratification as one would with a child, the patient's helplessness is decreased and the stage is set for the use of parentlike controls and direction (Goldfarb 1954). As a parent figure, the therapist uses both protective and controlling devices to counteract inordinate dependency and regression, but their effectiveness is essentially based upon the therapist's superior situation.

Turning now to family systems in this context, it is logical to assume that those best equipped to deal with dependency and regression not only have had long-standing patterns of reciprocity and mutual support, but also have a hierarchy of authority and power. The configuration of the Italian-American family is amenable to these outcomes because of its structural elaboration of both authority and nurturance elements in relationships. Nurturing stimulates a high level of need satisfaction on the part of the offspring, and the authority elements enforce these filial duties to make them obligatory. At the same time, the right to control can be transferred to the offspring to be used to modify the behaviors of the overly dependent parent. Since the offspring, however, has usually been dependent upon the parent and subservient to their authority, their status in the family would be changed to a great extent.

As some adjustments must be made in the power structure, the dependent member must surrender power, and reverting to a dependency status implies some reciprocal exchange (Emerson 1962). A dependent parent, then, must have something to give in return, whether financial remuneration, the bestowal of honor and prestige to the offspring, or even subjective rewards for repaying filial debts. In hierarchical family systems, the power and authority vested in the parental role consists of another resource that can be transmitted to the offspring in return for the right to be dependent. The exchange of power, in one respect, can be viewed as a lever to impel the child to a higher status. The offspring then assumes the superior position and acquires the right to control the behavior of the parent.

The Onset of Filial Maturity

In the clinical literature, this situation has been described as a role reversal in which a child becomes a parent to a parent. Margaret Blenkner (1965) concludes that this is a pathological rather than a normal condition and reflects neurotic and immature behaviors. The normal role, she maintains, is the filial role, not the parental role. The normative mandate of middle-aged children is to respond to the parent's need, so some response from the offspring is predictable. She describes a stage beyond Freudian theory's genital maturity to that of filial maturity. A filial crisis faces many individuals in their forties and fifties when, instead of receiving support from parents, they must now provide support to them. Successful resolution of this crisis comes from performing a filial role at a higher stage of maturity. In the process she describes, the child must complete his or her emancipation from the parent in order to help the parent. The filial crisis marks the end of childhood as one is now depended upon and dependable in meeting the needs of parents. The child responds to the parent as a mature adult.

Since Italian offspring in middle age are undoubtedly more dependent upon their parents than their contemporaries from other backgrounds, one can predict difficulties in reaching filial maturity. However, a reversal of the dependency and power relationship in most cases seems to emancipate the child from his or her dependency as well as the subordinate position. Italian families possess characteristics that favor the transfer of long-term patterns of authority and nurturance from parent to offspring. In fact there is some evidence of a decline in status among Italian elderly (Covello 1972; Cronin 1970).

Mrs. Cesta is a good example of one who is in the process of resolving the filial crisis. She and her husband are an attractive couple in their late thirties. Both have had some college education and have attained affluence through a jointly run construction company. They live on the outskirts of the city on a large plot of land where they built an additional house for her parents. His parents and numerous other relatives live a few miles away.

We had some difficulty in scheduling the interview because of Mrs. Cesta's father's illness. After numerous delays, the meeting finally took place, and she immediately began to discuss the recent problems arising from the illness:

> My parents are next door. It's super to have both of them alive, but on some days it's not so great. I have a dual role, watching over my parents and my children. Since I am an only child, I have a lot of responsibility.

> I chauffeur them every place, I check on them constantly. I must see Father all the time, for I'm the only one who has any control over him. He's getting cantankerous. He won't take his medicine or take care of himself. I must force him to be careful, so we argue a lot. My son tells me that I'm inconsistent. I preach respect all the time and then I yell at my father.

> Both sets of parents are very dependent upon us. They helped us a lot in the past, so now it's our turn. I don't think we can ever get away from this.

In regard to their own children, the Cestas are cognizant of current childrearing practices and pay lip service to their eventual independence, but the more traditional hierarchy persists. When asked about discipline, she was most emphatic in discussing the way she treats her sixteen-year-old son.

> If it comes to a point of a standstill, where talking doesn't work, I hit him or send him to his room. He has to treat us with respect. I'm proud of my husband; the children have to respect him no matter what he does. We are both conservative. We feel

*you should respect parents and old people whether they've
earned it or not. At school they don't teach this any more, so
sometimes I feel we are fighting a losing battle.*

Mrs. Cesta recognized the inconsistencies of her daily life. She is
attracted to the women's movement and even thinks of going to law
school; still these are not viable options since her husband and her parents are opposed. She finds great appeal in a life of freedom to travel,
to make new friends, or to take advantage of their recent financial success, yet her life is essentailly unchanged. In her view, the limitations
imposed by her parents' situation will only increase in the next few
years. She and her husband share these values and generally support
each other in performing the many duties both sets of parents require.
Nevertheless, she pointed to one advantage of her new stage of maturity. For the first time in her life, she feels more in control of things.

Other respondents showed similar dilemmas with parental authority.
Rather frequently, they reported that parents, when dependent, resorted to tears when they felt their needs were not being filled. On occasion, when the parent was present during the interview, she was
treated as a child, to be seen and not heard. Their errant, childlike behaviors were discussed in their presence as if they were not there, or
they were sent off to do some small task. Yet normatively the fiction
of parental authority was preserved.

Caring for elderly parents was occasionally referred to as
"babysitting." One woman looked back on the five years her mother
had lived with them after having a stroke:

*She couldn't talk, but she always tried to communicate. She
couldn't have lived that long in a nursing home. There would
have been no love or care. I put a hospital bed in the dining
room. We all pitched in to help. When we went out, my son*
babysat. *He liked to play with her. (Emphasis added.)*

Another respondent, after living in her parents' house for forty-five
years, finally moved to her own home out of desperation. She cared
for a sick mother during much of her early adulthood. After her mother's death, her father became increasingly dependent on her and was
making many demands of her at the time of the interview, a situation
that brought her to the point of tears. She went daily to prepare meals
and even to bake his bread, for he would only eat food prepared at

home. She handled all of his bills and gave him an allowance. In other words, her first step in reaching filial maturity was to move out of her father's house, yet she continued in a command position where she exercised much control over his activities.

When these duties can be shared with siblings, the situation is eased somewhat. One respondent described a solution when both parents became ill and dependent. When the need for nursing home placement loomed, the sisters decided they could not live with such an outcome, yet neither one could take care of both parents. So each one took a parent and initially had to deal with the parents' tears and sadness at being separated from each other and leaving their home of fifty years. In order to ease the strain of separation, the daughters acted as matchmakers and arranged a get-together at least twice a week. The respondent and her family went away once for a weekend and left the parents together in her home. She proudly reported that it was like a second honeymoon for them and that it was as if they were young newlyweds.

In these cases, no respondent consciously identified the exchanges of power and dependency taking place. Yet their newly achieved power, which gave them a feeling of competence, permeated the discussion. The fact that they were no longer so dependent upon the parent was a source of satisfaction as was the knowledge that the unilateral flow of service from parent to offspring was at last being reversed. Debts were being repaid, rewards were accruing in the form of power, and a feeling of competence was achieved with the move up the family hierarchy. The costs then, in terms of conflict and ambivalence, were balanced by the rewards.

In most Italian families the controlling devices usually operate at the covert level; parents rarely explicitly state the debts an offspring owes them. Usually the expectations of filial care so permeated the family life for years that it was not necessary to reaffirm them at the verbal level.

Likewise, the many caregiving activities conform to ongoing practices of mutual aid already typifying these families. The role reversal replicates the earlier parent-child relationship, although it is now being acted out in reverse. In families long accustomed to hierarchical structures with authority vested in one individual, the recently acquired power of the offspring is readily utilized to monitor and control the behaviors of the parents. The system of rewards and punishments can be used to prevent further regression and dependency. In other words, these controlled conditions not only resemble parental authority models, but also those described for dependency stages of illness.

These processes are inferred from interview data. The motivations no doubt operate at a deeper, psychological level not tapped by a social investigation. The power and dependency situation is usually not discussed, because it stems from a covert base where exchange and reciprocity are deeply embedded at the psychological level. Consequently, when asked directly about how such obligations were instilled, respondents usually replied, "It's the natural thing to do." "It comes from love, not obligation." "It never had to be stated," and so on.

Even in situations where considerable conflict arises among family members, the blame is often assigned other causes rather than to the realistic stresses that the caretaking creates. For example, the two sisters who shared the care of the parents had no major conflict over who was doing what. However, they were disputing vigorously the division of the proceeds from the sale of the parent's house, even though the joint care continued uneventfully. Our respondent blamed her brother-in-law for taking more of the proceeds than was his due. In another family, a year of caring for a dying mother by siblings ended with an outright rupture upon her death.

It is difficult to see how similar situations can develop without these ingredients of high affection, authority, and long-standing patterns of mutual support. Families that are more nucleated and geared to the autonomy of individual members generally do not have either the motivation or the resources to extend such comprehensive caregiving. Neither parents nor offspring have such high expectations that this is what one should do. Further, the families have few models to use and they receive few rewards for such altruism. There is less likely to be a power structure that can be utilized as a resource in exchange for dependency. Many families interviewed, of course, have not been faced yet with the situation of parental dependency. If the situation should occur, however, I conclude these characteristics of the majority of Italian Americans are more predictive of support than a more nuclear system where personal autonomy is stressed and hierarchical relationships are deemphasized.

Other Adjustments

There are some variants, however, to this model in cases of long illness and high dependency. One such type involves a daughter's great dependency upon her parents which was not reversed in their old age and final illness. In this case, the daughter had difficulty achieving maturity upon her parents' deaths.

Mrs. Richards is married to a non-Italian who works in a skilled blue-collar position. In their twenty-three years of marriage, they have lived in her parents' home where an apartment had been converted for their use. Two of her mother's sisters and their families lived on the same block. She described her marriage as very unhappy because her husband spent much of his time gambling. In the past, her parents always helped financially when his gambling debts accumulated.

A lifetime of dependence upon her parents was severed by her father's death seven years ago and ended with her mother's death five months before the interview. When her mother became ill, her two aunts on the block did everything for her. They cooked, cleaned, and took over the physical care of her mother and finally made all of the funeral arrangements. Mrs. Richards had little to do except provide companionship to her ailing mother. Because her aunts did everything, she had not had the opportunity to reverse the dependency situation and reach filial maturity. After her mother's death, she was lonely and unhappy and complained about the strong hold her mother had had over her.

> My mother and I were very close. We ate all of our meals together. She was a second mother to the children. You know how people sit around and talk about all of the difficulties they've had. Well, I have never had them, because my parents were always there. They took care of everything I needed.

To explain this bond and her suffering with its loss, she concludes:

> Italians are like that. It's hard for others to understand how we are. My mother was a good mother, but she was loud and dominant. If she said black was blue, I didn't question it. They said they never expected anything in return but love and respect. We did all we could because we wanted to. Maybe we felt some guilt, but it was more out of love. They probably suffocated me as a child. We were brainwashed about Italian things. In some

*ways, Mother was like a witch—she had a hold over me.
Though she never said anything, I could see the hurt in her eyes
if I did not conform.*

She described herself as a "doormat" who had always maintained
peace in the family, so she could never develop her own interests. Although her internal conflict was unresolved and her loneliness was om-
nipresent, she did concede that her husband was trying to reform and
take over more family responsibilities now that her parents were no
longer available. Thus, their marriage might become more supportive.
Nevertheless, the loss of a deeply embedded filial bond was difficult
for her to surmount. One explanation could be the lack of opportunity to reverse the dependency situation, leaving Mrs. Richards with
few resources to assume a role of power in her family of procreation,
even though she had achieved a long-delayed independence from
her parents.

There are other examples of depression and unhappiness with the
death of parents even after several years. In a few cases, they were associated with self-recrimination for failure in performing filial duties.
These examples were more often found in geographically mobile families where distance prevented them from fulfilling obligations. One such
respondent concluded that her mother might have lived longer if she
hadn't moved away. However, more often it was a situation similar to
Mrs. Richards's where no role reversal had taken place. It might be that
the resolution of the filial crisis plays an adaptive function in cases
where a strong symbiotic bond between parent and child existed
throughout the adult years and marriage of the offspring.

One might well ask about those cases where conflict and resentments
arose over the obligation to the parents. Such reports were rare when respondents were referring to one's own parents but quite common when
discussing in-laws. In such cases, one's biological parents were seen as
warm, understanding, undemanding, while one's in-laws were often
unforgiving, demanding, and unfair. Such judgments could reflect that
the use of projection is adaptive. The strains arising from excessive parental demands can arouse defenses that are projected upon in-laws
rather than on the parent. In other cases, conflict among siblings is di-
verted from the problem of caring for a parent to areas that pose no
threat to the parent's support.

Where hostility or resentment toward one's own parents was reported, several factors appeared to be associated with it. In some cases,

the parent had failed to perform his or her role properly in the respondent's childhood. Divorce or desertion were the most obvious sources. Other examples were traced to personality problems, where the parent was excessively demanding or dependent. Threats to the marriage were also elicited as cause for resentment. One respondent describes the problems with her mother as follows:

> I had her with me for five years. She almost broke up my marriage. She was nosey. She didn't know enough to mind her own business. She was not crazy about my husband, and she was always criticizing the children. We had her sleeping in the living room, so she was always into everything. I finally found a family who would take her in at reasonable rates. Now I call her daily and visit her once a week.

Generally these infrequent reports describe a parent who was unreasonable and demanding in the respondent's eyes. For example, one parent overtly reduced her son to guilt-laden helplessness when he didn't call her daily: "Here I am sick and you don't even call me." These complaints, expressed by a minority of the respondents, illustrate situations in which middle-aged children do not successfully resolve the crisis and reach a higher stage of maturity.

The last type of response involves a few respondents who rejected outright the notion of filial responsibilities and suffered no guilt or remorse for doing so. In these situations, the respondents were more assimilated and separated from the extended family and the Italian community. For example, Mrs. Paratore is college-educated and holds an important administrative job. She moved away from her home town early in her marriage, but her mother moved also to be near her after the death of her father. This was the mother's second choice after a difficult period living in her other daughter's home.

> Mother is a totally dependent person. It's like she's still eighteen years old. My father was the old-fashioned Italian man—very dominant. Mother was lost when he died.

> But Mother raised us in the American way. She wanted always to live in the better neighborhood in town where there were few Italians. We never had an opportunity to learn about these duties. I saw Mother suffering at the hands of her own mother. She said she didn't want it for us, but now when you get right down to it, she expects the Old World ways.

When she moved here, I never let her stay in our house. I got her an apartment right off, for I saw what it did to my sister. Now she sits staring at four walls or watches T.V. She expects me to call her every day, but I'm too busy. I only see her on Sundays.

Mrs. Paratore was hoping that her mother would eventually move back to the home town and live with her aunt, but she had few qualms about the present situation and expressed no guilt. She concluded that "I never got the message. It never rubbed off on me that I should take over completely the care of the parent." She attributed her attitudes to the fact that she had always felt far removed from the Italian community. She also described her own childhood as more typical of the permissiveness of Americans where she had considerable independence and personal freedom. The family of her childhood, by her reports, did not structurally elaborate the patterns of nurturance and control more typical of Italian families. In the intervening years, there were few expectations on the part of her parents that she should have obligations. At the time of the interview, there was no evidence that the situation was causing her undue stress.

Summary

This chapter has described various patterns of adaptation at the point of parental dependency, and factors associated with filial behaviors have been identified. Statistically, the strongest correlation points to the importance of nurturance and need fulfillment at any age as a prerequisite for the mobilization of a support system for the elderly parent. Also, a hierarchical power structure and delayed independence are characteristics of Italian families which are most likely indirectly related to filial bonds. In addition to these childrearing variables, the characteristics of the family network are also important, for nuclear families need the help of others when one member becomes dependent. The configuration described here has been part of long-standing family practices; they cannot be suddenly activated when a parent becomes sick and in need of help.

This analysis also suggests that the norms espoused by the respondents are not always consistent with their behaviors and thus reveal only limited insights. Consequently, I have attempted to illustrate what happens by looking at transition periods that require changes in authority, dependency, and caregiving patterns in hopes of illuminating the insights about the Italian family that we have presently. To do so, it was necessary to distinguish the more deeply embedded role structure from the set of expectations overtly stated.

I conclude that, irrespective of what one says or does, the relationship with one's parents is permeated by internalized commitments and obligations which influence the individuals in ways that are not revealed by interview techniques generally used by social scientists. What is revealed is an obligation to parents that has both explicit and implicit dimensions. Explicitly, parental obligation among Italian Americans is attributed to feelings of love, repayment, or a natural progression of events often attributed to being Italian. "It is something an outsider cannot understand." Implicit is the conclusion by our respondents that interdependence, nurturance, and social control underlie their conformity to parental expectations. Certainly, the world of debts and credits and the emotional baggage one carries as a result of socialization continue to play a central role at the later stages in the parent-child relationship.

These middle-aged offspring, however, have generally experienced a lifelong dependency upon the parents. Thus, in the assumption of the dominant position as they care for a dependent parent, their status in most cases changes more markedly than the norm. The concept of filial maturity has been used here to interpret the processes by which they have reached the point of being depended upon rather than being dependent upon and finally assume a position of maturity and authority in the family.

Chapter 12
Conclusion

Throughout this book I have attempted to map the workings of the Italian-American family through an exploration of the potential resources this family system has for serving the needs of its elderly members. This work rests on two assumptions. First, to understand the nature of the relationships between elderly and their middle-aged offspring, one must look at long-standing family processes and how needs are satisfied over the lifetime of the family cycle. Consequently, families in the middle stages of the cycle are an appropriate focus for study. At this stage, basic dilemmas have to be resolved in regard to the increased autonomy as children reach adulthood and the decreased autonomy of parents with the increasing likelihood of incapacity. One is a situation of increasing independence, the other of increasing dependence.

The second assumption concerns the need for comparison. Although there are numerous popular assumptions that some American ethnic groups have stronger family systems, there is still some uncertainty as to what the norm is for our society. We do know from large-scale surveys that few elderly are abandoned by their children. In fact, four-fifths of the elderly see an offspring at least weekly (Shanas 1979). However, we have less knowledge on variations in the quality of these relationships and the degree to which children can be called upon to provide real support in old age. Thus, it is important when one is researching one ethnic group to introduce a comparative perspective, so variations and the factors associated with them can be singled out. The families of Protestant, non-Italian origin and non-Italians who had married into Italian families provided this perspective.

In almost every area of family life, the Italians differed from the Protestants, whereas the intermarried families fell somewhere in between. Irrespective of whether we were dealing with blue-collar or white-collar families, the variable of ethnicity stood out as the greatest source of variation. While blue-collar, Protestant families and intermarried Italians resembled the class-based family model, in-married

Italians reversed the predicted pattern; both groups were more family-centered than the other groups. However, middle-class Italians were the most family-centered and also traditional in the patterning of family roles.

Before I discuss the dimensions of Italian families that create this high level of attachment, it is useful first to review the basic prerequisites that families need to function as a support system for elderly members who become dependent. One can view the situation of the elderly on a continuum where their needs vary greatly, but basically their needs fall into four categories: *social* needs for companionship and sociability; *economic* needs for some health costs and augmentation of retirement income; *service* needs for assistance in transportation, housekeeping, and so on; and *emotional* needs to promote a feeling of satisfaction and well-being.

At one end, those who are from sixty-five to seventy-five years might be in fairly good health and might actively participate in many of the activities they did in late middle age. Nevertheless, retirement and widowhood usually have exacted some toll on their social life, so that their reliance on their children to satisfy their social needs might have increased. Emotionally, they might have to rely on their children more to combat increasing discontent created by social losses. Economically, they might be secure as long as illness or inflation does not intervene. Since they are still fairly healthy, they do not need services as long as they can get about to shop or go to the doctor.

As the elderly move toward the other end of the continuum, increasing age and infirmity usually increase their need for help from others. As long as they live independently in the community yet have limited functioning, someone must be available to help. It is at this point that families must decide whether to use family solutions or seek outside assistance. Who will take a parent to the doctor if all sons and daughters work? Who will see that they do not become isolated from social contacts in an average weekday? And who shops for them and helps prepare their meals? For some elderly who reach the stage of complete dependency, when round-the-clock care is required, families must decide whether they have the resources to provide such dedicated support or whether a nursing home is the only solution.

Clearly, over the range of supports that might be required, families must meet basic criteria if they are not to be overtaxed in providing an adequate support system. Undue stress, conflict, or resentment would not serve the elderly well nor would minimal support which leaves them relatively unprotected. First, then, families must have a pool of accessible adults. Second, the costs—objective ones like money, or more subtle ones like emotional costs—should be kept to a minimum so that no one is overly burdened. Third, one member must be relatively freed from other commitments so that other priorities do not compete. Fourth, for a family support system to function well, particularly in satisfying emotional needs, caregivers must be motivated to extend themselves. Unwilling or begrudging helpers contribute little to life satisfaction of the elderly.

On the whole, Italian-American families meet these prerequisites to a greater degree than do the Protestant families in the study. As to the pool of accessible relatives, the Italian elderly have more who are likely to live nearby. Since they have a larger and more active kinship group, other relatives can relieve the primary caregiver from time to time. This situation helps to satisfy cost containment, for some relief of the strains provided by others prevents excessive costs from falling on one individual.

The third prerequisite is one member who is relatively freed from job commitments or his or her own nuclear family, so there is time and energy to devote to the elderly parent. Like many families today, Italian women are likely to work, so one cannot be certain that a daughter will be available without her having to give up her job. However, Italians do differ from others in one respect. If both husband and wife are of Italian background, both of them have been raised in families where respect and service to parents are the norm. Thus, one's marriage is less likely to pose problems in serving elderly parents. Children who are approaching adulthood in Italian families also generally facilitate rather than impede family caregiving, for filial behaviors are the approved ones they have learned in the course of their socialization. Efforts to help parents, in these cases, are reinforced by the norms of the primary group.

The fourth criterion, the motivational system that creates individuals who are willing and ready, is also more likely to be found in Italian families. Few individuals viewed these responsibilities as duty-bound obligations, insisting instead that they wanted to serve the parent as a natural expectation of their filial role. This dimension raises an important question: what are the underlying mechanisms in these families that instill these behaviors? A review of these processes and some interpretations are now in order.

Traditionalism and the Old-fashioned Way

We saw in the earlier chapters that Italian immigrants always placed a strong emphasis on primary relationships over secondary ones. From the earliest reliance on the *padrone* and the *paesano*, they tended to confine their experiences in America to a setting not totally unlike what they left behind in Italy. The most notable feature was the creation of primary relationships out of secondary relationships when practical necessity required it. Even before families were formed here, the godparent system provided quasi-kin relationships to alleviate situations ripe for anomie.

Once most Italian men had founded their own families in this country, the other institutionalized means of creating a primary community were either dropped or incorporated into family activities. Thus, godparents became family, and the *paesano*, always important to the immigrants, did not really survive as a significant basis of solidarity for the second generation. In any case, the immigrants created an insular social community where there was a basic distrust of outsiders. Their world was the Italian one, and all others were part of the American world. Even the Italian world was delimited, however, for the Italian way meant that family considerations superceded all others.

Italian ways were essentially what the elderly called the old-fashioned way. This concept referred to the priority of the family and its basic prerequisites: a good home, ample food, and respect and affection. Any action that threatened these was condemned, so that options for their children were somewhat limited if they posed a threat to what their parents valued. Since the Italian community was insular and made some efforts at excluding competing priorities, there was some success in transmitting features of the old-fashioned way to the offspring.

Second- and third-generation Italian Americans have many reservations about the ways of their parents and recognize the limitations it has placed upon them. However, when it comes to family concerns, they have preserved its chief characteristics. Normatively, the family *should* be the primary unit to the exclusion of others and the components that make it work are still reported to be respect and affection. Thus, traditional values on social control and the desired attachment to family remain discernible even without wholesale acceptance of the old-fashioned way.

Family-Centeredness and Role Continuities in Old Age

The solidarity of the Italian family is generally taken for granted. In Italy, the overriding loyalty is to family over other allegiances. Service to family means the subjugation of personal interests to that of the family. In fact, some commentators conclude that there is an inability to conceptualize a social role apart from the family. The strength of the family and its extensions is documented in this research. While most households today are nuclear in structure, for all practical purposes the extended family plays an important role in daily life, when Italians are compared to other groups.

When family roles are given the highest priority, there are fewer adjustments that have to be made in the transition to old age, as long as the family itself has not suffered serious depletions over time through geographic mobility or a transfer of allegiance to other primary relationships. When children, grandchildren, and other relatives remain nearby, retirement from a job or the death of a spouse does not decimate the social resources of the elderly Italian Americans. These blood relationships have usually remained in the vicinity and the patterns of sociability were set many years before. Thus, the age-related losses, such as widowhood or retirement, have less effect because Italian-American elderly have never relied heavily on age-segregated social networks. They have always been incorporated into their married children's activities just as they have incorporated their children into theirs. When the realities of old age finally become prominent, both elderly men and women continue to perform the roles that have always been of primary significance—their family roles. Consequently, there are fewer sharp breaks in role relationships than are described in the gerontology literature (Blau 1973).

One effect of this pattern, however, is the tendency of the elderly to avoid forming new friendships in old age. They usually shun more formal age-segregated associations in old age, such as senior citizen groups, so those whose social resources do become depleted through loss of family ties can become quite isolated.

Kinship Solidarity, the Sibling Bond, and Network Connectedness

Most activities take place in a group larger than merely parents and children. Italian Americans have an actively functioning kinship system which is the primary focus of solidarity for the nuclear family. The system itself is predatory and expansive and, in most of its activities, tends to pull in many relatives. Relationships are not allowed to wither through lack of contact because, through force of habit and the ritualization of occasions for high sociability, rarely a week goes by that relatives do not play a central part in the average family's activities. In this respect, Italian Americans are much more likely to socialize with cousins, aunts and uncles, nieces and nephews, than are non-Italians. Even if one intends to distance oneself from such an all-embracing family system, it is easier said than done.

An important source of kinship solidarity lies in the development of collateral relationships. Cousins are usually close friends because their parents have continued to maintain a close bond as brothers and sisters. In other words, sibling solidarity is exceptional in most Italian families, and this bond generally reaches out to pull in the offspring in the younger generation. It is easily accomplished, because the patterns of sociability were set long ago. One sees cousins weekly and often retains this bond in adulthood in a form more like friendship in contemporary society. Furthermore, when parents die, the bonds can usually transcend the primary linkage and persist in patterns of sociability.

Since relatives are Italian, the social network is ethnically contained. I should also point out that neighborhoods where our respondents live include other Italians. Although the average Italian may see many associates at work and socialize with friends and affinal relatives who are not Italian, the major portion of their time is spent with other Italians. These individuals are likely to share the same views on family life. Whether family responsibilities provide pain or pleasure, there are many others in the same boat. One can commiserate together or celebrate the positive features of Italian family life.

Even more important, however, is the effect that kinship-dominated, age-integrated, and ethnically contained networks have upon the persistence of ethnic values. When these friends and relatives share the same views on family matters and are in constant social contact, the network itself forms a normative consensus which perpetuates traditional values and acceptable ways of running family life. When one strays from these acceptable ways, sanctions are imposed that have some effect as long as one continues to associate with these primary relationships.

Escape Valves to Family Encirclement

Certainly anyone growing up in the American society cannot ignore the major value system that is at odds with the one described here. The middle-aged Italians are no exception; they tend to view the old-fashioned way with a great deal of amibivalence. They know that the idealized conceptions of their parents are not always compatible for them and their children if they are to get ahead. Many interviews prominently featured the respondents' inconsistencies in their evaluation of the Italian family: "They smother you." "Parents cling to you and won't let go." "They discourage achievement," and so on. These same interviews, however, also extol the virtues of the Italian family, the security, the love, and the support.

The costs imposed generally center on the limited options one has to family loyalties. Numerous respondents feel they could not escape the all-embracing demands, concerns, and attentiveness. However, there are some escape valves built into this family system which alleviate tensions produced by such a tightly bound system of primary relationships. Primarily, pressures can be reduced through the expression of emotions. Venting feelings of anger, rage, or love and sentiment are perfectly acceptable means of expressing oneself in the family circle. Furthermore, basic human nature is viewed as such that an individual has many faults over which he or she has no control, so that social controls are needed. Where these controls fail and individuals behave at odds with family expectations, the fault is usually assigned to the foibles of human nature, not to an individual's character deficiency. Thus one can be ambivalent, resentful, or erratic in behavior and this will usually be overlooked. Those who fail to meet the expectations of the family are usually not severely penalized as long as contact is maintained.

With this view, I believe it is easier to conform to the many expectations of Italian family life, because while expectations are high, they are not rigidly enforced. Rather, they are on a sliding scale where basic deficiencies in human nature are taken into account and few severe sanctions are imposed. Thus, the costs of family responsibilities are minimized for they are mediated through an environment where emotions can be expressed and forgiveness is usually forthcoming.

Socialization over the Family Circle

I have mentioned repeatedly that the primary ingredients in closely knit Italian families are a complex blend of affectual and hierarchical behaviors. Affectual behaviors serve to create close emotional bonds at the same time that they satisfy dependency needs. The controlling features in the hierarchy of family roles serve to enforce conformity. In this sense, these factors work together instrumentally to further family goals at the expense of individual ones. A child grows up in a secure environment where needs are well met. Where he or she might stray from parental expectations, the system of social control is set into action without reservation. The techniques of social control appear to impel individuals back into the family rather than into alternative relationships outside the family because of the noticeable affectional component. Family relations can be personally rewarding. Errant young people, however, must also face the many relatives who can step into the role of the parent and remind them of their responsibilities.

How these same processes operate later in the family cycle between elderly parents and their middle-aged offspring is more difficult to interpret. This problem is due to the fact that developmental theories of family processes are only now being extended to relationships at these later stages of the family cycle, so we do not have understanding of these processes parallel to those at earlier stages of the family. Yet when one looks at the examples presented in chapter 11, it is difficult to see how high filial devotion can exist without both affection and social control, important dynamics also in the earlier stages. However, unlike the earlier stages, the affectional and nurturing behaviors are somewhat at odds with societal values. In our country, one is expected to be independent and free from parental control in adulthood. Consequently, when situations arise that demand a choice between personal interests and family interests, the common cultural directive is to place priority on individual interests, a decision foreign to most Italians.

Where families do have strong controlling mechanisms at the same time that they provide security and affection, filial behaviors are greatly facilitated. In cases of real dependency, however, children are prone to reach a new stage of maturity which in one sense frees them from parental influence. Where offspring become the dispensers of control to their dependent parents, they have reached a stage of filial maturity. In this new status, they exert controls over their parents and expect them to conform. The high resources in most Italian extended families, combined with the psychological and social processes described here, appear to serve the elderly well.

In any case, in the average Italian American family, lifelong attachments have been created through high levels of nurturance and need fulfillment. Controls over the individual initially take the form of strict discipline techniques. However, in adulthood, these controls become more indirect. Few adult offspring are told they have to conform to parental expectations; the emotional bond, implanted earlier in life, generally operates without explicit exhortations. Since considerable expression of feelings is tolerated, an individual is not rigidly constrained; he or she does not have to be. The dependence of childhood has become an interdependence in adulthood where many loyalties competing with the family are excluded or minimized in importance. Furthermore, an elderly parent can resort to emotional expression rather than direct demands, and tears, sighs, and hurt expressions can be equally effective.

Further Directions

In the future, the family system described here will most likely face many changes. There are high rates of intermarriage among Italian young people. We have seen that intermarried families are as much like the Protestant families as they are like in-married Italian families. Although some in-married and out-married Italians seem worlds apart, an impression documented by significant statistical differences in kinship contact and patterns of childrearing, it is important to mention again that Italian Americans who marry out do not differ significantly in their relationship with their parents. They continue to perform the proper filial behaviors mandated by the old-fashioned way.

Theoretically, it is possible to map the changes intermarriage exerts. The first effect is in the social network. New friends and relatives by marriage come to play an important role in the life of the nuclear family. These contacts more often than not introduce new values which call into question the basic premises of the traditional Italian family. Marriages are likely to change from a segregated role system to one where companionship is the primary cement holding a couple together. This type of marriage can pose impressive barriers to fulfilling loyalties to parents, for the marriage is given highest priority. New values also change the way children are raised, so that ideas on discipline, nurturance, and independence training begin to change, and parental vigilance in enforcing conformity decreases.

This chain of events obviously has happened in many out-married Italians we interviewed, yet statistically we see that the bond to the parent remains strong. For this reason, I felt it necessary to explore the psychological effects of childrearing practices. I can only conclude that the long years of socialization create invisible loyalties to parents in any subculture (Boszormenyi-Nagy and Spark 1973). However, where these practices emphasize affection and dependence and have controlling mechanisms to enforce an attachment to families, as found in Italian families, then more concrete forms of attachment are manifested.

Policy Implications

Before one concludes from reading this book that a primary solution to the problems of the elderly in this country lies in family supports, several conclusions need to be emphasized. It is both economical and desirable for policy makers to think in terms of family solutions over outside forms of assistance. However, we do find that the high rates of intermarriage among Italian Americans most likely will mean the family type here will not be prevalent in another generation or two. Even if the changes described become stabilized, other hurdles are bound to appear.

For one thing, the economy today is not conducive to family supports. With inflation, it is necessary for Italian women to work even if they prefer following the more traditional domestic roles of their mothers. Since caretaking generally falls upon a working daughter, an elderly parent cannot always count on her support.

Furthermore, family size is smaller than in the days of the immigrants. There are simply fewer children to provide support. Most individuals marry today, so it is unlikely that a single child without other commitments will take over the care. When these daughters work and have children of their own, comprehensive care of a dependent parent is difficult. When there are few siblings to share in these services, Italian families like most others are likely to become overtaxed. Even if their values and their motivations indicate the best of intentions, they too must weigh their options and usually place their spouse and children's needs above their parents.

It must also be remembered that Italian Americans have experienced enough social mobility to have a toehold in the middle class. They are part of the nationwide system of rising expectations where life is expected to be better for them and for their children. Dividing or decimating the resources allocated to raising the standard of living in order to care for a parent must cause a revision in expectations. One cannot buy the house in the suburbs or send a child to college if the wife must quit her job to care for an ailing mother.

It bears repeating the story of Mr. Vito who has lived in a nursing home for six years. Certainly his children did not want to place him there. He tried to live with them, but first he couldn't adjust to the new neighborhood. Then when his health declined, the choice between the nuclear family's income and filial obligations presented itself. The best solution to all concerned was a move to a nursing home, not because of motivation but because of economic conditions.

Certainly, Italian Americans are highly motivated and do not need great incentives to assume the care of elderly parents, but they too can become overtaxed in the face of numerous obstacles. If the government would provide supports to the family supporters of the elderly, Mr. Vito might still be living with his son and daughter-in-law to the satisfaction of all.

It is important for public planners to be sensitive to variations in the American family system. Adherence to the prevalent assumptions that most white ethnics have melted into the working class will do little to enhance our understanding of potential family strengths. The family systems in some of these subcultures do have existing assets that serve their members well in old age under certain conditions. These assets do not have to be fostered through social reform measures; they already exist. It is their preservation that should be of central concern to policy makers.

References

Abramson, H. 1973. *Ethnic Diversity in America*. New York: John Wiley and Sons.

Adams, B. 1968. *Kinship in the Urban Setting*. Chicago: Markham.

————. 1971. "Isolation, Function and Beyond: American Kinship in the 1960s." In *Decade Review of Family Research in Action*, C. Broderick, ed. Minneapolis: National Council on Family Relations.

Alba, R. 1976. "Social Assimilation among American Catholic National Origin Groups." *American Sociological Review* 41:1030–1046.

Banfield, E. 1958. *The Moral Basis of a Backward Society*. New York: Free Press.

Barth, F. 1969. *Ethnic Groups and Boundaries*. Boston: Little, Brown.

Barzini, L. 1964. *The Italians*. New York: Atheneum.

Bell, D. 1975. "Ethnicity and Social Change." In *Ethnicity: Theory and Experience*, N. Glazer and D. Moynihan, eds. Cambridge, Mass.: Harvard University Press.

Berezin, M. 1972. "Psychodynamic Considerations of Aging and the Aged: An Overview." *American Journal of Psychiatry* 128:33–41.

Blau, Z. 1973. *Old Age in a Changing Society*. New York: New Viewpoints.

Blenkner, M. 1965. "Social Work in Family Relationships in Later Life." In *Social Structure and the Family: Generational Relations*, E. Shanas and G. Streib, eds. Englewood Cliffs, N.J.: Prentice-Hall.

Boszormenyi-Nagy, I., and Spark, G. 1973. *Invisible Loyalties*. New York: Harper and Row.

Bott, E. 1971. *Family and Social Network*. New York: Free Press.

Brody, E. 1981. "Women in the Middle and Family Help to Older People." *The Gerontologist* 21:471–482.

Butler, R., and Lewis, M. 1977. *Aging and Mental Health*. St. Louis: C. V. Mosby.

Campisi, P. 1948. "Ethnic Family Patterns: The Italian Family in the United States." *American Journal of Sociology* 53:443–449.

Castiglione, G. 1905. "Italian Immigration into the United States, 1901–1904." *American Journal of Sociology* 11:183–206.

Cath, S. 1972. "Institutionalizing an Elderly Parent: The Nadir of Life." *Journal of Geriatric Psychiatry* 5:25–46.

Child, I. 1943. *Italian or American? The Second Generation Conflict*. New Haven: Yale University Press.

Clark, M. 1969. "Cultural Values and Dependency in Later Life." In *Dependence and Old People*, R. Kalish, ed. Ann Arbor: University of Michigan, Occasional Papers in Gerontology.

Clark, M., and Anderson B. 1967. *Culture and Aging*. Springfield, Ill.: Charles C. Thomas.

Cohen, J. 1980. "Sex Roles in a Comparative Context: Some Observations on Jewish and Italian-American Women." *Journal of Comparative Family Studies* 11:233–248.

Cohler, B., and Grunebaum, H. 1981. *Mothers, Grandmothers and Daughters: Personality and Child Care in Three-Generation Families*. New York: John Wiley and Sons.

Cohler, B., and Lieberman, M. 1979. "Personality Change across the Second Half of Life: Findings from a Study of Irish, Italian and Polish Women." In *Ethnicity and Aging*, D. Gelfand and A. Kutzik, eds. New York: Springer.

Cordasco, F., and Bucchioni, E., eds. 1974. *The Italians: Social Background of an American Group*. Clifton, N.J.: Augustus Kelly.

Coser, R. 1974. "Authority and Structural Ambivalence." In *The Family: Its Structure and Functions*, R. Coser, ed. New York: St. Martins.

Covello, L. 1967. *The Social Background of the Italo-American School Child*. Leiden, Netherlands: E. J. Brill.

Cowgill, D., and Holmes, L., eds. 1972. *Aging and Modernization*. New York: Appleton-Century-Crofts.

Cronin, C. 1970. *Sting of Change: Sicilians in Sicily and Australia*. Chicago: University of Chicago Press.

Day, Helen. 1929. "Sicilian Traits." In *Gold Coast and Slum: A Sociological Study of Chicago's Near North Side*, H. Zorbaugh, ed. Chicago: University of Chicago Press.

Douglas, W. 1984. *Emigration in a Southern Italian Town*. New Brunswick, N.J.: Rutgers University Press.

Duncan B., and Duncan, O. 1968. "Minorities and the Process of Stratification." *American Sociological Review* 33:356–364.

Duvall, E. 1971. *Family Development*. Philadelphia: Lippincott.

Elder, G. 1974. *Children of the Great Depression*. Chicago: University of Chicago Press.

Emerson, R. 1962. "Power-Dependence Relations." *American Sociological Review* 6:31–41.

Femminella, F., and Quadagno, J. 1976. "The Italian American Family." In *Ethnic Families in America*, C. Mindel and R. Habenstein, eds. New York: Elsevier.

Firey, W. 1947. *Land Use in Central Boston*. Cambridge, Mass.: Harvard.

Fisher, S., and Greenberg, R. 1977. *The Scientific Credibility of Freudian Theory and Practice*. New York: Basic Books.

Foerster, R. 1919. *The Italian Immigration of Our Time*. Cambridge, Mass.: Harvard University Press.

Fullerton, G. 1977. *Survival in Marriage*. Hinsdale, Ill.: Dryden Press.

Gambino, R. 1974. *Blood of My Blood*. New York: Doubleday.

Gans, H. 1962. *Urban Villagers: Group and Class in the Life of Italian Americans.* New York: Free Press.

Gibson, G. 1972. "Kin and Family Networks: Overheralded Structure in Past Conceptualizations of Family Functioning." *Journal of Marriage and the Family* 34:13–23.

Giovannini, M. 1978. "A Structural Analysis of Proverbs in a Sicilian Village." *American Ethnologist* 5:322–333.

Glazer, N. 1981. "Culture and Mobility." *The New Republic*, July 4, 11: 29–34.

Glazer, N., and Moynihan, D. 1963. *Beyond the Melting Pot.* Cambridge, Mass.: M.I.T. Press.

———, eds. 1975. *Ethnicity: Theory and Experience.* Cambridge, Mass.: Harvard University Press.

Goldfarb, A. 1954. "Psychotherapy of the Aged." *Psychosomatic Medicine* 16:209–219.

Goode, W. 1963. *World Revolution and Family Patterns.* New York: Free Press.

Gordon, M. 1964. *Assimilation in American Life.* New York: Oxford University Press.

Greeley, A. 1974. *Ethnicity in the United States.* New York: John Wiley and Sons.

———. 1977. *The American Catholic: A Social Portrait.* New York: Basic Books.

Green, A. 1946. "The Middle-Class Male Child and Neurosis." *American Sociological Review* 11:31–46.

Hansen, M. L. 1952. "The Third Generation in America." *Commentary* 14:496.

Herberg, W. 1955. *Protestant-Catholic-Jew: An Essay in Religious Sociology.* New York: Random House.

Horowitz, I. 1975. "Race, Class and the New Ethnicity." *Worldview* 18:46–53.

Howe, I. 1977. "The Limits of Ethnicity." *The New Republic*, June 25:17–19.

Hunt, R. 1971. "Components of Relationships in the Family: A Mexican Village." In *Kinship and Culture*, F. Hsu, ed. Chicago: Aldine.

Ianni, F. 1961. "The Italo-American Teenager." *Annals of the American Academy of Sciences* 338:70–78.

Ianni, F., and Reuss-Ianni, E. 1975. "The Godfather is Going Out of Business." *Psychology Today*, December: 87–92.

Iorrizo, L., and Mondello, S. 1971. *The Italian Americans.* New York: Twayne.

Isaacs, H. 1975. "Basic Group Identity: The Idols of the Tribe." In *Ethnicity: Theory and Experience*, N. Glazer and D. Moynihan, eds. Cambridge, Mass.: Harvard University Press.

Johnson, C. 1976. "The Principle of Generation among Japanese in Honolulu." *Ethnic Groups* 1:13–35.

———. 1982. "Sibling Solidarity: Its Origin and Functioning in Italian-American Families." *Journal of Marriage and the Family* 44:155–168.

———. 1983. "Dyadic Family Relations and Social Supports." *The Gerontologist* 23:377–383.

Juliani, R. 1973. "Origin and Development of the Italian Community in Philadelphia." In *The Ethnic Experience in Pennsylvania*, J. Bodnar, ed. Youngstown, Pa.: Bushnell.

Kennedy, R. 1952. "Single or Triple Melting Pot? Intermarriage Trends in New Haven, 1920–1950." *American Journal of Sociology* 58:56–59.

Kerkoff, A. 1965. "Nuclear and Extended Family Relationships." In *Social Structure and the Family: Generational Relations*, E. Shanas and G. Streib, eds. Englewood Cliffs, N.J.: Prentice-Hall.

Kitch, L., and Egon, M. 1976. "The New Pluralism: From Tolerance and Neglect." *Ethnicity* 3:378–387.

Kluckhohn, F., and Strodtbeck, F. 1961. *Variations in Value Orientations.* New York: Harper and Row.

Kohn, M. 1969. *Class and Conformity: A Study of Values.* Homewood, Ill.: Dorsey.

Komarovsky, M. 1962. *Blue Collar Marriage.* New York: Random House.

Lalli, M. 1969. "The Italian-American Family: Assimilation and Change." *Family Coordinator* 18:44–48.

Lasch, C. 1979. *The Culture of Narcissism.* New York: Warner Books.

LeVine, R. 1973. *Culture, Behavior and Personality.* Chicago: Aldine.

Levy, D. 1943. *Maternal Overprotection.* New York: Columbia University Press.

Lieberson, S. 1963. *Ethnic Patterns in American Cities.* New York: Free Press.

Litwak, E. 1965. "Extended Kin Relations in an Industrial Democratic Society." In *Social Structure and the Family: Generational Relations*, E. Shanas and G. Streib, eds. Englewood Cliffs, N.J.: Prentice-Hall.

Lopata, H. 1978. "Contributions of Extended Families to the Support System of Metropolitan Widows: Limitations of the Modified Kin Network." *Journal of Marriage and the Family* 40:355–364.

Lopreato, J. 1970. *Italian Americans.* New York: Random House.

McClelland, D., Pandlesbacker A., and de Charmes, R. 1955. "Religious Training and Other Sources of Parental Attitude toward Independence Training." In *Studies of Motivation*, D. McClelland, ed. New York: Appleton-Century-Crofts.

McDonald, J., and McDonald, L. 1964. "Chain Migration, Ethnic Neighborhood Formation and Social Network." *Milbank Memorial Fund Quarterly* 42:82–97.

McLaughlin, V. 1971. "Patterns of Work and Family Organization: Buffalo Italians." *Journal of Interdisciplinary History* 2:229–314.

Majoribanks, K. 1972. "Ethnicity and Learning Patterns: A Replication and an Explanation." *American Journal of Sociology* 63:477–481.

Mindel, C., and Habenstein, R., eds. 1976. *Ethnic Families in America.* New York: Elsevier.

Monticelli, G. 1967. "Italian Emigration: Basic Characteristics, and Trends with Special Emphasis on the Post-War Years." *International Migration Review* 1, no. 3:10–24.

Moss, L., and Thomson, W. 1959. "The Southern Italian Family: Literature and Observation." *Human Organization* 18:354–364.

Munnichs, J., and van den Heuvel, W., eds. 1976. *Dependency or Interdependency in Old Age.* Netherlands: Martinus Nijihoff.

Nelli, H. 1967. "Italians in Urban America: A Study in Ethnic Adjustment." *International Migration Review* 1:38–55.

———. 1970. *The Italians in Chicago, 1880–1930: A Study in Ethnic Mobility.* New York: Oxford University Press.

———. 1980. "The Italians." In *Harvard Encyclopedia of American Ethnic Groups*, S. Thernstrom, ed. Cambridge, Mass.: Harvard University Press.

Neugarten, B., and Weinstein, K. 1964. "The Changing American Grandparent." *Journal of Marriage and the Family* 26:199–204.

Novak, M. 1972. *The Rise of the Unmeltable Ethnics.* New York: Macmillan.

———. 1974. "The New Ethnicity." *Center Magazine* 7, no. 4:18–25.

Odenkrantz, L. 1919. *Italian Women in Industry.* New York: Russell Sage.

Paglia, C. 1976. "Reflections on Being Italian in America." *A New Day* 1:8.

Palisi, B. 1966. "Patterns of Social Participation in a Two-Generation Sample of Italian Americans." *Sociological Quarterly* 7:667–678.

Papajohn, J., and Spiegel, J. 1975. *Transactions in Families.* San Francisco: Jossey-Bass.

Parsons, A. 1969. *Belief, Magic and Anomie.* New York: Free Press.

Parsons, T. 1949. "The Social Structure of the Family." In *The Family: Its Function and Destiny*, R. Anshen, ed. New York: Harper and Row.

———. 1953. "Illness, Therapy and the Modern Urban American Family." *Journal of Social Issues* 13:13–31.

———. 1958. "Social Structure and the Development of Personality." *Psychiatry* 21:321–340.

———. 1965. "The Normal American Family." In *Man and Civilization: The Family's Search for Survival*, S. Farber, ed. New York: McGraw-Hill.

———. 1975. "Some Theoretical Considerations on the Nature of Change of Ethnicity." In *Ethnicity: Theory and Experience*, N. Glazer and D. Moynihan, eds. Cambridge, Mass.: Harvard University Press.

Pearlin, L. 1970. *Class, Context and Family Relations.* Boston: Little, Brown.

Pisani, L. 1959. *The Italians in America: A Social Study and History.* New York: Exposition Press.

Psathas, G. 1968. "Ethnicity, Social Class and Adolescent Independence from Social Control." In *Permanence and Change in Social Class*, W. Lane, ed. Cambridge, Mass.: Schenkman.

Rabkin, J., and Struening, E. (n.d.). "Ethnicity, Social Class and Mental Illness." Institute on Pluralism and Group Identity. Working paper series no. 17.

Rosen, B. 1959. "Race, Ethnicity, and the Achievement Syndrome." *American Sociological Review* 24:47–60.

Rosow, I. 1967. *The Social Integration of the Aged*. New York: Free Press.

Rossides, D. 1976. *The American Class System*. Atlanta: Houghton-Mifflin.

Rubin L. 1977. *Worlds of Pain: Life in Working-Class Families*. New York: Basic Books.

Russo, N. 1969. "Three Generations of Italians in New York City: Their Religious Acculturation." *International Migration Review* 3:3–16.

Savitsky, E., and Sharkey, H. 1973. "The Geriatric Patient and His Family: Study of Family Interaction in the Aged." *Journal of Geriatric Psychiatry* 5:3–19.

Schneider, D., and Smith, R. 1973. *Class Differences and Sex Role in American Kinship and Family Situations*. Englewood Cliffs, N.J.: Prentice-Hall.

Schooler, C. 1976. "Serfdom's Legacy: An Ethnic Continuum." *American Journal of Sociology* 81:265–286.

Sears, R., Rau, L., and Alpert, R. 1965. *Identification and Childrearing*. Stanford: Stanford University Press.

Seeley, J., Sims, R., and Loosely, E. 1956. *Crestwood Heights: A Study of Suburban Life*. New York: Basic Books.

Shanas, E. 1979. "Social Myth as Hypothesis: The Case of the Family Relations of Older People." *The Gerontologist* 19:3–9.

Shanas, E., and Streib, G., eds. *Social Structure and the Family: Generational Relations*. Englewood Cliffs, N.J.: Prentice-Hall.

Shanas, E., Townsend, R., Wedderburn, D., and Friis, H. 1968. *Old People in Three Industrial Societies*. New York: Atherton.

Silverman, S. 1968. "Agricultural Organization, Social Structure and Values in Italy: Amoral Familism Reconsidered." *American Anthropologist* 70:1–20.

Slater, P. 1961. "Parental Role Differentiation." *American Journal of Sociology* 67, no. 3:296–311.

———. 1963. "On Social Regression." *American Sociological Review* 28:339–364.

———. 1970. *The Pursuit of Loneliness*. Boston: Little, Brown.

Smith, J. 1977. "The Immigrant Family and Cultural Change: Two Generations of Italians and Jews in Providence, Rhode Island." Paper presented at the Joint Conference of the American Italian Historical Association and the American Jewish Historical Society, Waltham, Mass.

Stein, H., and Hill, R. 1973. "The New Ethnicity and the White Ethnic: The

Psychocultural Dynamics of Ethnic Irredentism." *Canadian Review on Nationalism* 1:81–105.

Stein, R. 1971. *Disturbed Youth and Ethnic Family Patterns.* Albany, New York: SUNY Press.

Stone, E. 1978. "It's Still Hard to Grow Up Italian." *New York Times Magazine,* December 17.

Strodtbeck, F., McDonald, M., and Rosen, G. 1957. "Evaluation of Occupations: A Reflection of Jewish and Italian Mobility Differences." *American Sociological Review* 22:546–553.

Sussman, M. 1965. "Relationships of Adult Children with Their Parents." In *Social Structure and the Family: Generational Relations,* E. Shanas and G. Streib, eds. Englewood Cliffs, N.J.: Prentice-Hall.

———. 1976. "Family Life of Old People." In *Handbook of Aging and the Family,* R. Binstock and E. Shanas, eds. New York: Van Nostrand.

Sussman, M., and Burchinal, L. 1962. "The Kin Family Network in Urban Industrial America." *Journal of Marriage and the Family* 24:231–240.

Suttles, G. 1968. *The Social Order of the Slum.* Chicago: University of Chicago Press.

Thernstrom, S., ed. 1980. *Harvard Encyclopedia of American Ethnic Groups.* Cambridge, Mass.: Harvard University Press.

Treas, J. 1977. "Family Support Systems for the Aged: Some Social and Demographic Considerations." *The Gerontologist* 17:486–491.

Troll, L. 1971. "The Family in Later Life." In *Decade of Family Research and Action,* G. Broderick, ed. Minneapolis: National Council of Family Relations.

Troll, L., and Smith, J. 1976. "Attachment through the Life Span: Some Questions about Dyadic Bonds among Adults." *Human Development* 19:156–170.

Ulin, R. 1968. "Ethnicity and School Performance: An Analysis of the Variables on Italo-Americans." *California Journal of Educational Research* 19:190–197.

Vicoli, R. 1974. "The Italian Americans." *Center Magazine* 7, no. 4.

Ward, D. 1971. *Cities and Immigrants: A Geography of Change in Nineteenth Century America.* New York: Oxford University Press.

Ware, C. 1935. *Greenwich Village, 1920–1930.* New York: Houghton-Mifflin.

Wechsler, H., Demone, H., Thim, D., and Kasey, E. 1970. "Religious Differences in Alcohol Consumption." *Journal of Health and Social Behavior* 11:3–8.

Williams, P. 1938. *South Italian Folkways in Europe and America.* New Haven, Conn.: Yale University Press.

Wood, V., and Robertson, J. 1978. "Friendship and Kinship Interaction: Differential Effect on Morale of the Elderly." *Journal of Marriage and the Family* 40:500–505.

Yancey, W., Ericksen, E., and Juliani, R. 1976. "Emergent Ethnicity: A Review and Reformulation." *American Sociological Review* 41:391–403.

Young, M., and Willmott, P. 1957. *Family and Kinship in East London*. London: Routledge and Kegan Paul.

Zax, M., Gardner, E., and Hart, W. 1967. "A Survey of the Prevalence of Alcoholism in Monroe County, New York." *Quarterly Journal of Studies on Alcoholism* 28:316–317.

Index

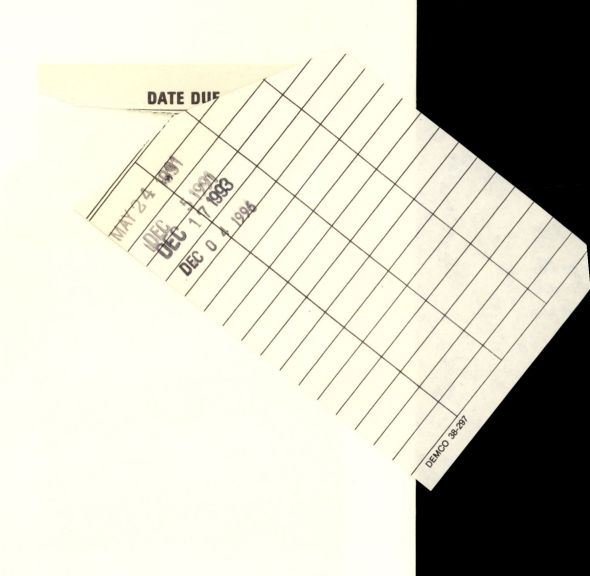